Russian Literary Journals, Dostoevsky, and Tolstoy in St. Petersburg, 1877

REACTING TO THE PAST is an award-winning series of immersive role-playing games that actively engage students in their own learning. Students assume the roles of historical characters and practice critical thinking, primary source analysis, and argument, both written and spoken. Reacting games are flexible enough to be used across the curriculum, from first-year general education classes and discussion sections of lecture classes to capstone experiences, intersession courses, and honors programs.

Reacting to the Past was originally developed under the auspices of Barnard College and is sustained by the Reacting Consortium of colleges and universities. The Consortium hosts a regular series of conferences and events to support faculty and administrators.

NOTE TO INSTRUCTORS: Before beginning the game, you must download the game materials, including an instructor's manual containing a detailed schedule of class sessions, role sheets for students, and handouts.

To download these essential resources, visit https://reactingconsortium.org/games, click on the page for this title, then select "Game Materials."

Russian Literary Journals, Dostoevsky, and Tolstoy in St. Petersburg, 1877

LINDA M. MAYHEW

BARNARD

The University of North Carolina Press

Chapel Hill

© 2025 Reacting Consortium, Inc.
All rights reserved
Manufactured in the United States of America

ISBN 9781469691381 (pbk.: alk. paper)
ISBN 9781469691398 (epub)
ISBN 9781469691404 (pdf)

Cover art: *Arrest of a Propagandist* (1892) by Ilya Repin. Courtesy Wikimedia Commons.

For product safety concerns under the European Union's General Product Safety Regulation (EU GPSR), please contact gpsr@mare-nostrum.co.uk or write to the University of North Carolina Press and Mare Nostrum Group B.V., Mauritskade 21D, 1091 GC Amsterdam, The Netherlands.

Contents

List of Illustrations / vii

1. INTRODUCTION / 1

Brief Overview of Game / 1

Prologue / 2

Basic Features of Reacting to the Past / 4

    Game Setup / 4

    Game Play / 4

    Game Requirements / 5

    Controversy / 5

    Counterfactuals / 6

2. HISTORICAL BACKGROUND / 7

Chronology / 7

The Foundation of Saint Petersburg / 8

Religion in Russian Culture / 11

The Crimean War and Alexander II's Great Reforms / 13

Censorship under Alexander II / 15

Literacy in the Nineteenth Century / 16

The Populists / 16

Violence and Revolution / 18

The Woman Question / 19

The Slavophiles / 21

Literary Journals and Other Publications / 22

3. THE GAME / 27

Major Issues for Debate / 27

Rules and Procedures / 28

    Meetings / 28

    Objectives and Victory Conditions / 29

    Special Events / 29

    Advice on Debating in Character / 30

    Tips for Analyzing Literature / 30

Assignments / 31
   Speeches / 31
   Publishing / 31
   Journal Editors / 31
   Censors / 34

4. FACTIONS AND ROLES / 35

Factions / 35
   Populists / 35
   Slavophiles / 35
   Westernizers / 36

Journals / 36
   Notes from the Fatherland / 36
   Messenger of Europe / 36
   Russian Messenger / 36

Brief Outline of Each Role / 37
   Journal Editors / 37
   Censors / 37
   Populists / 37
   Slavophiles / 38
   Westernizers / 38
   Indeterminates / 39

5. CORE TEXTS / 41

Selections from "Regulations on the Press: The Reign of the Sovereign Alexander II, April 1865" / 41

Vissarion Belinsky, "A Letter to Gogol" / 51

Selections from Nikolai Dobrolyubov, "What Is Oblomovism?" / 57

From Gleb Uspensky, "A Village Diary" / 63

Selections from Alexander Herzen, *The Bell* / 71

Selections from Nikolai Chernyshevsky, "The Aesthetic Relations of Art to Reality" / 81

Selections from Elena Andreevna Shtakenshneider, *Diary and Memoirs (1854–1886)* / 85

Pyotr Lavrovich Lavrov, "Foreword to the First Edition" and "Letter One: Natural Science and History" in *Historical Letters* / 94

Nikolai Nikolaevich Strakhov, "Comments on Contemporary Literature" / 99

Selections from Fyodor Dostoevsky, *The Diary of a Writer* / 102

Selections from Prince Vladimir Petrovich Meshchersky, *Recollections* / 109

Selections from Leo Tolstoy, *Anna Karenina* / 116

Fyodor Dostoevsky, "The Grand Inquisitor" / 123

Acknowledgments / 137

Appendix: Russian Names / 139

Notes / 141

Bibliography / 147

Illustrations

FIGURES

Map of St. Petersburg, 1893 / 9

Table of contents in the *Russian Messenger* 133 (January 1878) / 23

Title page of the *Messenger of Europe* 2 (1876) / 25

TABLES

1. Schedule and assignments due for a standard game / 32
2. Schedule and assignments due for a compressed game / 33

> # Russian Literary Journals, Dostoevsky, and Tolstoy in St. Petersburg, 1877

1 Introduction

BRIEF OVERVIEW OF GAME

In *Russian Literary Journals, Dostoevsky, and Tolstoy in St. Petersburg, 1877,* students with roles as editors, writers, or social activists explore the intersection of literature and politics through literary journals. These "thick journals" contain a range of materials, including both serial novels and nonfiction work, sometimes with a political subtext meant to escape the attention of censors. Writers must contend for publication space in literary journals while navigating the politics of censorship and authoritarianism. Amid the intellectual divides of Populists, Slavophiles, and Westernizers, these authors must find allies to help them achieve their publication and political goals. Editors, on the other hand, seek to uphold their publishing goals and meet the censors' approval. They have the power to decide whose articles and novels to publish. Work from major writers like Fyodor Dostoevsky and Leo Tolstoy will certainly be their first choice, but pieces from minor writers will also be reviewed. Social activists will attempt to shape everyone's political views through debate, pamphlets, and essays.

Authors have the option of writing in a variety of styles: poetry or prose, feuilletons, literary criticism, or historical or political essays. Each writer's work will be presented at Elena Shtakenshneider's literary salon, followed by discussion and negotiations for publication. Themes include the relationship between art and social issues; the role of women; access to education; the Russian Orthodox Church; and means for achieving political and social change.

While each author struggles to find a journal to publish their writing, each editor must sell enough copies and subscriptions to ensure the journal's survival. An unsuccessful journal will shut down, but a successful journal will shape Russia's literary and political future. The editor of the surviving journal will have a chance to meet with Tsar Alexander II and persuade him to either create a constitutional monarchy, maintain the strength of the monarchy and the Russian Orthodox Church, or restructure the country's political and social systems.

PROLOGUE

January 1877

I splurged on a carriage to take me from my editor's office by the train station to my house at the other end of Nevsky Prospect. I am, after all, soon to be a published writer. After so many rejections, copying my work over and over to show different editors or ask acquaintances to pass along, what a joy to finally have my own editor! I can feel my heart pounding, flying into my throat, and my hands and feet are tingling. I haven't been paid, of course. First-time authors rarely receive any compensation. But if I am successful, in the future, I will be paid. I needed to take the carriage so I could hurry home and begin work on the next chapters of my novel, *The Train to Petersburg*. I don't want to give anything away, but my work consists of a series of stories about female figures on the train traveling to St. Petersburg for very different reasons and how their lives overlap. My novel will include all classes of women, those working in factories as well as the nobility. The train was one place they came together, albeit in different cars. My editor seemed uninterested in politics, one way or another. "This journal focuses on stories that are well written, but entertaining, captivating. Your story about the connection between the Princess and her maid is charming, just what I like," he said. He probably thought stories about women, especially ones written by a woman, were safe. I didn't want to anger him and lose my opportunity to see my words in print, but I plan to describe the tensions between classes. I am still figuring out the best way to approach this topic so both my editor and the censors will approve.

I arranged my skirts across the seat, allowing the ribbons to peek out from underneath my heavy coat. The carriage bounced along the cobblestones, past the Passazh, the four-story department store with expensive hats, fans, and other fine clothing. Once I was a paid writer, I could afford one of the fine garments at the Passazh. Looking to the other side of the street, to the Our Lady of Kazan Cathedral, I remembered not everyone had money for carriages or embellished dresses, but they dreamed of other things: an apartment, food, or just a decent night's sleep. The Cathedral Square was quiet, but at the courthouse today, the trial for the people, mostly factory workers, who demonstrated in this very spot last December is starting. Many demonstrators had been arrested—not only by the police but also by passersby, and nearby merchants, who jumped in to quell the parading workers with their signs of "Liberty." I heard that the organizers escaped, but the ones who were arrested were treated brutally, beaten before being taken away. Even the women who were demonstrating were treated roughly, bruised from getting hit and shoved.

As we continued down the street, past the majestic St. Isaac's Cathedral, the driver turned a corner and stopped in front of my apartment. I pulled some coins out from my black fur muff to pay him and scurry inside. Even after the short ride, my eyes were watering from the cold, and I could feel the snowflakes on the tips of my eyelashes when I blinked.

The apartment was warm, thanks to our servant Masha, the windows sealed against drafts and the stove sending out waves of warmth. She helped me unwrap my frosted coat and hung up my hat and muff, before setting out some food for me. She placed some bread, boiled meat, and cabbage salad on the dining room table. I could barely swallow the tea, much less eat, with my stomach flying up into my heart from excitement.

"Did Ivan Petrovich mention when he would be home?" I asked.

"He said he had appointments this evening and would arrive home late, Natalia Alekseevna."

I nodded. This meant, since it was Tuesday, that I was free to go to Elena Shtakenshneider's salon. I enjoyed my husband's company, but I did like to go out in society by myself, free to talk with whomever about whatever I wanted. Despite my independent streak, I wasn't one of those short-haired women concerned about the woman question. Luckily for me, my husband's work as a clerk often kept him out late.

The hour was early, much too early to arrive at the salon. I decided to keep on the dress that I'd worn to meet with the editor and sat down to read. The January edition of *Russian Messenger*, a thick journal, had arrived from Moscow. The essay on "The University Question: Shortcomings in the Current Condition of Our Universities" intrigued me, but I was anxious to read the latest installment of Tolstoy's *Anna Karenina*. I could only pray that readers would find my work equally captivating.

Later that evening, I walked to Elena Shtakenshneider's. The temperature was cold, nearly ten degrees below freezing, but we hadn't had much snow this year, so the ground was dry. I entered her home, surveying the large open room. There were some familiar faces but no one I knew well. Dostoevsky sat on a plush brown couch, looking straight ahead with a stony glare while a young man in a coat with sleeves stopping inches above his wrist talked into his ear. I had seen Dostoevsky at Elena Shtakenshneider's before, though we'd never been introduced. I'd never dreamed of conversing with him. His writing was too penetrating, his face too austere. Not just Dostoevsky's, but everyone's mood seemed somber tonight. Perhaps we all were thinking of the trial taking place for the demonstrators this week. Regardless of one's politics, the increased frequency of demonstrations and the bringing of dissenting voices to trial would change all of our lives.

Two young women approached the piano, one sitting down to play and the other standing to sing. The music was lighthearted and made the atmosphere a bit more cheerful. I moved over to the samovar for a cup of tea and a cake. I usually knew several other guests at the salon and spent hours chatting about the latest journals with them. But this evening, I didn't recognize anyone, so I stepped back near the wall to observe the room, finally free from working to find editors or sympathetic authors to help me get published. As the women's music ended, someone shouted out, "Let's have a reading! Dostoevsky, read Pushkin for us!" He shook his head slightly and continued to glare sullenly, apparently not even flattered by the request. I had never heard him give a reading despite both our regular visits to the salon, but everyone always gushed about his animated and compelling recitations of poetry. The young man speaking to Dostoevsky jumped up and strode to the center of the room, standing in front of the piano. "Pushkin's 'The Bronze Horseman,'" he announced.

I saw Dostoevsky raise his eyebrows—disapproval or skepticism, perhaps? The young man began, his voice flowing over the room like a deep river:

> A wave-swept shore, remote, forlorn:
> Here stood he, rapt in thought and drawn
> To distant prospects. Broad and chartless
> The river ran, along it borne
> A lonely skiff, rough-hewn and artless.
> Darker against the marshy green
> Of moss-grown banks appeared some mean
> Log huts: the poor Finns' habitation;
> And forests which had never seen
> The mist-veiled sun's illumination
> Were live with whispers.
> And he thought:
> "From here the Swede is ill-protected:
> A city on this site, to thwart His purposes, shall
>   be erected.
> For here we may, by Nature blessed,
> Cut through a window to the West
> And guard our seaboard with conviction."[1]

The powerful poem, speaking of Peter the Great's fateful decision to build his city on this very spot, reverberated through the room and stoned us all into silence. I can't swear it, but the edges of Dostoevsky's mouth spread outward, almost in a smile. Finally, one person started to clap, then the entire room burst into applause. The young man tugged on the cuffs of his shirt, blushing as he quickly moved out of the center of the room. I saw him walking toward me, to the samovar. Despite his inspiring reading, I was not any more interested in talking to him than Dostoevsky was. Suddenly eager to see my husband and share the news of my upcoming publication, I gathered my things and headed home, hoping to arrive there first and greet him at the door.

BASIC FEATURES OF REACTING TO THE PAST

This is a historical role-playing game. After a few preparatory lectures, the game begins, and the students are in charge. Set in moments of heightened historical tension, it places you in the role of a person from the period. By reading the game book and your individual role sheet, you will find out more about your objectives, worldview, allies, and opponents. You must then attempt to achieve victory through formal speeches, informal debate, negotiations, and conspiracy. Outcomes sometimes differ from actual history; a debriefing session sets the record straight. What follows is an outline of what you will encounter in Reacting and what you will be expected to do.

Game Setup

Your instructor will spend some time before the beginning of the game helping you understand the historical context. During the setup period, you will use several different kinds of material:

- The game book (what you are reading now), which includes historical information, rules and elements of the game, and essential historical documents.
- A role sheet, which provides a short biography of the historical person you will model in the game as well as that person's ideology, objectives, responsibilities, and resources. Some roles are based on historical figures. Others are "composites," which draw elements from a number of individuals. You will receive your role sheet from your instructor.

Familiarize yourself with the documents before the game begins and return to them once you are in role. They contain information and arguments that will be useful as the game unfolds. A second reading while in role will deepen your understanding and alter your perspective. Once the game is in motion, your perspectives may change. Some ideas may begin to look quite different. Players who have carefully read the materials and who know the rules of the game will invariably do better than those who rely on general impressions and uncertain memories.

Game Play

Once the game begins, class sessions are presided over by students. In most cases, a single student serves as some sort of presiding officer. The instructor then becomes the GM (the "game master" or "game manager") and takes a seat in the back of the room. Though they do not lead the class sessions, GMs may do any of the following:

- Pass notes
- Announce important events
- Redirect proceedings that have gone off track

Instructors are, of course, available for consultations before and after game sessions. Although they will not let you in on any of the secrets of the game, they can be invaluable in terms of sharpening your arguments or finding key historical resources.

The presiding officer is expected to observe basic standards of fairness, but as a fail-safe device, most games employ the "podium rule," which allows a student who has not been recognized to approach the podium and wait for a chance to speak. Once at the podium, the student has the floor and must be heard.

Role sheets contain private, secret information that you must guard. Exercise caution when discussing your role with others. Your role sheet probably identifies likely allies, but even they may not always be trustworthy. However, keeping your own counsel and saying nothing to anyone is not an option. To achieve your objectives, you must speak with others. You will never muster the voting strength to prevail without allies. Collaboration and coalition building are at the heart of every game.

Some games feature strong alliances called factions. As a counterbalance, these games include roles called indeterminates. They operate outside of the established factions, and while some are entirely neutral, most possess their own idiosyncratic objectives. If you are in a faction, cultivating indeterminates is in your interest, since they can be persuaded to support your position. If you are lucky enough to have drawn the role of an indeterminate, you should be pleased; you will likely play a pivotal role in the outcome of the game.

Game Requirements

Students playing Reacting games practice persuasive writing, public speaking, critical thinking, teamwork, negotiation, problem solving, collaboration, adapting to changing circumstances, and working under pressure to meet deadlines. Your instructor will explain the specific requirements for your class. In general, though, a Reacting game asks you to perform three distinct activities:

Reading and writing. What you read can often be put to immediate use, and what you write is meant to persuade others to act the way you want them to. The reading load may have slight variations from role to role; the writing requirement depends on your particular course. Papers are often policy statements, but they can also be autobiographies, battle plans, newspaper articles, poems, or after-game reflections. Papers often provide the foundation for the speeches delivered in class. They also help to familiarize you with the issues, which should allow you to ask good questions.

Public speaking and debate. During a game, almost everyone is expected to deliver at least one formal speech from the podium (the length of the game and the size of the class will determine the number of speeches). Debate follows. It can be impromptu, raucous, and fast paced. At some point, discussions must lead to action, which often means proposing, debating, and passing a variety of resolutions. GMs may stipulate that students must deliver their papers from memory when at the podium, or they may insist that students begin to wean themselves from dependency on written notes as the game progresses.

Wherever the game imaginatively puts you, it will surely not put you in the present. Accordingly, the colloquialisms and familiarities of today's college life are out of place. Never open your speech with a salutation like "Hi guys" when something like "Fellow citizens!" would be more appropriate.

Always seek allies to back your points when you are speaking at the podium. Do your best to have at least one supporter second your proposal, come to your defense, or admonish inattentive members of the body. Note passing and side conversations, while common occurrences, will likely spoil the effect of your speech, so you and your supporters should insist upon order before such behavior becomes too disruptive. Ask the presiding officer to assist you. Appeal to the GM as a last resort.

Strategizing. Communication among students is an essential feature of Reacting games. You will likely find yourself writing emails, texting, attending out-of-class meetings, or gathering for meals. The purpose of frequent communication is to lay out a strategy for achieving your objectives, thwarting your opponents, and hatching plots. When communicating with fellow students in or out of class, always assume that they are speaking to you in role. If you want to talk about the "real world," make that clear.

Controversy

Most Reacting games take place at moments of conflict in the past and therefore are likely to address difficult, even painful, issues that we continue to grapple with today. Consequently, this game may contain controversial subject matter. You may need to represent ideas with which you personally disagree or that you even find repugnant. When speaking about these ideas, make it clear that you are speaking in role. Furthermore, if other people say things that offend you, recognize that they too are playing roles. If you decide to respond to them, make it clear you are doing so using the voice of your role. If these efforts are insufficient, or the ideas associated with your particular role seem potentially overwhelming, talk to your GM.

When playing your role, rely on your role sheet and the other game materials rather than drawing upon caricature or stereotype. Do not use racial and ethnic slurs even if they are historically appropriate. If you are concerned about the potential for cultural appropriation or the use of demeaning language in your game, talk to your GM.

Amid the plotting, debating, and voting, always remember that this is an immersive role-playing game. Other players may resist your efforts, attack your ideas, and even betray a confidence. They take these actions because they are playing their roles. If you become concerned about the potential for game-based conflict to bleed out into the real world, take a step back and reflect on the situation. If your concerns persist, talk to your GM.

Counterfactuals

While this game is historically based, a few details have been changed.

All these writers probably never met in the same room at the same time. Although many of them did know each other, Dostoevsky and Tolstoy never met. They were, however, familiar with each other's work.

Tolstoy did not live in St. Petersburg; he lived primarily in Yasnaya Polyana. He did visit Moscow. After visiting St. Petersburg in 1861, he didn't go back until 1878.

Nekrasov, editor of *Notes of the Fatherland,* and the censor Alexander Nikitenko both died from old age by 1878. They would have most likely been too ill to attend any literary salons in 1877.

Katkov resided in Moscow. The *Russian Messenger* was published in both St. Petersburg and Moscow.

Praskovia Ivanovskaia was stationed in Odessa, not St. Petersburg in 1877. She did, however, attend the Alarchinsky courses in St. Petersburg in the early 1870s, hold Populist values, and work as a typesetter, as she does in this game.

2
Historical Background

CHRONOLOGY

1849 Members of the radical Petrashevsky Circle, including Dostoevsky, are denounced. They are accused of reading Belinsky's banned "Letter to Gogol" and circulating copies of this and other banned works. They are sentenced to death. While they stand in front of the firing squad, the execution is stayed, and they are exiled to a hard labor camp in Siberia.

1855 Crimean War begins.
Nicholas I dies.
Alexander II's reign begins.
Repeals of Nicholas I's restrictions on travel abroad and the number of students attending universities.

1856 Peace of Paris ends Crimean War.
Coronation of Tsar Alexander II.

1857 Tolstoy's first trip to Western Europe.

1858 Treaty of Aigun signed, establishing much of the modern-day borders between China and Eastern Siberia, while giving Russia some access to the Amur River.

1859 Dostoevsky returns from Siberian exile.

1860 Treaty of Peking signed, giving Russia full control of the Primorye territory in Siberia. With these rights, Russia could access the sea directly through the Amur River, important for naval outposts and trade routes.

1861 Serfs emancipated by decree of Tsar Alexander II.

1863 *Russian Messenger / Russkii Vestnik* is founded by Mikhail Katkov.

1864 *Zemstvo* reforms and judiciary system reforms.

1866 First assassination attempt on Alexander II. Dostoevsky completes *The Gambler* and *Crime and Punishment*.

1867 Assassination attempt on Alexander II in Paris.
Russia sells Alaska to the United States for $7,200,000.

1869 Tolstoy completes *War and Peace*.

1870   Municipal reform reorganizes town governments according to many *zemstvo* practices.

1872–73   Three Emperors' League established (Russia-Romanovs, Germany-Hohenzollerns, Austria-Hungary–Hapsburgs).

1874   Alexander II visits London.

Thousands of young radicals asked to leave their studies in Switzerland and return home. They take jobs in villages, some hoping to start a revolution.

1875   Three Emperors' League collapses over issue of Turkey and the Balkans.

Rebellion sweeps the Balkans, beginning with insurrection against Turkish rule in Herzegovina and Bosnia.

1876   Intellectual and political group Land and Freedom gains momentum as a Populist revolutionary group.

In spring, St. Petersburg intelligentsia stage a large protest at Chernyshev's funeral, a student who died in prison.

Turkey violently suppresses uprising in Bulgaria and declares war on the Porte of Serbia and Montenegro, causing a sense of Pan-Slavism to spread from intellectual circles to the Russian public. Five thousand Russian volunteers, from all social classes, join the Serbian army.

Revolutionary ideology takes hold among the St. Petersburg working class. On December 6, workers, joined by intelligentsia, stage a demonstration on Kazan Cathedral square. Police arrest many of the protestors, but the organizers, who were also involved with Land and Freedom, escape.

1877   In April, Russia declares war on Turkey.

THE FOUNDATION OF SAINT PETERSBURG

There is nothing to compare with Nevsky Prospect, at least not in St Petersburg, where it embodies everything. There is no end to the glamour of this street—the belle of our capital city! I know that not one of its pale and high-ranking residents would exchange Nevsky Prospect for the world. Not only the twenty-five-year-old who sports a splendid moustache and a remarkably well-tailored frock coat, but even the individual with white bristles sprouting from his chin and a head as smooth as a silver dish, even he is ecstatic about Nevsky Prospect. As for the ladies! Oh, Nevsky Prospect is even more of a delight to the ladies. Indeed, is there anyone it doesn't delight? The moment you step onto Nevsky Prospect there is an air of pure conviviality.
—Nikolai Gogol, "Nevsky Prospect"

This young man belonged to a class of people which constitutes quite a strange phenomenon among us, and he belongs as much to the citizens of St Petersburg as a person who appears in our dreams does to the real world. This exceptional social group is very uncommon in this city, where everyone is either a civil servant, a merchant or a German craftsman. He was an artist. Is that not indeed a strange phenomenon? A St Petersburg artist! An artist in the land of snow, an artist in the land of the Finns, where all is wet, plain, level, pale, grey and misty. These artists have nothing in common with Italian artists—proud, passionate like Italy itself and its sky—on the contrary, these are mostly kind, meek folk, timid, easy-going, quietly enjoying their art, drinking tea with a couple of friends in small rooms, modestly discussing their favourite topic and showing no interest at all in anything else. They are always inviting some old beggar woman to their place, making her sit for a good six hours in order to commit her pathetic impassive countenance to canvas.
—Nikolai Gogol, "Nevsky Prospect"

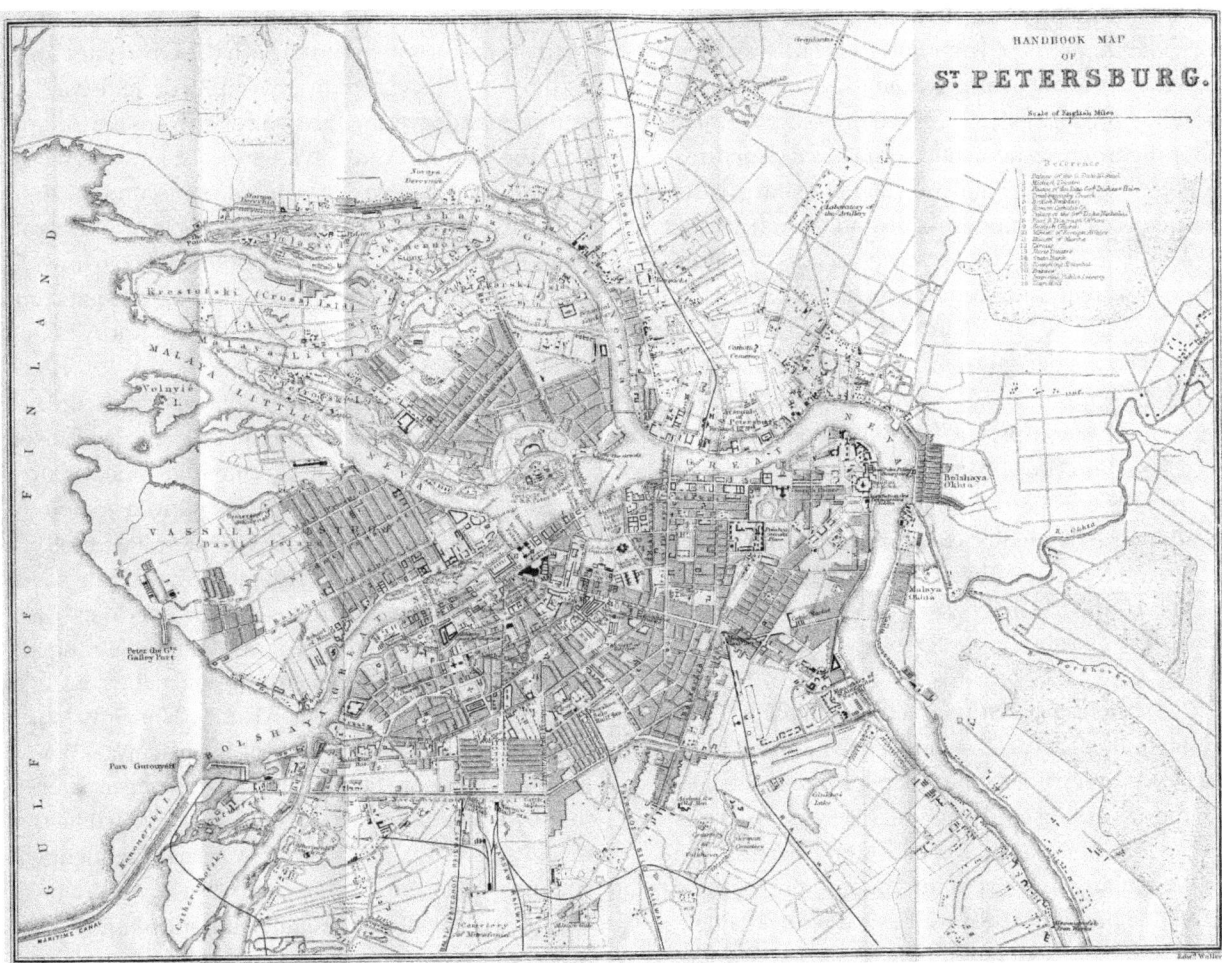

Map of St. Petersburg in John Murray, *Handbook for Travellers in Russia, Poland and Finland* (Paris 1893), University of Texas Libraries.

The heat in these streets was stifling. The stuffiness, the jostling crowds, the bricks and mortar, scaffolding and dust everywhere, and that peculiar summer stench so familiar to everyone who cannot get away from St. Petersburg into the country, all combined to aggravate the disturbance of the young man's nerves. The intolerable reek from the public houses, so numerous in that part of the city, and the sight of the drunken men encountered at every turn, even though this was not a holiday, completed the mournfully repellent picture.
—Fyodor Dostoevsky, *Crime and Punishment*

All these new ideas, reforms, theories, have penetrated to us in the provinces, but to see the whole picture and see it clearly, one must be in the capital.
—Fyodor Dostoevsky, *Crime and Punishment*

According to legend, Peter the Great handpicked the site of his new city, St. Petersburg, marching through the swamplands with his troops until he planted a flag at the perfect location. In reality, Russian troops built a fort along the Neva River, prized for its access to the Gulf of Finland and waterways around Northern Europe, that would allow them to defend the territory from invaders. The city grew up around the fort, later named the Peter and Paul Fortress. Peter, however, was not present when the troops began building the fortress; he arrived only six weeks later, after the troops established some basic structures.[1]

Peter the Great established St. Petersburg with the particular goal of modernizing and westernizing Russia. The city's plans increased access to Europe, opening direct water routes from the Neva to Western Europe. Visually, its canals and classical architecture mimicked the designs in Amsterdam, Venice, and Paris. Geographically, however, the swamps and marshes that comprised the space provided few, if any, benefits. The absence of raised ground and the many inlets and streams caused frequent flooding. Trade routes were blocked six months out of the year, when the Neva was frozen. Most of the water was brackish, and the fresh water was contaminated with parasites, like giardia, which plague the water supply to this day.

Constructing the city was a difficult, life-consuming process. The landscape required builders to drive sixteen-foot-long oak piles into the soil to support building construction. Peter the Great ordered tens of thousands of serfs and prisoners to St. Petersburg to assist in the construction of the city. The men had only the most basic tools available, although many used their bare hands to dig and move soil. Peter's willingness to expend lives in the construction of St. Petersburg enabled it to be one of the fastest built cities in history. A mere nine years later, in 1712, Peter the Great proclaimed St. Petersburg the new capital of Russia.

Many of the nobility and bureaucrats were required not only to relocate to the capital city but also to pay for their new homes. Most resented this obligation when the city was first built, as they saw Petersburg as a provincial outpost and considered Moscow the true center of Russian culture. But the lower classes who traveled to St. Petersburg for work considered living and working in the new capital a life-changing opportunity. As more people moved to St. Petersburg, the city transformed into a cosmopolitan and manufacturing center. The Industrial Revolution brought a wealth of factories, workshops, and markets that sprouted up in both the city center and its outskirts, disregarding any zoning or land-use controls, and layering the skyline with smoke. Along with the factories came in an increase in workers, many of whom were emancipated serfs, and inexpensive, crowded housing. The city was rumored to be the unhealthiest in Europe, but it was also one of the larger cities. Residents were numbered at 300,000 in 1800 with the population swelling to approximately 1 million in 1890.[2]

St. Petersburg was the main administrative and primary military center, but industrial growth caused the increase in populations. In the mid-nineteenth century, St. Petersburg factories employed 20,000 workers, half of them in textiles. By 1867, factories employed 34,500 workers with 36 percent of them in textiles, 29.4 percent of them in metalworking, 10.4 percent in paper and printing, and the remaining in chemical, food, and tobacco; tanning, tallow, and soap; and other miscellaneous areas.[3] In comparison to other Russian cities, specifically Moscow, St. Petersburg had more factories that employed greater numbers of people. For example, in 1913, each factory in St. Petersburg employed an average of 213 people, whereas in Moscow the average was 147. Additionally, in St. Petersburg, foreigners financed more of these companies, especially in the field of electrical equipment, led by the German-owned Siemens and Allgemeine Elektrizitat Gesellschaft establishments.[4]

While factories employed many people, they did not provide the only job opportunities in the capital city. People worked in various areas of commerce, including the Nevsky Prospect department store Passazh and markets with stalls selling manufactured and handmade goods. Gostiny Dvor, also on Nevsky Prospect, had 500 outlets and sold higher quality items, whereas the Aleksandrovsky Rynok facing the Fontanka Canal had 768 stalls. Apraskin Market, nearby on Sadovaia Street, had nearly 500 stalls and sold furniture, produce, and clothing. Other jobs outside of factory work included construction, driving, and domestic servanthood. All these jobs were more than an eight-hour day, with people laboring up to fifteen or nineteen hours during the summer months when St. Petersburg stayed light for most of each day.[5]

The growing merchant class comprised a middle class of sorts. These bankers and brokers were not always accepted by the rest of St. Petersburg society with its established elite classes of nobility, high ranking bureaucrats, and military officers. The upper class enjoyed a rich and lavish lifestyle of theater, music, and balls that started late in the afternoon at a private home and lasted until the early morning, with a banquet partway through the evening to sustain the attendees.[6]

RELIGION IN RUSSIAN CULTURE

Influenced by the European Enlightenment, Peter the Great not only reshaped Russian cities and the military but also restructured the Russian Orthodox Church according to Western ideals. Christianity came to Russia in the tenth century, when Prince Vladimir of Kievan Rus selected Russian Orthodoxy among Islam, Judaism, Catholicism, and Orthodoxy as the nation's new official religion, replacing pagan practices. From this point, official Russian religious structures answered to the Greek patriarch even after Constantinople fell to the Turks in 1453 and the center of Eastern Christianity came under the rule of the Muslim sultan. In 1589, an independent Moscow Patriarchate of the Russian Orthodox Church was founded, separating Russia from Eastern Orthodoxy. In 1721, Peter created the Holy Synod, an administrative institution, to lead the church. This reorganization placed the church squarely under the tsar's rule, as the head of the Holy Synod was a layperson that the tsar appointed.

Most Russians identified with Russian Orthodoxy in terms of its cultural practices, rather than having a deep knowledge of its theology. Practitioners valued **tserkovnost'**—rituals, altars, relics, and icons that were interwoven into their daily lives, whereas doctrine and theoretical teachings that rationalized and analyzed life were secondary. This sense of community arose not simply from visiting the shared space of a church but from participating in the shared practices and rituals with religious meaning that occurred outside of the church.

Tserkovnost': Often translated as "churchism" or "ecclesiasticism," Russians use this word to refer to their attachment to religious practices. There are many philosophical discussions on the meaning of "tserkovnost," but the concept generally includes: "1) a nondiscursive, experientially based knowledge as a way of relating to the holy; 2) a reverence for and sense of the sacred and its expression in symbolic (liturgical

HISTORICAL BACKGROUND 11

forms); and 3) a communal orientation or collective spirit that sees the faith as a fundamental shared phenomenon."[7]

These community-building practices included a range of traditions. The Orthodox calendar, for example, gave structure to many practitioners' lives, providing guidelines for marriage, burials, and naming babies. The church's practices also influenced a variety of social events for different social classes, ranging from official ceremonies for nobility and the military to baptisms and funerals at local parish churches. Icons depicting both individual saints and biblical scenes were particularly powerful symbols that connected religion to many aspects of people's lives, informing them of sacred stories and rituals.

Within the church itself, there was a social hierarchy that included both monks and priests, with some positions requiring one to be highly trained while others required only rudimentary skills. In the nineteenth century, the role of monasteries and *startsy*—church elders—became prominent in the church. *Startsy* were especially popular among well-educated clerics dedicated to the teaching of church fathers. Many *startsy* resided in monasteries throughout Russia. Although monasteries were not new to Russia, they grew in popularity throughout the nineteenth century. One-third of Russian monasteries in the late nineteenth century were less than 100 years old. Optina Pustin, a monastery outside of Moscow, attracted many believers, including both the educated and the illiterate and women as well as men. Both Dostoevsky and Tolstoy, among many other writers, traveled to Optina Pustin to consult with the elder there, who later became known as Saint Ambrose. Many believe that Dostoevsky based the monastery in *Brothers Karamazov* on Optina Pustin and Father Zosima on Saint Ambrose.

While Russian Orthodoxy was the predominant religion in Russia, there were several religious minorities. Most notably, within the Russian Empire there was a Jewish population restricted to living in the **Pale of Settlement** on the western edges of Russia. Living culturally and physically separate lives from Russian Orthodox Christians, Jews spoke a different language—Yiddish—and relied upon the Jewish laws in the Talmud and Shullan Arukh to guide their daily rituals. They celebrated the Sabbath on Saturday instead of Sunday and wore dark, modest clothing.[8] Up until the 1860s, Jews received permission to live in St. Petersburg only if they served in the military or the police force. Part of Alexander II's Great Reforms (see more below) allowed Jews, especially merchants, artisans, and students, to cross the boundaries of the Pale of Settlement. As the economy modernized and public transportation advanced, the Jewish population became less fixed, as people migrated and integrated into larger Russian cities, such as St. Petersburg and Moscow. Some learned Russian and dressed to blend into big city life. Others went as far as forging passports and changing their names in order to assimilate more fully into Russian culture.

Pale of Settlement: a region created in 1791 by Russian empress Catherine the Great in an attempt to keep Jews out of Russia. The borders changed over the years, but the area occupied all of present-day Belarus, Moldova, and Lithuania, large parts of Ukraine and Poland, and some territory now in Western Russia. The Pale was no longer enforced after the Russian revolution of 1917.

In the 1860s and 1870s, as Jews migrated away from the Pale of Settlement into different parts of the Russian Empire, crown rabbis were tasked with documenting vital events such as birth, marriages, and deaths. The information was then transferred to the provincial governor for documentation and preservation in the state archive. But the recordkeeping was inconsistent in St. Petersburg and Moscow, as well as in other regions of the empire, making population statistics inaccurate and complicating the state's ability to govern.

THE CRIMEAN WAR AND ALEXANDER II'S GREAT REFORMS

Despite the diversity of organized religions in the Russian Empire, many Russians connected Orthodoxy to their sense of national identity. In fact, the perception of Russian Orthodox practitioners as Russian nationals, regardless of their actual residence, led to the Crimean War in October 1853. This conflict between Russia and an alliance of France, Britain, and the Ottoman Empire erupted over the rights of Christian minorities in the Holy Land, which was then controlled by the Ottoman Empire. Concerns about religious rights of Russian Orthodox practitioners and the expansion of the Muslim empire initiated the war. At the same time, Nicholas I was concerned with protecting trade routes through the Black Sea and markets in the Near East. Prince Menshikov traveled to Constantinople at the request of Nicholas I to advocate for the Orthodox citizens. The negotiations failed as the Turks refused to permit Russian interference, and Prince Menshikov returned home. Nicholas I attempted compromise after his emissary's departure, but Turkey declared war, forming an alliance with France, Great Britain, and Austria.

The allies focused the majority of their military efforts on the Crimean Peninsula. A decisive moment came in 1854 during a yearlong battle at the Russian naval base in Sevastopol, on the Black Sea. Notable literature from both sides describes the war—Leo Tolstoy, then an artillery officer, published *Sevastopol Tales* (1855), whereas Alfred Lord Tennyson wrote "Charge of the Light Brigade" (1854). The prolonged battle also influenced nursing, as Florence Nightingale established a new style of war hospital and worked with Russian and French women to modernize nursing practices. Russian forces abandoned Sevastopol in September 1855, blowing up the military weapons and fortifications. The following year, Nicholas I died. Alexander II took over the throne and quickly moved to make peace. As part of the Treaty of Paris, Russia agreed to make the Black Sea a neutral zone without any navy or fortifications. Russia also ceded its position as protectorate of the Orthodox followers in the Ottoman Empire.

The Crimean War humiliated Russia, highlighting the country's need for military, political, and social reform to match the standards of other powerful nations. After ending the Crimean War, Alexander II gradually addressed these concerns through his Great Reforms. While many believed that Alexander II was as conservative as his father, he was actually very moderate. His series of reforms ended feudalism and reshaped the judicial system, local assemblies, the military, and censorship, all of which democratized Russia politically and economically.

Liberating the serfs in 1861 made a powerful impact on Russian society. In the first half of the nineteenth century, the number of serfs shrank from 58 percent of the population to 44.5 percent in 1860. In fact, serfdom became unfeasible for economic reasons: Gentry had accumulated enormous debts, and some landholders struggled to feed their serfs. Political groups from opposing perspectives—Slavophiles, Westernizers, Populists—all supported the abolition of serfdom for moral reasons. In fact, when Alexander II decreed the emancipation of serfs, no one opposed this decision. Groups did debate, however, the most effective means of emancipation. The gentry argued for a reform structure that would benefit them—some wanted more land and others wanted money for freeing their serfs. Alexander II insisted that serfs receive some of the land they worked.

Although freed, serfs continued to work within their peasant communes. The government reinforced the commune system when reappropriating the land after emancipation, selling the property that serfs worked on to the commune rather than to individual workers. The government then provided loans to be repaid over a period of forty-nine years so the freed serfs could purchase the land.

Local assemblies, or *zemstvos*, underwent dramatic transformation in 1864 through Alexander II's reforms. Under the new system, members of towns, peasant communes, and individual landowners indirectly elected members, without any class restrictions, for the district assemblies. Delegates to the larger provincial assembly were then selected from these district representatives. The zemstvos made decisions on how to handle a variety of issues at the local level: education, healthcare, road development, and emergency procedures. Later, in the 1870s, Populists in particular sought involvement with the zemstvos as they hoped to make connections with the peasant communes. Zemstvos were especially successful regarding healthcare and education, with the assemblies voting to provide free medical care and surgery starting in the second half of the nineteenth century, well before most European countries.

Alexander II's judicial reforms of 1864 transformed the courts from a secretive class-based procedure into an independent branch of government with public hearings. Under Nicholas I, there were a variety of courts for different types of crimes. Cases were often passed from one court to another, dragging out for years, even decades. Those with connections could take advantage of loopholes in the law, while citizens unable to pay bribes or call upon acquaintances didn't have these options. The accused and the judges never saw each other, as all evidence in a court case was presented to the judge in written format. Nearly half the judges were illiterate and depended upon the court secretary to read the evidence and write up the decision.[9] Under the new system, a justice of the peace oversaw minor hearings while a jury tried grievous offenses. Radicals viewed these reforms as politically significant, as the open trials allowed for greater freedom of expression. Socially, the new judicial system allowed a new class of lawyers to emerge. To serve on a jury, citizens needed to meet a specific set of criteria. Those who met the criteria were included on a list compiled by September 1 each year by the Special Provisional Commissions for each district. Only citizens between the ages of twenty-five and seventy, who had resided in the district for at least two years, were included on the list. Priority was given to justices of the peace, judges, and civil servants, as well as elected officials.[10]

The **Nechaev Trials** in 1869 were the first public political trials under the new system, but later trials, such as the "Trial of 193" and "The Fifty," received significantly more public attention. The first group of 193 people was tried for demonstrating in front of Kazan Cathedral. The second group of fifty was part of the "Going to the People" movement and was charged with attempting to educate the rural population. The trial of "The Fifty" made an impression on the Russian public, especially radicals, as the accused spoke eloquently about the inhumane prison conditions they endured before coming to trial. Their testimony brought these problems into the public light, shocking the educated public with the government's severe response to a seemingly harmless crime.

Nechaev Trials: The court case accused Sergei Nechaev and some accomplices of killing a member of his organization, the revolutionary group "The People's Retribution." Nechaev fled to Switzerland, but sixty-seven members of his organization were tried and convicted. In 1872, the Swiss police extradited him to Russia, where he was finally tried and sentenced to twenty years in the Peter and Paul Fortress. He died while imprisoned in 1882.

CENSORSHIP UNDER ALEXANDER II

The zemstvos and the judicial system reforms allowed citizens to speak more openly in public, but restrictions on free speech remained. The many intelligentsia who traveled to Europe noticed a palpable difference in an atmosphere where they did not fear arrest or exile for voicing their opinions. Russian citizens needed to guard their spoken words, never knowing who might be listening, and all written materials were still subject to the censors' approval before publication. In the beginning of the nineteenth century, under Alexander I, censorship did not pose overbearing restrictions on Russian publications. In fact, many nineteenth-century Russians viewed censorship as a set of principles to guide public debate rather than restrictions on their speech and thought. Writers, literary critics, and professors dedicated to supporting and shaping the future of Russian journalism and literature often served as censors. Toward the middle of the century, under Nicholas I, radical groups such as the Decembrists in 1825 and the Petrashevsky Circle in 1848 were arrested and either executed or exiled for speaking out against the tsar and the Russian political system. In response to the radical activity, Nicholas I tightened up censorship starting in 1848, bringing in "the age of censorship terror."[11] Under the stricter policies, a secret committee, led by Dmitri Petrovich Buturlin (1790–1849), reviewed all published materials and punished any censors, editors, and authors who failed to follow the secret rules. Censors, knowing they were being watched, read between the lines and blocked the publication of any nuance that aroused their suspicions.

Tsar Nicholas I's goal was to avoid giving authors rules to navigate and work around—and he succeeded, causing confusion among the literary world until his death in 1855.[12]

While periodicals faced an uphill battle during Nicholas I's reign, struggling to figure out what they could and could not publish, these publications resumed their prominence and rapid development in the mid-1850s when Alexander II took the throne.

Less than a year after Alexander II ascended, he eliminated the Buturlin Committee in 1855 and eased some of the censorship rules and regulations.[13] In particular, Alexander II permitted all journals and newspapers to report on the government's domestic and foreign policies that occurred prior to 1855. But the content nonetheless remained under the government's control, as journals were not allowed to publish articles debating current affairs and were expected to show support for the government's initiatives.

In 1863, Alexander Golovnin, head of the Ministry of Public Instruction, proposed revamping the censorship process. Censors throughout the empire were overwhelmed with the amount of material to review. Thirty-nine censors assisted by twenty-three clerks reviewed 6,669 periodical issues and 1,884 books in 1863. Another fifteen censors and six clerks read thousands of books imported from abroad.[14] After two years of deliberation, the state announced the **Temporary Rules of 1865**, which dictated publishing and remained in effect until 1905 (selections from these rules are included in the game book readings).

Temporary Rules of 1865: Under this set of laws, journals moved from a prepublication review to a postpublication review with censors evaluating work after printing and before distribution. Any censorship concerns would go to court, where the government and the editor could both argue their cases. Many editors, however, remained skeptical of this new system and continued to show the manuscripts to censors before publishing.

Changes to military service, the last of Alexander II's Great Reforms, took place in 1874. Under the new system, all Russians, not just the lower classes, were required to serve in the military. The length of required service was shortened from twenty-four years to six, and a military reserve was created. Illiterate recruits received an elementary education, filling gaps for schooling in rural areas.

LITERACY IN THE NINETEENTH CENTURY

The changes under Alexander II were significant, but Russia was still not on equal footing with Western Europe politically, economically, or socially. Providing education for young men in the military improved literacy, as there wasn't any systematic schooling provided throughout Russia in the nineteenth century. Upper-class families hired tutors, but children from lower-income families were taught through an unstructured combination of churches and the state. Many rural families pulled their sons out of school to help with planting and harvesting crops. Their daughters were often not sent to school at all, as they were needed at home year-round to help with cooking, sewing, cleaning, and caring for younger children. The 1897 census estimated the literacy of Russia at 21 percent. In the 1860s, literacy was at about 6 percent in rural areas, while industrialized areas, such as Moscow Province, boasted a literacy rate of 70 percent.[15]

THE POPULISTS

Through the 1870s, as the Populists became increasingly influential, they argued for personal freedom for both genders and all classes. Peter Lavrovich Lavrov (1823–1900) and Nikolai Konstantinovich Mikhailovsky (1842–1904) shaped much of the Populist thinking. In Lavrov's *Historical Letters* (1870), he explored the role of the individual in history, arguing that "critically thinking individuals" would bring about social progress, including social and economic justice.[16] Mikhailovsky, a critic and editor connected with *Notes from the Fatherland*, wrote "What Is Progress?" (1873), arguing that social progress depended upon the social development of each individual person. The whole person could develop in a just society, which, for Russia, would be based on the socialist principles of the *mir* (peasant commune).[17] As the Populists strengthened, tensions with the tsar's regime increased, and the government ordered all Russians studying abroad in Switzerland to return home in 1873, hoping to remove them from the influence of radical Russians who had emigrated. Many of the returning students moved to rural areas, serving as teachers or doctors. Some sought to contribute to society, while others plotted to bring about revolution. The students attempting to radicalize the peasants as part of the Going to the People movement, encouraged by Lavrov, were largely unsuccessful. Being from urban middle- and upper-class families, the students didn't realize that the peasants were devoted to their tsar, whom they saw as a beneficent father figure. The peasants, in fact, reported and helped arrest the Populist students attempting to spread socialist ideals.

In contrast, urban factory workers were open to socialism and the idea of revolution. In the second half of the nineteenth century, St. Petersburg was in the process of transforming into an industrial center. Factories produced guns, locomotives, and warships. The number of smokestacks grew along Schlüsselburg Road, emitting clouds that clung to the skyline. By the 1870s many rural workers and former serfs traveled to St. Petersburg searching for jobs in these factories and living on the outskirts of town, in the growing slum area. Living conditions were dismal for this class, with workers housed in cellars polluted with standing water and human waste. Running water was rare, found in only one of fourteen buildings in the Aleksandro-Nevskaia borough, while the Vyborg section had only one spigot to serve fifty-one buildings.[18]

Along with crowded and worsening living conditions came other problems, including crime and disease. By 1870, nearly 7,000 infants were abandoned each year, 100 people were arrested daily for crimes ranging from panhandling to murder, and 30,000 Petersburg residents per year contracted syphilis. City water came from the Neva and its tributaries, which were polluted with factory waste. People were cautioned against drinking unboiled water. Well-off families did not have access to cleaner water, but they did have access to better food options, such as imported French wines and other delicacies and confections. Restaurants along Nevsky Prospect or at the luxurious Europa or Astoria hotels, where elite citizens would dine, all cost many times what a factory worker made.[19]

In the early 1870s the working-class Populist movement existed on a very small scale in St. Petersburg. But there was a constant flow of revolutionary philosophy in the city, and after 1874, these ideas expanded. Instead of university students trying to educate others about socialism, the workers themselves took the initiative to educate their fellow laborers and organize meetings or demonstrations. The intelligentsia considered the urban workers and peasants as part of the same class. But these groups saw themselves differently. The workers generally looked down upon peasants who hadn't made any attempt to educate themselves or improve their living conditions. The St. Petersburg workers shaped the agenda of the Populist group Land and Freedom and planned strikes throughout St. Petersburg in the 1870s. In a manifesto written in 1876, they stated their goals to return agricultural lands to the workers and break up the Russian Empire. The manifesto read:

Our demands can be brought about only by means of a violent revolution. The methods to prepare this and bring it about are, according to us: (1) Agitation—to be carried out both by word and above all by deed—aimed at organizing the revolutionary forces and developing revolutionary feeling (revolts, strikes; in general, action is in itself the best way to organize revolutionary forces). (2) The disorganization of the State. This will give us some hope of victory, in view of the strong organization which will be created by agitations in the early future.[20]

St. Petersburg workers followed through with their plans for action on December 6, 1876, when they, along with intelligentsia, staged their first protest on Kazan Cathedral square. They asked a clergy member to arrange for a funeral service to give the demonstration an appearance of legality. Although they initially believed 2,500 people would participate, only a few hundred workers arrived. They were, however, joined by many intellectuals and students who supported their fight for economic justice and social equality in Russia. Police arrested many of the protestors, but the organizers, who were also the founders of Land and Freedom, escaped. At the trial, the court separated the workers and the intelligentsia, assigning them disproportionate sentences. Workers received light sentences, were ordered to retreat and repent in monasteries, or were exiled to Siberia. Intellectuals, on the other hand, were sentenced to ten to fifteen years of hard labor, considered a heavy punishment at the time. Because the intelligentsia were so influential, the court punished them more harshly in an attempt to thwart the Populist movement.

Between 1873 and 1877, authorities arrested 1,611 revolutionaries. The statistics show that the majority of those arrested were young, upper-class men with university educations. Of those arrested, 425 went on to trials. Of those tried, only 42 were more than thirty years old. In terms of social class, 147 were nobles, 90 were clergy, 58 were sons of high officers, 11 were soldiers, 65 were peasants, and 54 were bourgeois.

Most were either Russian or Ukrainian, while 23 were Jews, 10 were from the Caucuses, and 6 were foreigners. While this was a rather homogenous group, the numbers indicate the beginnings of a movement that included a range of social classes, such as clergy and peasants, a result of the Going to the People movement.[21]

VIOLENCE AND REVOLUTION

While the Populists of Land and Freedom believed they could bring about change through a combination of empowering the working class and disorganizing the state with demonstrations and strikes, other revolutionaries pushed for terrorist acts—specifically the assassination of the tsar and other public officials—to achieve their radical goals. From their point of view, liberalism, Alexander II's Great Reforms, and other constitutional reforms were the enemy, as they slowed down social progress and kept the Russian Empire from being rebuilt.[22]

In the 1860s, Nikolai Ishutin, a university student and charismatic leader, led one particularly impactful terrorist group in Moscow called Organization. This group concealed Hell, a smaller group with secret membership. The purpose of Hell was to direct Organization in their terrorist goals of assassinating members of government and land-owning classes, ultimately planning to assassinate the tsar. Ishutin falsely represented this group as the only Russian section of a European Revolutionary Committee that planned to assassinate monarchs throughout Europe. The randomly selected assassins of Hell were required to follow a specific code of behavior that Ishutin designed. The assassins were required to socialize outside of revolutionary circles, even reporting people to the secret police to maintain their cover. On the day of the assassination, they were supposed to disfigure their faces to avoid recognition. After carrying out the assassination, they would poison themselves. A note in their pocket would explain the reasons for their actions. After one assassination, another member of Hell would continue the group's efforts.[23]

Dmitri Karakozov, a member of Hell, grew impatient with planning and decided to take matters into his own hands. On April 4, 1866, as Alexander II took his regular afternoon walk in the Summer Gardens, Karakozov took aim and shot at the tsar. Karakozov failed to hit the tsar or anyone else. While Alexander II climbed into his carriage and went about the rest of his day, Karakozov was chased down and tackled by a young peasant.[24] After being arrested, Karakozov (who had not followed any of Ishutin's protocols) gave the police the address of Ishutin's apartment in Moscow. Ishutin and all the members of Organization were arrested. Karakozov was executed for his crime, while Ishutin and the other terrorists were exiled to Siberia.[25] Although this group did not succeed in their goals, radical Populists throughout the 1860s and 1870s perpetuated the idea that terrorism was a necessary step in building a socialist Russia.

THE WOMAN QUESTION

Women, regardless of class, had similar obligations of marriage and motherhood placed upon them and struggled for independence and access to education. Although Russian women retained their rights to property even after marriage, both laws and cultural norms required women to obey the men in the family, whether that was a husband, brother, or father. They were expected to marry, bear children, and obey their husbands. Noblewomen often bore more children than their peasant counterparts, having children every sixteen to twenty-four months. The increase is attributed to noblewomen's better health and tendency to use a wet nurse, rather than breast feed their own babies, a practice that offered some birth control, albeit an unreliable option.[26]

Starting in the 1860s, the woman question became a popular topic of debate among both men and women in intelligentsia circles. Legally, both sexes were nearly equal, but social traditions dictated women's employment and education opportunities. Women, for example, could inherit and own property, and marriage law did not favor one sex over the other. But permission from a husband or father was needed for a woman to seek employment, while a male representative cast the ballot for women when voting for officials. The radical group of nihilists, a term popularized in Ivan Turgenev's *Fathers and Sons* (1862), focused on individual freedom and encouraged women to pursue their dreams, whether that meant getting an education, avoiding marriage, or seeking employment. Nihilist ideals were more reactionary than philosophical as they didn't have any intellectual underpinnings but simply rebelled against social conservatism. Nihilists did have a noticeable appearance: male nihilists often had long hair and wore soiled clothes, while women cut their hair short and wore plain clothes without crinolines and parasols.[27] In their debates, writers, many of them male, advocated for women's rights and the freedom to pursue their personal goals.

Influenced by this discussion, many young noblewomen left home, striking out on their own as they sought jobs or traveled abroad, particularly to Switzerland, where they could enroll at universities. Many of these same women later became involved in the revolutionary movement.[28] Their level of activity was impressive on its own but even more so considering the challenges women faced in getting access to higher education and their subjugation to male family members. The women involved in revolutionary activities did, however, participate primarily in supporting roles, rather than as leaders. For example, Sergei Nechaev, one of the first radical leaders tried under Alexander II's reformed judicial system, didn't support equality as most liberals and radicals did. In fact, he openly showed his bias against women, writing in his Revolutionary Catechism that some women were most useful when working as slaves of men, while others should follow rather than lead, and a select few women, when pushed, would either become true revolutionaries or die.[29]

In the 1870s, women received increased opportunities for education, shaping both their thinking and their ability to influence revolutionary circles. Starting in 1859, women were allowed to audit lectures at Russian universities. In 1869, the government initiated the Alarchinsky courses in St. Petersburg for women interested in non-degree-granting coursework in higher education. These courses became an opportunity for young women to befriend and network with like-minded thinkers, who later worked together to support Populists and revolution. In 1872, Moscow State University opened a program to train women as secondary school teachers, the Ger'e Higher Women's Courses, with 140 women enrolling each year. In 1878, University Courses for Women, based on the Ger'e model, opened in Kazan, Kiev, Moscow, and St. Petersburg, providing the first accredited four-year, university-level courses for women in Europe.[30]

The educational and political path of Sophia Lvovna Perovskaya illustrates the challenges and the dreams of a female revolutionary from the intelligentsia. Born into an aristocratic family, her father held several prestigious political positions, serving as the vice-governor of Pskov and Tarida provinces and the governor of St. Petersburg. Her traditionally minded father demanded conventional behavior. When the family moved to St. Petersburg, Sophia enrolled in the Alarchinsky courses and joined a reading circle of other young, liberally minded women. The group's discussions focused on women's rights: independence from men, political involvement, and freedom from domestic duties, such as marriage and childrearing. Several women, including Sophia, opposed romantic relationships, as they believed this bond prevented them from acting independently and pursuing political goals. The group of women didn't limit their studies to political philosophies, though, also taking classes in mathematics. Sophia, apparently, was especially talented in this field.

A domineering father, Lev Perovsky considered his daughter's behavior inappropriate and threatened to lock her in the house and keep her from associating with her friends. As a result, she left home, living first with her friends in St. Petersburg, then moving to Kiev, and eventually returning to St. Petersburg when her father finally agreed to provide her with the identity papers necessary for her to live on her own. He refused to allow her back into his house.

Inspired by her political readings, Sophia was determined to take action. She learned how to give vaccines from a country doctor, then traveled to rural areas persuading peasants to be vaccinated for smallpox. Once gaining their trust, she attempted to share revolutionary propaganda with them. Like so many who had participated in the Going to the People movement, she found this endeavor fruitless. Once she vaccinated as many people as possible, she returned to St. Petersburg and rejoined her reading group, now known as the Chaikovsky Circle. She and her friends began to realize their goals from their Alarchinsky days, living in a coed apartment for practical, not romantic, purposes. In 1874 the Third Department, the Russian secret police, learned of the Chaikovsky Circle's revolutionary agenda and arrested its members, including Perovskaya. She did not stay imprisoned long, though, as her father used his money and connections to bail her out. Although she briefly reconciled with her father, she sought her independence and got trained as a medical aide with the intention of avoiding future revolutionary activity.

Fate, however, had other plans in store for her. She appeared as a defendant at the Trial of 193, which tried nearly 4,000 intelligentsia for their participation in Going to the People. Although Sophia was acquitted, she could not ignore those who were prosecuted and staged several successful rescues. The police caught up with and arrested her, sending her by train to St. Petersburg for imprisonment and trial. Perovskaya escaped by drugging the guards with poisoned tea and jumping off the train; she then caught a different train, continuing on to St. Petersburg to reconnect with revolutionary circles while living undercover.[31]

THE SLAVOPHILES

Slavophile nationalists countered the Populist movement, highlighting the monarchy and Russian Orthodoxy as central to Russian national identity, with some advocating for a Pan-Slavic nation that unified Russia with her Slavic neighbors in Eastern Europe. This turn toward Europe represented a shift in Russian foreign interests, which had focused on expansion into Siberia and Central Asia since the end of the Crimean War. In 1867, Russia founded Vladivostok, serving as Russia's outpost on the Pacific Ocean, and sold Alaska and the Aleutian Islands to the United States, realizing they could not defend this territory. In 1875, Russia ceded all the Kurile Islands to Japan in exchange for full control of Sakhalin Island.[32] In Central Asia, General Mikhail Cherniaev seized Tashkent in 1865. Russia continued the campaign in Central Asia, forcing states to give up their own foreign policies in order to preserve internal autonomy.[33]

Meanwhile, nationalist movements grew among Balkan Slavs in the 1870s as they began to protest Turkish rule, restrictions on education, and increased taxes. The Turks responded powerfully and violently, putting down rebellions in Bosnia and Herzegovina in 1875 and quelling an uprising in Bulgaria in 1876. Later that year, the Turks declared war against Serbia and Montenegro. Many Russians, particularly proponents of Pan-Slavism, supported the Slavic nations' efforts to break away from the Turks. They donated money, collected funds, gathered weapons and other supplies, and volunteered to fight in their armies. Alexander II sought a diplomatic solution, as did the British. A European Conference, held in Constantinople, attempted to negotiate peace, but the Turks rejected the Russian and British proposals.[34] As a result of this failure, on April 24, 1877, Russia declared war on Turkey. In the official declaration of war, Alexander noted that the war was both necessary and moral, defending Christians residing in Turkey, preserving Russian honor, and ultimately, creating peace between nations.[35] Russians, many of whom embraced Pan-Slavism, showed their support for their Balkan neighbors. Both nobility and peasants volunteered to fight in the Serbian army, led by the same General Mikhail Cherniaev who'd established his name in Central Asia. Although he had retired from the military in 1874 and taken a position as editor and publisher of the daily newspaper *Russian World*, his dedication to the Pan-Slavic movement motivated him to return to battle, albeit against Alexander II's wishes.

LITERARY JOURNALS AND OTHER PUBLICATIONS

Throughout these debates in the nineteenth century, literary and popular publications played an important role in entertaining and educating Russians. The publishing industry expanded rapidly in the second half of the nineteenth century, growing from 2,085 published titles in 1860 to 7,366 in 1887.[36] Whereas there were only 16 daily and biweekly periodicals and 92 weekly ones in 1860, these numbers increased to 79 and 121, in 1870, and 126 and 124, in 1880, respectively.[37] Changes in technology made this possible, as powered machines replaced hand presses in the 1860s and 1870s, while other advances made it possible to bind pamphlets and books in-house rather than sending them out or letting readers do this themselves.[38]

Literary journals with their political and historical articles, as well as serialized novels, generally appealed to an educated crowd in the middle and upper classes. Writers and editors involved in journals formed a tight community, often praising or attacking each other through published works, while socializing in literary circles. Memoirs and autobiographies were also a popular genre throughout the nineteenth century, and many women writers published in this area, although often under a pseudonym to protect themselves against any social retaliation from friends or family members mentioned in the text or from those who didn't approve of women publishing. While not everyone had access to higher education, any literate person could pick up a journal and absorb articles on history, poetry and novels, and opinion pieces.

At the same time, many other types of publications were available. Popular literature intended to appeal to lower-class people grew as literacy increased in Russia. Publishers in this field tended to be entrepreneurial and willing to take risks, as were the urban and rural peddlers who carted their publications and sold them throughout Russia. Literature of the Lubok was based on religious and folkloric prints with sayings underneath them, telling tales of saints' lives,

ОГЛАВЛЕНIE

ТОМА СТО ТРИДЦАТЬ ТРЕТЬЯГО

ЯНВАРЬ.

	Стр.
Происхожденiе человѣка по Геккелю. *И. Ѳ. Цiона*.....	5
Княжна ***. Трагедiя въ октавахъ. *А. Н. Майкова*.....	72
Критика отвлеченныхъ началъ. Гл. X—XI. *В. С. Соловьева*.....	103
Очерки современной исторической литературы. *Р.*.....	133
Въ Сербiи 1876—1877. Записки добровольца. Гл. I—III. *В. В. Яшерова*.....	18
Скрежетъ зубовный. Романъ. Часть первая. *В. Г. Авсѣенка*.....	226
Турцiя и турецкiе дѣятели. *Н. В. Щербаня*.....	308
Никшичъ. (Изъ Ненадовича.) Стихотворенiе. *Н. Боева*	366
Не Горахъ. Разказъ. Глава. LIX—LXIV. *Андрея Печерскаго*.....	370
Царевичъ Алексѣй. Трагедiя въ четырехъ дѣйствiяхъ. *Д. В. Аверкiева*.....	408
Точность никогда не излишня. (По поводу главы объ устройствѣ учебныхъ заведенiй въ *Полицейскомъ правѣ* профессора Бунге.) *X*.....	469
По поводу романа Альфонса Додэ „Набабъ". *Г*.....	487

Table of contents in the *Russian Messenger* 133 (January 1878). Works include "In Serbia 1876–1877: Notes from a Volunteer," by V. V. Yasherov, and "On the Mountains: A Story," by Andrei Pechersky.

military expeditions, and characters from fairy tales while appealing to readers in both rural and urban settings. Illustrated magazines, detective serial novels, and daily newspapers were also widely produced and read by people from all classes.[39]

Literary journals, like all publications, were subject to censorship rules and the Temporary Rules of 1865 discussed earlier. Typically, each literary journal had one censor assigned to review and supervise its publication. But literary journals were not examined as closely as political journals, and for this reason, many writers turned to literary journals to share their political views. Vissarion Belinsky (1811–48) played a crucial role in the formation of Westernizer values. He was dismissed from the University of Moscow after three years and never received a degree. He primarily educated himself through readings and social circle discussions. Not long after leaving the university, he published his "Literary Musings," considered the beginning of Russian intelligentsia journalism. Belinksy argued for a new, modern type of writing that reflected real life and promoted social values, shaping the realistic school of literature in Russia. While abroad in 1847, and free from Russia's censorship, he wrote his famous letter in response to writer Nikolai Gogol's recent defense of Russian autocracy, serfdom, and the church in *Selected Passages from Correspondence with Friends* (1847). Belinsky's call for writers to be leaders against nationalism and for human dignity became a fundamental essay for progressive activists. More journalist and critic than creative writer, Belinsky's "Letter to Gogol" and other writings were a powerful influence on the Russian public, supporting both Westernizers and radicals, questioning tradition, and encouraging efforts to improve the world.[40]

While Alexander II relaxed publication rules, there were still restrictions. Writers, following Belinsky's example, traveled to Western Europe where they could publish politicized works in the free press. Others, like the prominent journalist **Alexander Herzen** (1812–70), emigrated to Europe altogether. Herzen left Russia in 1847, living first in Switzerland and eventually settling in London. The Russian government alternately ordered him to return home and forbade him from reentering Russia; even overseas the Third Department constantly followed him. In London, he developed his career as a revolutionary journalist. He published his Russian language journals, *The Polar Star* and *The Bell* (1856–67), at his own expense and ensured they were distributed widely, albeit illegally, throughout Russia. Like everyone else, Russian officials (even the tsar) read *The Polar Star* and *The Bell*, claiming it was necessary to know the enemy.

Alexander Herzen: A moderate socialist, acquainted with and influenced by Marx and Engels, Herzen argued for reforms in the Russian government, especially emancipation of the serfs, and critiqued public officials, but he never supported the violent actions of extreme radicals. Herzen's style was as revolutionary as his content. His journals introduced Russian language editorials, as Herzen opened each issue with a summary, examination, and response to current events in Russia. While he needed to rely on others for on-the-ground information about Russia, Herzen managed to investigate situations and collect data that allowed him to expose misconduct among Russian officials.

Herzen's incendiary writings were just one element making up a hotbed of debates and ideas in the 1860s. During this decade, in the age of Alexander II's Great Reforms, writers, intellectuals, and activists publicly discussed emancipation of the serfs, education for women and the poor, and sexual freedom. Nikolai Gavrilovich Chernyshevsky's (1828–89) ideas were at the heart of many radical, nihilist discussions in the early 1860s that argued for atheism, faith in humanity and science, socialism, and equal rights for women and people from all social classes. A writer for the journal *The Contemporary*, he was first recognized for his master's essay "The Aesthetic Relations of Art to Reality" (1853), where he set the groundwork for realist creations, claiming beautiful art portrays beautiful nature. In 1859, Chernyshevsky took the role of coeditor for *The Contemporary*, along with Nikolai Alekseevich Nekrasov (1821–78). As the journal became increasingly radical, well-known liberals such as Ivan Sergeyevich Turgenev (1818–83) and Ivan Aleksandrovich Goncharov (1812–91) disassociated themselves from the journal and were replaced by newer, unknown writers like Mikhail Evgrafovich Saltykov-Shchedrin (1826–29). Under Nekrasov, who was a talented poet, and Chernyshevsky, *The Contemporary* became the widest circulating journal in nineteenth-century Russia. But its left-leaning tendencies and willingness to publish politically oriented work attracted the attention of censors. In 1862, the journal was closed for eight months, and Chernyshevsky was imprisoned for his involvement in student and worker protests. While in the Peter and Paul Fortress, Chernyshevsky wrote his novel *What Is to Be Done?* (1863), which tells the tale of a young woman embracing her independence, told from a socialist perspective. When *The Contemporary* reopened in 1863, it published the novel, passing by two censors who each thought the other would suppress it.[41] Chernyshevsky's work influenced an entire generation of radicals, but his exile to Siberia in 1864 meant he was no longer involved with journalism or publications.

Amid these social debates of the 1860s, there was a shift among literary journals. Some journals survived,

Title page of the *Messenger of Europe* 2 (1876).

like *Notes from the Fatherland*, open since 1818, while others closed down, most notably *The Contemporary* and *Russian Word*, both in 1866. Their closures paved the way for new journals, such as *Messenger of Europe*, revived in 1866, while *Russian Messenger*, opened in 1856, increased in popularity. *Time*, another new journal, was founded and edited by Fyodor Dostoevsky and his brother Mikhail in 1863.[42] *Time* didn't follow any political lines; rather, it promoted a mystical Populism that drew on both Slavophile values and ideals of the people. In 1863, *Time* was suppressed for an article on the Polish question written by Nikolai Nikolaevich Strakhov, a philosopher and critic. The Dostoevskys argued the censor had misread the article, and eventually, they were allowed to reopen a new journal, *Epoch*. The second journal, however, never thrived or received the number of subscribers *Time* had. Dostoevsky, having gone bankrupt, closed it in 1864.[43] By the 1870s, the publication of Russian journals became more stable.

During this time, the second half of the nineteenth century, realistic fiction dominated the Russian literary scene. The roots of Russian realism are found in some of the literary greats of the early nineteenth century: Nikolai Gogol, Mikhail Lermontov, and Alexander Pushkin, novelists and poets, as well as Vissarion Belinsky. Realist literature explored the range of human emotions and experiences, covering the wealthy and the impoverished, the evil and the virtuous, and everything in between. The writing style had a journalistic quality, consisting of simple and straightforward sentences from the perspective of a neutral observer. Narrative structure was often less relevant; instead, detailed character development or exploration of ideas made up the content of a realist novel.[44] Settings tended to be contemporary, as authors could only observe and portray familiar subjects.

Tolstoy and Dostoevsky were among the most popular writers, although Dostoevsky received much of his recognition in the early twentieth century, well after his death. Tolstoy was a well-established and highly regarded author by the 1870s, having completed his historical *War and Peace* (1865–69). When he began this novel, he planned to write about the Decembrists but then decided he needed to study the previous generation in order to understand the revolutionary group. The success of *War and Peace* made Tolstoy attempt another historical novel, going even further back to Peter the Great. But the novel never came together, and in 1873, Tolstoy began writing *Anna Karenina*. Because the writing went so well for the first several months, Tolstoy initially planned to publish the first part of his novel as a book, rather than in a journal. Mikhail Katkov, editor of *Russian Messenger*, agreed to publish the first part of *Anna Karenina*. Katkov had in that same year printed 3,600 copies of Tolstoy's collected works in an eight-volume set, 1,000 of which sold in the first year. In the end, however, Tolstoy decided to allow *Russian Messenger* to publish the novel in a serial format as this was more lucrative, and he needed the funds to purchase land near one of his estates. The first installments appeared in 1875 and were eagerly read by the public. Katkov was less enthusiastic, asking Tolstoy to tone down the description of Vronsky and Anna's sexual relationship, but the author refused.[45] By early 1877, the majority of the novel had been published, with the exception of the concluding chapters and the epilogue.

In 1871, Dostoevsky returned to Russia after having lived abroad for several years to avoid his creditors. All between 1865 and 1871, he published *Notes from the Underground*, *Crime and Punishment*, and *The Idiot*. For four of these years, from 1867 to 1871, he was living abroad in genteel poverty. Once on stable financial footing, he returned home and paid for the publication of *The Possessed* (1873), inspired by Nechaev's revolutionary circle. The novel received excellent reviews. Dostoevsky remained involved with the publication of journals during the time, taking the position of editor for Prince Meshchersky's *The Citizen* in 1873 and also starting his own publication *A Writer's Diary* in 1876.[46] Toward the end of the decade, Dostoevsky began plotting out *Brothers Karamazov*, although the first section was not published until early in 1879.

Alongside the stories of journals opening and closing, writers were striving to finish and publish works, find both financial and artistic success, and negotiate political views with the rules of censorship. Such are the lives of all the characters in this game.

3
The Game

MAJOR ISSUES FOR DEBATE

Through this game, you will explore the role of the writer in society and the responsibility of art to social issues. Can literature and art shape politics? Is there a point where aesthetic ideals and political values intersect? Or does the idea of "art for art's sake" provide greater benefits to the artist and their work?

The discussion of the role literature plays in society will draw in many of the political debates of the time. These debates will address the monarchy, education, religion, the role of women in society, and Western European influences. Players may share their opinion on these topics either explicitly or implicitly. A feuilleton or analytical essay will allow characters to speak openly about their opinions on a topic. Writers who wish to speak directly about political concerns cannot necessarily speak freely, especially if they want to critique the current system—the Third Department, spies, and censors are paying attention and can report you to the authorities. A story or poem offers characters the opportunity to address issues directly or indirectly, or they could ignore social issues altogether. This brings the writers back to the predominant question of the game: Are art and social issues connected?

Specifically, in playing this game, you will learn to do the following:

1. Analyze Russian literature from the late nineteenth century, placing it in a historical, political, social, and/or aesthetic context and use this analysis in classroom debates, speeches, and essays.
2. Express familiarity with prominent figures, including writers, editors, and activists, in late nineteenth-century Russia to strategize and achieve victory objectives.
3. Demonstrate an understanding of major philosophies in prerevolutionary Russia—Slavophilism, Populism, and Westernization—in persuasive arguments.
4. Understand the challenges of making your voice and opinion heard in an autocracy and learn to

negotiate these restrictions to achieve your character's goals.
5. Identify social and political conditions that lead to revolutionary movements.
6. Write across a variety of styles, including traditional essays, journalism, and creative writing.
7. Produce well-organized and confident speeches (no reading from laptops; only notecards may be used).

RULES AND PROCEDURES

Meetings

The game consists of two different types of classes: Literary Evenings and Publication Days. Each class opens with a five-to-ten-minute meeting with the editors, during which editors and writers will have the opportunity to discuss publications and philosophies. Authors and editors should also reach out to the censors to determine their position on literary journals. At this time, editors may set up contracts with authors for work they think will contribute to their journal's success.

Literary Evenings will be hosted in the home of Elena Shtakenshneider, famous for her St. Petersburg literary salon. These social events are a time for authors and critics to present works in progress, such as feuilletons, poems, or short stories, with the hope of impressing the public or editors. Critics may comment on recently published works or on relevant social issues. These are somewhat counterfactual events in that not all these writers knew each other or socialized—Dostoevsky and Tolstoy, for example, were never introduced, although they once attended the same musical performance and certainly read each other's work. But the salons do accurately reflect that many writers, with different backgrounds and perspectives, came together to discuss political, philosophical, and literary ideas.

Elena Shtakenshneider will moderate these discussions. To speak, one simply needs to stand up at their seat. Anyone who stands up will have the opportunity to speak, but Elena Shtakenshneider has the authority to ask people to finish up speeches so everyone's voice may be heard or to interrupt a heated discussion to keep her salon peaceful and orderly.

On **Publication Days**, editors will present journals. A censor must approve all the material prior to publication. Editors may suffer consequences for publishing unapproved content. On Publication Days, everyone will be able to review the journals and subscribe to their favorites. These subscriptions determine a journal's success (or failure). Each journal purchase costs 1 coin, whereas a subscription costs 3 coins. After receiving all the orders, the editors must pay printing costs, which are the number of members in each faction plus three. If a journal survives, there will be a die roll to determine its success.

Objectives and Victory Conditions

The primary goal of each editor is to produce a successful journal that reflects their aesthetic or political values. Writers of both fiction and nonfiction need to seek out editors who will publish their work. While there are natural alliances between certain editors and writers, they won't always agree. Censorship provides an additional layer of complexity, especially for politicized writing. Radicals must find a way to comment on society without attracting the attention of censors or the Third Department, the tsar's secret police.

Each editor will produce one to two editions of their journal, depending on the game length. Successful journals will sell quickly and receive subscriptions. Journals with not enough subscriptions or enough "popularity" (based on a die roll) will shut down. Editors of popular journals will have the power to support a particular cause, which could be anything from purchasing weapons to funding a new literary journal.

The editor of the most successful literary journal and its associated writers win the game. Each journal must receive enough subscriptions or sell enough individual copies to pay printing costs. Even if the journal meets its financial obligations, a die must be rolled to determine if the journal received enough positive reviews from the public to survive.

The winning editor has a chance to accomplish any political objectives by earning a meeting with the tsar. The editor must write a persuasive memo to the tsar with the signatures of all members in the related faction and at least two indeterminates.

Each character will also have the opportunity for an individual win or loss, as role sheets give specific objectives that must be met.

Special Events

Starting a New Journal

For a variety of reasons, some characters may want to start a new journal. They may have a unique creative vision, or they may have trouble publishing in one of the existing journals. Whatever the reason, any character may start a new journal provided they can demonstrate to the GM that they have the necessary support. To start the journal, the editor must make a down payment for the publishing cost. This is typically half the amount due at the time of publication. Consult with the GM for the exact cost.

Arrests

Writers and editors who challenge authority could be thrown into jail at the Peter and Paul Fortress, like the Decembrists or Dostoevsky and members of the Petrashevsky Circle in the first half of the nineteenth century. Prisoners may not pitch their work to editors; journals that publish the work of prisoners will be scrutinized.

Game players may also be thrown in jail for violating particular rules of the game. For example, breaking character or referencing current events is cause for imprisonment. This happens at the game master's discretion.

Trials

Anyone accused of conspiring against the tsar or propagating radical views will be subject to a trial by jury to determine guilt or innocence. As engaged members of Russian society, you have the power to call for a trial. To do this, provide the game master with evidence of the crime. If approved, the GM will ask for volunteers to temporarily take on the roles of prosecutor and defender, as none of the characters in this game are lawyers. Speeches during the trial may be eligible to count as one of the required assignments in your role. The GM will also assemble a jury by randomly drawing names from the approved list of eligible jury members (Jews and women may not be included). To avoid serving as a member of the jury, you may pay someone to serve in your place, although they must be eligible.

Assassination Attempts

If the radicals accrue enough influence and resources (defined in their role sheets and by the GM), they may make an assassination attempt on conservatives or nobility. Nobility, such as Tsar Alexander II, are not characters in the game but may still be assassinated. A die roll will determine the outcome of this attempt.

Coins

Each character starts with 1 ruble (1 coin) to spend. Characters may earn additional coins for especially successful readings or thoughtful comments or questions during Literary Evenings. Rubles may then be used to purchase a single copy of a journal (1 ruble) or to get an annual subscription (3 rubles). After printing copies of the journal and selling subscriptions, each editor will need to pay printing fees. The exact amount will be set by the game master (see Publication Day details for the formula). The remainder may be used to offer contracts to or simply pay the writers.

Violence

This is a tumultuous time in Russia with frequent protests, demonstrations, and acts of violence. Whenever these types of events occur, symbols or colors you are wearing may affect the outcomes. The double-headed eagle insignia shows support for Alexander II and his regime, whereas the Land and Freedom symbol shows support for Populists. Other factions or characters may ask you to show support for them by wearing particular symbols or colors.

Advice on Debating in Character

Each student brings their own worldview and set of beliefs to the game and their interpretation of their role sheet. When creating an argument, set aside your personal beliefs and represent the values outlined on the role sheet to the best of your ability. Some role sheets will ask students to argue in support of reprehensible ideas, espousing violence, misogyny, or xenophobia. If your role sheet asks you to make these arguments, quoting passages (appropriately cited, of course) from relevant documents in the game book is a good strategy—as it is in any situation. This also makes it easier to argue in support of issues that you personally disagree with and clearer to your audience that you are speaking in your nineteenth-century Russian role.

If listening to these arguments challenges you as a guest at the literary salon, remember that you are listening to a perspective from nineteenth-century Russia, not the personal beliefs of your peers. If appropriate for your role sheet, you might find it meaningful for your victory objectives to address these ideas while you are in character. In fact, including your opponent's perspective and pointing out its flaws is an effective means of building an argument, and this applies to all roles.

Confronting these difficult ideas helps us understand people's lives and the literature from this period. If you are finding any debate topics challenging for any reason, please consult with the game master. When the game ends, there will be a postmortem session when you can discuss difficult topics from the game and reflect on them from a contemporary perspective.

Tips for Analyzing Literature

While you likely have studied literature before, here are some suggestions for including literary analysis in a Reacting to the Past essay or speech:

- Summarize and describe the passage. Who are the characters, what is the setting, what events are happening, and what is the topic of conversation?
- Consider point of view. Who is the narrator? Is the passage written from a particular character's perspective? Does the narrator seem sympathetic or judgmental toward any characters?
- Make connections. How does this passage connect to the ideas of the game? Does it reference any philosophies described in the game book? What about historical events? Does it remind you of any speeches given during gameplay?

- Evaluate the language. You may be reading texts in translation, but the translator and the original author chose their words very carefully. Are there any specific terms mentioned? Is there any repetition of words or colors—perhaps different shades of blue like azure, turquoise, or navy? Are there particular types of images that repeat? For example, a countryside setting might have various descriptions of trees or grass to compare.
- Reflect on your character. After looking at the passage from your own perspective, review your role sheet and consider how your character might react to the text. Does it connect to any of their interests or goals?
- Quote phrases or sentences. In keeping with the adage "show don't tell," support your analysis with a few carefully chosen phrases or sentences from the text.

ASSIGNMENTS

Speeches

Most characters will give two formal speeches. Formal speeches may not be read word for word from a paper, phone, computer, or tablet. Two to three index cards, with some hints, are allowed. Typically, speeches will be a modified version of a writing assignment, lasting three to five minutes. Students who exceed their allotted time may be cut off by hostess Elena Shtakenshneider.

Publishing

Each student must publish two texts. One must be a review of a recently published work of fiction or poetry, commenting on its social relevance or aesthetic value. The second may be either a creative work or a historical or political essay. Each role sheet will provide further details.

Certain writers will have finished pieces they want to publish in journals. They may augment or delete parts of essays or novels when appealing to editors for publication. In this case, their "review" should detail the changes and underlying reasons.

Censors have the power to edit or even eliminate certain works.

Writings not selected for publication can circulate independently.

Journal Editors

Editors may appoint successful writers as coeditors to help publication. Their choices may steer the publication in a particular direction.

Editors may provide financial backing to writers to create their own publication.

Editors can edit selected articles and choose to publish certain chapters from a novel and not others.

Editors are liable for any legal issues connected with journals.

Each journal publication should include a letter from the editor in which the editor comments on the contents, highlighting important works and/or themes.

TABLE 1 Schedule and assignments due for standard game

Session (fifty-minute class)	Material	Assignments due
1. Introduction / game setup	Discussion of historical context.	
2. Introduction / game setup	Discussion of background readings.	
3. Introduction / game setup	Discussion of background readings.	
4. Meeting with editors / Literary Evening, May 1877	a. Informal discussion between authors and editors about publishing opportunities. b. Authors present works of fiction, feuilletons, or critiques of existing works. c. Debate themes: What is the role of religion in society? Should Russia continue or withdraw from the Russo-Turkic War?	Authors and critics present and make pitches for their work.
5. Meeting with editors / Literary Evening, June 1877	a. Informal discussion between authors and editors about publishing opportunities. b. Authors present works of fiction, feuilletons, or critiques of existing works. c. Debate theme: Should literature be for aesthetic purposes or social commentary?	Authors and critics present and make pitches for their work.
6. Meeting with editors / Literary Evening, July 1877	a. Informal discussion between authors and editors about publishing opportunities. b. Authors present works of fiction, feuilletons, or critiques of existing works. c. Debate theme: What are the rights of peasants and urban workers in society?	Authors and critics present and make pitches for their work.
7. Publication Day, August 1877	a. Journals published and sold. b. Censors must approve journals before publication. c. Subscription opportunities.	a. Editors present their journals. b. Censors present on publishing decisions. c. Authors and critics may respond.
8. Meeting with editors / Literary Evening, October 1877	a. Informal discussion between authors and editors about publishing opportunities. b. Authors present works of fiction, feuilletons, or critiques of existing works. c. Theme: the woman question.	Authors and critics present and make pitches for their work.
9. Meeting with editors / Literary Evening, December 1877	a. Informal discussion between authors and editors about publishing opportunities. b. Authors present works of fiction, feuilletons, or critiques of existing works. c. Theme: a trial or other topic (Elena Shtakenshneider or GM chooses).	Authors and critics present and make pitches for their work.

12. Meeting with editors / Literary Evening, January 1878	a. Informal discussion between authors and editors about publishing opportunities. b. Authors present works of fiction, feuilletons, or critiques of existing works. c. Debate theme: What social structure best serves Russia?	Authors and critics present and make pitches for their work.
13. Publication Day, March 1878	a. Journals published and sold. b. Censors must approve journals before publication. c. Subscription opportunities.	a. Editors present their journals. b. Censors present on publishing decisions. c. Authors and critics may respond.
14. Postmortem		

TABLE 2 Schedule and assignments due for a compressed game

Session (fifty-minute class)	Material	Assignments due
1. Introduction / game setup	Discussion of historical context.	
2. Introduction / game setup	Discussion of background readings.	
3. Introduction / game setup	Discussion of background readings.	
4. Meeting with editors / Literary Evening, May 1877	a. Informal discussion between authors and editors about publishing opportunities. b. Authors present works of fiction, feuilletons, or critiques of existing works. c. Debate theme: Should literature be for aesthetic purposes or social commentary?	Authors and critics present and make pitches for their work.
5. Meeting with editors / Literary Evening, October 1877	a. Informal discussion between authors and editors about publishing opportunities. b. Authors present works of fiction, feuilletons, or critiques of existing works. c. Debate theme: religion, the woman question, or workers/peasants.	Authors and critics present and make pitches for their work.
6. Meeting with editors / Literary Evening, December 1878	a. Informal discussion between authors and editors about publishing opportunities. b. Authors present works of fiction, feuilletons, or critiques of existing works. c. Debate theme: What social structure best serves Russia?	Authors and critics present and make pitches for their work.
7. Publication Day, March 1878	a. Journals published and sold. b. Censors must approve journals before publication. c. Subscription opportunities.	a. Editors present their journals. b. Censors present on publishing decisions. c. Authors and critics may respond.
8. Postmortem		

Most editors will give a version of their "letter from the editor" as a formal speech on Publication Days. This is their chance to interest their audience in its contents and "sell" their journal.

Censors

The censors will announce rules for publication. These rules may include certain ideas or words that they will not approve in publication. They may, of course, censor anything else as needed.

At the opening of each Publication Day, censors will give a speech describing their censorship choices.

4

Factions and Roles

FACTIONS

Populists

Most Populists are members of the revolutionary organization Land and Freedom, fighting for social justice and social equality in Russia. A socialist system will bring equal rights to all Russians, giving the emancipated serfs the opportunities for education and the freedom promised under the emancipation act. Starting in 1874, many young Narodniki, or Populists, joined the Going to the People movement. They dressed in peasant clothing and went out to the villages, hoping to educate peasants in reading and writing while learning the ideals of a simple and pure life. Some worked as cobblers, plowmen, fisherman—often getting fired because they weren't good at their jobs—while others served as doctors and teachers. From a revolutionary perspective, the movement was a massive failure. The peasants were loyal to the tsar and believed that he wanted to protect them and their interests. In fact, peasants who caught wind of subversive or revolutionary ideas were likely to report offenders to the authorities. After several years, many Populists, frustrated and disillusioned, returned home to the city with the goal of promoting the revolution on familiar territory. Those who stayed were not so lucky—the Third Department arrested nearly 4,000 Narodniki living in the provinces, attempting to keep them from spreading disquiet.

While many Populists argue that education of the public is the most important element for bringing about reform, there are rumors of an offshoot organization called The People's Will that seeks to reform Russia by assassinating the tsar and other powerful leaders, thus destroying the current political system.

Slavophiles

This group promotes peace and harmonious unity, the essence of Russian Orthodoxy, a monarchical leader, and communal peasant culture. Slavophiles are primarily conservative nobility. This ideology is not new; in the 1830s, the Slavophile philosophy emerged in opposition to the trend of Westernizers. At the time of its origins, though, the group sought to preserve certain elements of Russian culture that they considered native, such as Russian Orthodoxy and the tsar.

The West, guided by the Roman Catholic Church and Protestantism, has chosen rationality over the Orthodox harmony. Peter the Great, who attempted to modernize Russia with the introduction of Western ideals, was mistaken. Slavophiles plan to heal Russia by generating a return to native principles. Then, they will cure the West by promoting harmony over individualism and rationalism.

Westernizers

In the tradition of Peter the Great, Westernizers hope to modernize Russia through increasing political and cultural connections with Europe. First and foremost, this group supports the monarchy, hoping the tsar continues his path of reforms. At the same time, they believe the tsar should maintain his current level of power, although a larger, less exclusive group of advisors would benefit him. As Konstantin Kavelin writes in 1855, Westernizers appreciate the "complete necessity of retaining the unlimited power of the sovereign, basing it on the widest possible local freedom."[47]

Members of this group come from a variety of backgrounds. Some may be gentry, while others may be merchants, doctors, well-off, or impoverished. The prominent leaders of this group, Belinsky (1811–48) and Herzen (1812–70), represent diverse classes and embrace religious views ranging from atheism to Orthodoxy. Yet they all admire the West and want to integrate European ideals into Russian society.

JOURNALS

Notes from the Fatherland

The editor, Nikolai Nekrasov, is politically radical. But the journal is not limited to works with a radical perspective, if only because that will not pass by the censors. The journal is also known for its artistic excellence, as the editor strives to include literature of the highest artistry.

Messenger of Europe

Mikhail Stasiulevich, the editor, wanted to create an apolitical journal in this time of hotly contested debates so that scholars could focus on research and education and avoid the debates connected to politics and literary criticism. But the journal's popularity has made it difficult to avoid politics, so instead, he has chosen to include as many perspectives as possible, always looking for the liberal middle ground.

Russian Messenger

The *Russian Messenger* is not just any journal: It is the most popular journal in Russia, publishing the works of notable writers such as Dostoevsky and Tolstoy. This journal is also known for reflecting the conservative ideals of the editor, Mikhail Katkov, showing support for the tsar, and promoting Slavophile nation-building efforts.

BRIEF OUTLINE OF EACH ROLE

Journal Editors

Mikhail Nikiforovich Katkov, editor of the *Russian Messenger*. Known as an outstanding editor, Katkov is also personally disliked by many writers for his extreme conservative and nationalist views. He also tends to edit the work of even the most talented writers with a heavy hand, sometimes publishing the changes without consulting the author. He supports the Russian Orthodox Church, values the tsar (although not necessarily his liberal-minded reforms), and opposes foreign influence in Russia.

Nikolai Alekseevich Nekrasov, editor of *Notes from the Fatherland*. Although he doesn't always agree with the Populists, he does feel a moral obligation to use this literary journal for social commentary. Before he became the editor in chief of *Notes from the Fatherland*, he was co-owner and editor of *The Contemporary*, founded by none other than the father of Russian literature, Alexander Pushkin (1799–1837). Under his leadership, *The Contemporary* became Russia's leading journal, publishing works by great writers and philosophers such as Dostoevsky, Turgenev, and Chernyshevsky. Closely watched because of its radical tone, *The Contemporary* was shut down by the authorities in 1861 following an assassination attempt on Tsar Alexander II.

Nekrasov is also well-known as a writer, not just an editor. His last work, the epic poem *Who Can Be Happy and Free in Russia?* (1876) about peasants, was recognized for both its content and rhyme scheme.

Mikhail Matveevich Stasiulevich, editor of *The Messenger of Europe*. Stasiulevich graduated from St. Petersburg State University's prestigious philology department in 1847 and then, as a professor of history, served as a personal tutor for Tsarevich Nikolai Alexandrovich from 1860 to 1861. Although his work typically focused more on history than politics, he got involved when St. Petersburg State University and the government decided to prosecute the student protestors speaking out against state restrictions and police brutality in the mid-1860s. Angered by the bureaucracy, Stasiulevich and several colleagues quit their professorship positions in protest. At this point, he founded *The Messenger of Europe*, hoping to create an apolitical journal in this time of hotly contested debates.

Censors

Alexander Vasilievich Nikitenko. Born a serf in 1804, Alexander Nikitenko was an outstanding grammar school student, but he could not move on to gymnasium, much less university, because of his social class. He educated himself, going on to tutor, albeit illegally without teaching certification, for wealthy families. In 1824, he traveled to St. Petersburg, where Kondraty Ryleev, a member of the revolutionary group the Decembrists, helped free him from serfdom and helped him enroll in St. Petersburg State University. Just one year later, in 1825, several Decembrists were arrested and executed, his dear friend Ryleev among them. As a result of this event, his views became more moderate. In 1833, he became a censor, recognizing the power of literature as a civic force and hoping to mediate between literature and the tsar.

Ivan Ivanovich Nordstrem, a censor working for the Russian State. He admires literature and writers but values his position as a censor. Friendly with many of the talented writers, as well the editors of literary journals, his primary allegiance is to the tsar and his regime. No matter what friendships he holds dear, he cannot endorse any criticism of Alexander II, either in writing or conversation.

Populists

Alexander Engelgardt. He currently lives in exile, in his family estate in Batishchevo, Gorogobuzhskii District, Smolensk Province. He spends his day writing letters for literary journals on peasant life and farming practices, while conducting agricultural experiments. His wife Anna Nikolaevna Engelgardt and three children reside in St. Petersburg, although they occasionally come to visit.

Praskovia Semyonovna Ivanovskaia. Trained as a typesetter, she is a key figure in publishing pamphlets, journals, and other materials that support the Populist cause. Born into an impoverished family in the

Tula Province, she attended a church boarding school thanks to the support of a family friend. In 1873, she moved to St. Petersburg and enrolled in the Alarchinsky classes for young women. After receiving teacher certification, she worked in Odessa for several years and has now returned to St. Petersburg.

Avdotya Panaeva. A radical woman writer and well-connected with the Populists and with St. Petersburg literary circles, she frequently publishes in *Notes from the Fatherland* under a pseudonym.

Mikhail Evgrafovich Saltykov. Born into a family of impoverished gentry, he pursued a career in government service, rising to the prominent role of vice-governor. Despite his apparent commitment to bureaucracy and the tsar's regime, he holds radical political views. After living in exile from 1848 to 1855 (while still employed by the government), he returned to St. Petersburg to begin a second career as a journalist and author. His ideals come through in his writing and work with radical journals, such as *The Contemporary* (now closed) and *Notes from the Fatherland*. He is widely known to publish under the pseudonym N. Shchedrin.

Varvara V. Timofeyeva. A well-traveled woman, she works on the editorial staff of several journals, becoming especially close to Fyodor Dostoevsky while on staff with his *Diary of a Writer*. Growing up in St. Petersburg high society as the daughter of Lev Perovsky, the civilian governor of St. Petersburg, she encountered radical views while traveling in Geneva. Returning home, she traveled to rural areas of Samara Province. After learning to give smallpox shots, she traveled around the area administering the vaccination in villages. Now back in the city, she lives a modest lifestyle residing in a house with other members of her circle.

Gleb Ivanovich Uspensky, known for his short stories and journalistic essays on rural Russian life. Some of these stories are based on his hometown of Tula, while others are inspired by travels around Russia.

Sophia Smirnova. A staff writer for *Notes of the Fatherland*, she travels in artistic circles. She published several novels throughout the 1870s: *Small Fire* in 1871, *Salt of the Earth* in 1872, and *Strength of Character* in 1876. In 1877, she marries Nikolai Sazonov, a well-known actor in the Alexander Theater in St. Petersburg, but continues to publish under her maiden name.

Slavophiles

Ivan Sergeevich Aksakov. Based in Moscow, he is the leading spokesman of Slavophilism.

Ivan Alexandrovich Goncharov, a famous novelist, known for *Oblomov* (1859) and *The Precipice* (1869). He's also worked as a censor to support the development and publication of Russian literature.

Prince Vladimir Petrovich Meshchersky. A wealthy member of the nobility, he is a supporter of the tsar and a devout member of the Russian Orthodox Church. He earned the name "Prince Full Stop" after publishing an article that stated, "It is necessary to bring the fundamental reforms [initiated by Alexander II with the liberation of the serfs in 1861] to a full stop."

Nikolai Nikolaevich Strakhov. A literary critic and philosopher, Strakhov has worked on several literary journals, following Dostoevsky from *Time* to *Epoch*, before finally settling on a job at the St. Petersburg Public Library. His thoughtful critiques of both Dostoevsky and Tolstoy have earned him recognition as a critic. He promoted Dostoevsky as a talented author when other critics ignored his work. He also proofread *Anna Karenina* for Tolstoy before he submitted it for publication.

Nadezhda Stepanovna Sokhanskaya, a Russian short story writer and autobiographer who wrote about the Ukraine under the pen name Kokhanovskaya.

Westernizers

Elena Ivanovna Apreleva. First receiving recognition from the literary world for her criticism of serfdom based on Turgenev's *A Hunter's Notes*, Elena Apreleva went on to write essays and translations. She worked for several literary journals, starting her own journal for children *Family and School* in 1872. She now resides primarily in Paris, where she meets frequently with her literary mentor Turgenev, who has helped her get published in literary journals such as St. Petersburg's *Messenger of Europe*.

Anna Engelgardt, one of the first women to work in publishing and with literary journals and a strong advocate for women's rights. Currently a staff member of *Messenger of Europe*, she works primarily as a translator. She is proficient in foreign languages, including English, German, French, and Italian. In 1877, she published the first Russian-German dictionary in collaboration with her father, the well-known Russian-French dictionary author Nikolai Makarov.

Afanasy Afanasevich Fet, born out of wedlock as Afanasy Shenshin to a German woman and a Russian nobleman. Because the courts would not recognize him as Shenshin's biological son, he was not able to use his family name or claim rights of the nobility. Finally, in 1873, Alexander II responded to his appeal and issued a royal edict granting him use of the name Shenshin and the rights associated with that name. He was educated at a German boarding school as a youth and returned to Russia to study at Moscow State University; he then served in the military. Fet (his pen name) has many connections in the literary world, being a close friend of Ivan Turgenev and married to the sister of literary critic V. P. Botkin.

He is best known for lyrical poetry collections published in the 1850s. In the sixties, he backed away from writing, not wanting to give in to the radical critics pressuring writers to include political messages in their work. Instead, Fet prefers to create poetry about love and nature, valuing artistic style above all else.

Nikolai Semyonovich Leskov. After traveling extensively throughout Russia for a private business, Leskov began pursuing a career in journalism in 1860, based in St. Petersburg, and started to write fiction, receiving recognition for *Lady Macbeth of Mtsensk* (1865) and *Cathedral Folk* (1875). Much of his work has been published in *Russian Messenger*, although he broke with Katkov over editorial differences. A believer in literature with a social message, Leskov is friends with many conservatives and a suspected employee of the Third Department Section. But the conservatives have lately become suspicious of Leskov for criticizing the Russian Orthodox Church in his stories "Episcopal Justice" and "The Unbaptized Priest."

Ivan Sergeevich Turgenev. Called "the American" as a student at St. Petersburg State in the 1830s, he is critical of Russian culture and admiring of Western European lifestyles. He received wide literary recognition for his *A Hunter's Notes* (1852), which exposed the cruelty of serfdom. Because of his critique, Nicholas I and the censors became suspicious of his intentions, and the secret police began following him. The situation worsened in 1852 when he referred to Nikolai Gogol as a "great author," even though a censor had forbidden mentioning this satirist's name. Because of this, Nicholas I ordered a month-long imprisonment, followed by permanent exile to his estate. When Alexander II took the throne, he granted Turgenev permission to travel again. Alexander not only enjoyed *A Hunter's Notes*, but he also found the work influential in his decision to free the serfs. Since then, Turgenev's work has mixed reviews. He's spoken about a new project, *Virgin Soil*, concerning the Populists. While he travels regularly to both Moscow and St. Petersburg for readings, he lives primarily in Paris.

Indeterminates

Fyodor Mikhailovich Dostoevsky, a popular writer known for his thought-provoking novels including *Crime and Punishment* as well as *The Idiot* and *The Possessed*. He is also well-known for his powerful poetry readings. Although he has a radical background, having been associated with the Petrashevsky Circle and sentenced to hard labor in Siberia, he has been deeply connected to the Russian Orthodox Church since his return in 1854. Dostoevsky also has poor health, suffering from emphysema and epilepsy, occasionally having seizures.

Alexander Ostrovsky. Without a doubt, he is the most prolific writer of this generation. Since 1847, he has produced nearly one play each year. He is best known for works that describe the daily life of merchants in cities and the provinces.

Ilya Efimovich Repin. A realist artist, he is called the "Rembrandt of Russia" and the "Tolstoy of Art." His paintings, often of Russian peasant and rural areas, are well-known in both Europe and Russia. His work has been shown at the Salon in Paris from 1874 to 1876 and at the Wanderers' Society in St. Petersburg. Repin comes from a humble background as a low-ranking military settler, one step above a serf. After being educated at the Imperial Academy, he received a Large Gold Medal, a six-year traveling scholarship. These funds allowed him to pay off the taxes owed to the state and become classified as a free artist, while supporting six years of travel throughout Europe.

Vladimir Sergeevich Solovyov, called a "holy fool" for his unique philosophy of Sophia, the Eternal Feminine—a synthesis of God, humanity, and nature. He is especially close friends with Dostoevsky, critics saying the famous writer modeled Alyosha in *Brothers Karamazov* after him. Some people mistake him for a priest, often dressed in black with long flowing hair, and kneel down in front of him for a blessing.

Elena Andreevna Shtakenshneider, the hostess of a well-known literary salon that gathers weekly at her St. Petersburg home. Born with a crooked spine, she requires crutches to walk. Her family had strong connections with the court, and even though they never expected her to marry, they did want to secure her position in society, so her mother started a literary salon, which Elena Andreevna now hosts. She is known for her moderate perspective, often jumping in to bridge the difference between two opposing sides in a heated debate at her salon.

Count Lev Nikolaevich Tolstoy. Tolstoy is widely acknowledged as the greatest Russian writer of the time, and most other writers strive to achieve his success and receive his accolades. His political and spiritual values vacillate, as he has studied and embraced beliefs from both radical and conservative perspectives at one time or another. The publication of *War and Peace* (1869) cemented his revered position in Russian literature. In the early 1870s, inspired by a rash of suicides, he undertook a new novel that incorporated current social issues—*Anna Karenina*. Readers adored *Anna Karenina*, eagerly snapping up copies of *Russian Messenger* to read the first installment in April 1875. But the publication has not gone smoothly. According to gossip, the famed author and Mikhail Katkov, the editor of *Russian Messenger*, had a disagreement about the depiction of intimacy in the novel. Then, despite the novel's acclaim, Katkov refused to publish the epilogue of *Anna Karenina*.

Alexandra Volkova, one of very few women who have accrued massive wealth through entrepreneurship, owning and operating her own independent vodka factory, Gothard Martini, since 1874. Mockingly called "Pot house sage" and her business ridiculed as "Liquor dealer's Jew trick" by various members of the nobility, Alexandra Volkova is nonetheless a successful Jewish businesswoman. She is part of a rising middle class, bridging the gap between the noble, elite class and the peasants. Although investing in similar fields as merchants and nobility, she is part of the taxpaying population, like the peasants, and therefore looked down upon by the upper classes.

5
Core Texts

Selections from "Regulations on the Press: The Reign of the Sovereign Alexander II, April 1865"

The following rules dictated publication for all print materials and listed fines for violations. Although these rules were intended to be temporary, they were in effect until 1905. This text has been abbreviated from its original version.[1] Italic ellipses in brackets indicate the author's omissions.

Source: Charles A. Ruud, *Fighting Words: Imperial Censorship and the Russian Press, 1804–1906*, with a new introduction (Toronto: University of Toronto Press, 2009), 237–52.

No. 41988, 6 April

The Personal Imperial Decree handed down to the Senate—*Concerning the granting of certain [measures of] relief and convenience to the national press.*

Wishing to grant the national press all possible relief and convenience, we deem it right to make the following changes in and additions to the censorship decrees in force during the present temporary position of our judicial branch and henceforth until such time as subsequent instructions in the experiment are handed down:

I. The following are exempted from preliminary censorship:

a In both capitals:
  (1) all periodical publications appearing to date whose publishers themselves announce their desire [for exemption];
  (2) all original writings consisting of no fewer than 10 printed signatures; and
b In all localities:
  (1) all governmental publications;
  (2) all publications of academies, universities, and educational organizations and establishments;
  (3) all publications in ancient classical languages and translations from these languages;
  (4) drafts, plans, and maps.

41

II. Those periodicals and other publications, writings and translations freed from preliminary censorship in which occur violations of the laws are subject to judicial prosecution; furthermore, in the event that a dangerous orientation is discerned in periodical publications, they are subject to administrative penalty according to the laws especially established for this purpose.

III. The management of censorship and press affairs is generally concentrated in the Ministry of the Interior under the higher supervision of the minister in the newly-established Chief Administration for these affairs.

IV. The operations of the existing decree do not, at the present time, apply to:

- *a* writings, translations and publications and portions thereof which are subject to Ecclesiastical Censorship according to the decrees and orders now in effect. These decrees and orders will continue to be carried out on presently existing principles, as will foreign censorship;
- *b* periodical and other publications of prints, drawings, and other pictorial representations with or without texts which are subject to the operation of censorship regulations also [based] on existing principles.

Having affirmed along with these [regulations] those changes and additions which, in consequence of the above-stated measures, must be included in the details of the regulations now in effect concerning the press, we ask the Governing Senate to issue an order for the promulgation of this, Our Will, so that it would take effect as of September 1 of the current year.

No. 41990, 6 April

The imperially approved opinion of the Council of State. *Concerning certain changes in and additions to censorship regulation now in effect.* The Council of State in the Department of Laws and in General Meeting has examined the presentation of the Minister of the Interior concerning these changes in and additions to the details of the regulations now in effect concerning the press which are necessary to conform with the Imperial Will as revealed in the decree of 6 April of this year (41988), and *has proposed* the enactment of the following regulations:

I. Concerning the Chief Administration of Press Affairs.

1 The Chief Administration of Press Affairs consists of:
   (1) the Head of the Chief Administration, and
   (2) the Council of the Chief Administration.
2 To the Chief Administration are attached:
   (1) the Office;
   (2) special Censors of dramatic works; and
   (3) clerks with special commissions.
3 The Head of the Chief Administration is appointed and dismissed by Imperial decree [handed down to] the Governing Senate upon recommendation of the Minister of the Interior.
4 The Council of the Chief Administration under the chairmanship of the Head of the Administration consists of the Chairmen of Censorship Committees on hand in St Petersburg and of members appointed and dismissed by Imperial decrees of the Governing Senate upon recommendation of the Minister of the Interior.
5 The Office of the Chief Administration is administered by the Managing Director assisted by aides under the direct supervision of the Head of the Chief Administration.
6 The Managing Director and his aides and the clerks with special commissions are hired and dismissed on the orders of the Minister of the Interior, but the office clerks and workers are hired and dismissed by the Managing Director of the Chief Administration on whose discretion depends their number and distribution of salary.
7 The concerns of the Chief Administration of Press Affairs are:
   (1) supervision of the operations of the Censorship Committees and special Censors in both domestic and foreign censorship; settlement of their disagreements and questions and

examination of complaints brought against them;

(2) supervision of works published by the press which come out without censorship permission; detection in them of violations of established regulations; institution of judicial prosecution when this was not done by subordinate authorities, and of matters concerning warnings to periodical publications exempted from preliminary censorship;

(3) matters concerning the openings of printing-houses, lithographies, etching works, and institutions producing and selling printing accessories, and supervision of these establishments as well as the book trade.

8 The Council of the Chief Administration of Press Affairs is subordinate to the general directives governing all Councils of the Ministries.

9 In the event that they discover violations of the regulations concerning press matters, all other administrative institutions apply to the Chief Administration through their superiors for prosecution of the guilty.

II. Concerning the periodical press.

1 The following are considered to be periodical publications:
   (1) newspapers and magazines published in separate issues, folios, or pamphlets;
   (2) collections or anthologies of new, original, or translated writings or articles of various authors published more than twice a year under one general title.

2 Supplements forming part of newspapers or magazines are considered as supplements only if they are not sold separately or in subscription or as separate pamphlets or numbers. Any publication having the character of a separate magazine or newspaper and one which may be bought separately, on subscription, or as individual pamphlets or issues is not considered a supplement to another periodical publication even though it might bear the same title as the periodical, and that is why all conditions of publication established by present regulations must be observed by each of the two publications separately.

3 The following are not relevant to the collections mentioned in article 1:
   (1) collections of previously printed writings and translations, for example, anthologies;
   (2) collections of historical documents;
   (3) all types of dictionaries.

4 Anyone wishing to publish a new periodical publication in the form of a newspaper, magazine, or collection is obliged, at the present time, to ask permission to do so from the Minister of the Interior on whom depends the permission for the release of such a publication either without censorship or on condition of preliminary censorship.

5 Petitions concerning permission are to be submitted to the Chief Administration of Press Affairs and must contain the following information:
   (1) the name or title of the publication, the table of contents, date of publication, and price of subscription;
   (2) the name and address of the publisher and editor-in-chief, and, if there are several of the above, the name and address of each of them;
   (3) the printing-house in which the publication is to be printed.

6 To the petition must be appended the following:
   (1) the identity papers of both the publisher and the editor-in-chief or, if there are several of the above, of each of them;
   (2) a written and personally signed statement of the editor-in-chief that he assumes the responsibility for the supervision of the publication or a part thereof, signifying which part.

7 If the publisher and editor-in-chief are the same person, this must be mentioned in the petition.

8. If anyone undertakes to publish any periodical publication without obtaining lawful permission, or if anyone includes in his magazine an article which exceeds the limits of the program established for the publication (article 17, point 2), he is liable to a fine not exceeding 50 rubles for each number or article, even if the published numbers or articles do not contain any unlawful material.

9. Anyone who has obtained permission through proper channels to put out a periodical publication has the right to undertake its publication within a year of receiving permission. In the event that this time expires, the publication is considered ineligible and the permission granted is considered void.

10. Any periodical publication which has already appeared but which, for whatever reason, does not come out in the course of the year is considered discontinued and new permission is required to renew its publication.

11. In the event of the transfer of a periodical publication from one publisher to another, the Chief Administration must be informed of it in good time and the notification must be signed by both the former and present publishers. For a change of editor, permission must be obtained according to the procedure mentioned in articles 4–7. Those guilty of violations of these regulations are liable to a fine not exceeding 100 rubles; transfer of a publication or replacement of an editor are considered invalid if done without permission.

12. The responsible editor will forfeit his position:
    (1) if he becomes subject to the loss or reduction of his rights of status or if he comes under police surveillance on orders of the court;
    (2) if he loses his civil rights for any other reasons whatsoever;
    (3) if he travels abroad without informing the Chief Administration or if he does not return at the summons of the Administration or some other authority.

13. The publisher must notify the Offices of the Governors General in the capitals and the Offices of the Provincial Governors in other localities concerning the transfer of a publication from one printing-house to another.

14. Permission for each periodical publication is issued by the Chief Administration in the form of certificates in duplicate. Without producing this certificate, no printing-house has the right to undertake the typesetting and printing of a periodical publication. One copy of the certificate remains in the printing-house for as long as the printing of a publication continues; if, however, a publication is subject to a deposit, the printing-house must demand a receipt when the deposit is paid before it begins typesetting and printing.

15. Publishers of periodical publications which are exempted from preliminary censorship measures are required to pay the deposit to the Chief Administration.

16. The deposit is paid according to the following scale:
    (1) for a daily newspaper or a newspaper appearing not less than 6 times a week—5,000 rubles;
    (2) for all other periodical publications—2,500 rubles.

17. The following are not required to pay a deposit:
    (1) periodical publications appearing with the permission of preliminary censorship;
    (2) publications the contents of which, in conformity with approved programs, are purely educational, economic, or technical;
    (3) governmental publications and publications of academies, universities, and educational organizations and establishments.

18. The deposit is paid to the Chief Administrator of Press Affairs in accordance with the wishes of the publisher, either in cash, or in Russian government credit notes which are considered at their nominal value upon receipt, or in stocks and bonds which are acceptable as deposits in transactions involving government contracts

and sales. The holder receives interest-bearing coupons on the dates prescribed for the issuance of such bonds.

19. The deposit covers fines imposed on a periodical publication. If the fine is not paid within the specified time, a corresponding sum is deducted from the deposit in cash or through the sale of credit notes at the going rate of exchange. In the latter case, ordinary expenses connected with the sale are also deducted from the deposit.

20. The part of the deposit deducted in payment for the prescribed fine must be repaid up to a fixed amount under threat of the discontinuation of the publication if this is not done.

21. Publications which appear more than twice a month are given two weeks from the date of the court decision to repay the deposit; regarding publications appearing less frequently, repayment must be made at least a day before the publication of the pamphlet due to appear after the fine is levied.

22. In the event that a publication is discontinued, the deposit is returned to the publisher not earlier than a year from the date of the appearance of the last number of the publication.

23. Each separately published number of a newspaper, each copy of a magazine, or each issue of a collection must bear the following information: the names of the publisher, editor-in-chief, and printing-house, and the price of subscription; if the publication has been examined by the censor ahead of time, the permission of the censor must also be printed. Those guilty of a violation of this regulation are liable to a fine not exceeding 25 rubles for each number, copy or issue.

24. Those guilty of falsifying the names of the publisher, editor-in-chief, subscription price, or censorship permission on a publication are subject to imprisonment for the term determined in vol. 15, part 1, article 42 [The Code of Law].

25. Periodical publications exempted from preliminary censorship are submitted by the publishers to the Censorship Committee at the following times:
    (1) copies of each number of a newspaper or publication in general which appears not less than once a week are submitted at the time of the final printing of that number;
    (2) copies of each issue of a publication appearing less frequently than once a week are submitted not later than two days before its distribution to subscribers or its release for sale. In fulfilment of this regulation the publishers are issued notices indicating the stated times for the submission of their copies. Those guilty of not submitting their copies are liable to a fine not exceeding 100 rubles.

26. Any periodical publication is obliged to print without delay and free of charge an official refutation or correction of information appearing in the publication without change in or comment on the text and with no objections to the text itself.

27. If information concerning a private individual appears in a periodical publication, the said publication cannot refuse to accept refutations or corrections submitted by that individual.

28. A refutation or correction submitted by a private individual must be printed without delay in the same script and in the same section as the original information; in addition, no charge [is levied] if such refutations or corrections do not take up more space than twice the length of the article to which they are an answer. A refutation or correction must be signed by the individual submitting it in his defense.

29. The Minister of the Interior is granted the right to issue warnings to periodical publications with reference to the articles giving cause for such warnings. A third warning results in the suspension of the publication for a period which is determined by the Minister of the Interior at the time he issues the warning, but which does not exceed 6 months. This regulation is applied with equal force to periodical

publications controlled by governmental or educational institutions.

30 If, after a third warning the Minister of the Interior deems it necessary to discontinue a publication irrespective of a preliminary suspension of a periodical publication for a specific time, he will submit a proposal concerning this action to the First Department of the Governing Senate.

31 A periodical publication receiving a warning is obliged to print it without changes or objections at the beginning of the first issue to appear after the warning has been issued.

32 A discontinued publication may not be reinstated without the personal permission of the Minister of the Interior.

33 For failure to print the following in a periodical publication: If the publisher fails to print a court decision or an administrative warning or refutations or corrections submitted by the Government or by private individuals within 3 days in a daily publication, and in the following number of a monthly publication, he is liable to a fine of 25 rubles for each number published after the fixed date when the publication appears more than once a month, and 100 rubles per number when it appears once a month or less often for as long as the submitted decision, warning, refutation, or correction are not printed; and if the decision, warning, refutation, or correction are not printed within three months, the publications will be discontinued on the order of the Chief Administration of Press Affairs.

III. Concerning printing-houses, lithographic works, etching works, and establishments producing and selling printing equipment, and also concerning the book trade.

A Concerning printing-houses, lithographies, and etching works.

1 Under the control of the Chief Administration of Press Affairs, the supervision of printing-houses, lithographies, and etching works (and also of establishments producing and selling printing equipment and of the book trade) is undertaken in the capitals by special Inspectors attached to the Offices of the Governors General, and in the provinces by Clerks under special commission designated by the Governors.

2 Those wishing to set up printing-houses, lithographies, etching works, or other establishments for printing written and pictorial material must get permission for this from the Governors General in the capitals and from the provincial governor in other localities. At the same time they are obliged to:

(1) produce, in cases stipulated by the regulations governing taxation for the right to engage in trade and other business, a certificate prescribed by these regulations;

(2) indicate the number and size of the rapid printing machines and presses which they propose to have in their establishment.

3 The permission granted to open a printing-house or another establishment mentioned in the previous article remains in force for two years; if, however, the establishment is not brought into production by the end of that time, new permission is needed for it to open.

4 Transfer of a printing-house, lithography, or etching works from one individual to another is allowed only with the permission of the authority which is also responsible for granting permission for their opening.

5 Whoever inherits a printing-house, lithography, or etching works must either fulfill the demands of article 2 or turn over the establishment to someone else under the same conditions within 6 months.

6 Any printing-house, lithography, or etching works opened or taken over from another individual by anyone at all without permission of the responsible authority is considered clandestine, and those guilty of opening or maintaining such an establishment are liable to a fine not exceeding 300 rubles and detention of

not more than 3 months, or to imprisonment for a term defined as not more than 3 months, or to imprisonment for a term defined by vol. 15, part 1, article 42, for the first and second degree of this type of punishment, or to one of these punishments at the discretion of the court.

7 Proprietors of establishments are obliged to report any changes in the number and size of their rapid printing machines and presses to the Office of the Governors General in the capitals and to the Offices of the provincial governors in other localities. Those who fail to do so are liable to a fine not exceeding 50 rubles.

8 Anyone wishing to possess a small, hand-operated printing press for personal use must ask permission to do so from the Governor General in the capitals and from the provincial governor in other localities. A violation of this condition puts the guilty party under the same liability as that which rests on those maintaining clandestine printing-houses.

9 Each printing-house, lithography, and etching works must have a ledger, each page of which is initialed by Inspectors of book printing in the capitals, and, in other localities, by clerks especially designated for this task by the provincial governors. In this ledger is noted any work intended for printing along with an explanation of whether it is being printed without preliminary submission to censorship or with the permission of the latter, and with evidence, in each case, of the number of copies and the format of the publication. Those guilty of non-fulfilment of this regulation are liable to a fine not exceeding 50 rubles.

10 Entries in the ledger as well as works already completed and those which are in production may be verified at any time by the individuals mentioned in the preceding article.

11 Offices which acquire hand-operated printing-presses for office needs must bring this to the attention of the individuals mentioned in article 9.

12 When the printing of any publication is finished and prior to the distribution of the publication, printing-houses, lithographies, and etching works are obliged to submit the number of copies designated by censorship Regulations to the local Censorship Committee which will then issue a receipt to this effect. The only exceptions to this regulation are office notices and writings which have as their subject community or domestic requirements, such as: wedding and various other invitations, visiting cards, matters of etiquette, price-lists, notices of sales of goods, or of change of address, etc. A printing house, lithographic works, or etching works is held accountable for the printing of such writings only in the event that their form conceals some other material foreign to these subjects.

13 A work printed or lithographed without preliminary censorship may be released for publication (with the exception mentioned in the preceding article) no sooner than three days after receiving notification that the Censorship Committee has received the required number of copies. Those guilty of not fulfilling this regulation are liable to a fine not exceeding 100 rubles specifically for a breach of this regulation.

14 In the extraordinary circumstance when, because of the seriousness of the harmful influence envisaged by the distribution of an illegal work or periodical publication, seizure cannot be postponed until a court verdict for it has been handed down, the Council of the Chief Administration and the Censorship Committee are given the right to suspend immediately the appearance of such a work, but they must have instituted court proceedings against the guilty party at the same time.

15 Each copy that is released by the printing house, lithographic works, or etching works must bear the name and address of the printer, lithographer, or etcher and, if the work was subject to preliminary censorship, the approval of the censor. Those guilty of non-fulfilment of this

[regulation] are liable to a fine not exceeding 50 rubles.

16 Those guilty of falsifying the name of the printer, lithographer, or etcher are subject to imprisonment for the term defined in vol. 15, part 1, article 42.

17 Those guilty of printing a work subject to preliminary censorship without the permission of the censor are liable to a fine not exceeding 300 rubles and detention of not more than 3 months, even though the contents of the printed work contain nothing illegal.

18 Also subject to such punishment is the owner of a printing house who allows the printing of a periodical publication without getting from the publisher the certificate or receipt required by article 14 of the regulations governing periodical publications.

19 Whoever is guilty of reprinting a work forbidden by the court and entered in the catalogue of forbidden books is liable, in addition to the confiscation of the whole publication, to a fine not exceeding 300 rubles and to detention of not more than 3 months.

B. Concerning establishments producing and selling printing equipment.

20 Permission to set up establishments for the production and sale of printing equipment is given to all individuals without discrimination who have the right to practice a trade or vocation. The permission is granted on the basis of the Regulations governing industries and factories and on the basis of the Regulations governing trade and vocation.

21 Every establishment producing or selling printing equipment must have a ledger, each page of which is initialed by clerks on whom falls the responsibility of dealing with printing-houses as stated in article 9. Into this ledger is entered any sale conducted in the factory or in a store along with a note of the name, rank, and address of the buyer. Those guilty of non-fulfilment of this [regulation] are liable to a fine not exceeding 50 rubles.

22 Within the Empire, printing-presses and types may be sold only to printers; furthermore, types may also be sold to individuals who have received permission to possess a hand-operated printing-press. Those guilty of non-fulfilment of this regulation are liable to a fine not exceeding 100 rubles.

23 Verification of the ledger in factories and stores which produce and sell printing accessories is carried out on the basis of article 10.

24 In the event that presses, rapid printing-presses, and types are imported from abroad, customs officials must immediately inform the Offices of the Governors General if the goods are shipped to the capitals, and the Offices of the provincial governors if they are shipped to other places, along with information about the quantity of the shipment and the name of the receiver to whom the shipment is being sent through customs. This information is forwarded by the Offices to the individuals mentioned in article 9.

C Concerning the book trade.

25 Private individuals as well as joint-stock companies or associations are allowed to establish bookstores, shops, and reading-rooms according to the procedure set out for the opening of printing-houses, lithographies, and similar enterprises. Those guilty of non-fulfilment of this [regulation] are liable to a fine not exceeding 100 rubles.

26 Individuals who receive the right to establish a bookstore or shop or a reading-room are obliged to declare the exact locations of these establishments and the person running them in each case to the Offices of the Governors General in the capitals and to the Offices of the provincial governors in other localities.

27 Anyone without discrimination is allowed to sell or deliver approved books and various periodical publications in separate issues, not in shops, but on the streets and squares with the proviso that those wishing to sell or deliver [these materials] have the permission of the

local police authorities to conduct such trade, in addition to the certificate prescribed for such trade by the current regulations. Those guilty of non-fulfilment of this [regulation] are liable to a fine not exceeding 25 rubles.

28 Bookstores, shops, and reading rooms have the right to keep in stock and sell or loan all approved publications printed in Russia in Russian or in foreign languages and, of those publications printed abroad in Russian or in foreign languages, all those which are not included in the general catalogue of forbidden books. This regulation also applies to those delivering books or selling them in the streets and squares.

29 If the proprietor of a bookstore, shop, or reading room, and this applies to street-sellers and book retailers [as well], keeps for sale and distribution such books or publications listed in the general catalogue of forbidden books or if these materials have been duly banned by the local police, he is liable to a fine not exceeding 250 rubles.

30 If a book which is initially permitted is subsequently banned, booksellers and proprietors of reading rooms are not held responsible for its distribution so long as it has not been entered in the general catalogue of forbidden books, or so long as the local police have not duly banned it.

D *Concerning the court in matters of the press.*

1 Those held responsible for holding printed or lithographed works, prints, etc., may be: the author, the publisher, the typographer or lithographer, the bookseller, and the editor. The measure of responsibility of each of the above mentioned individuals is determined by the court which examines the degree of complicity in the transgression on the precise basis of vol. 4, part 1, articles 13–17.

2 The individuals mentioned in the preceding article are called before the court in the following order:

(1) the author, in all cases in which he does not prove that his work was published without his knowledge or consent;

(2) the publisher, in the case in which the name or address of the author is unknown or if the latter lives abroad;

(3) the printer or lithographer, when neither the author nor the publisher is known or when their place of residence is not evident or when they live abroad;

(4) the bookseller, in the case in which the copy of the work does not bear the name and address of the printer or lithographer.

3 In the cases when publishers, printers, and booksellers abrogate their direct responsibility on the basis of the preceding article, they may be prosecuted as accessories to offenses and misdemeanors of the press, depending on the circumstances, if it is proved that they wittingly participated in the publication and distribution of the printed matter while being aware of the criminal intention of the chief offender.

4 In any case, responsibility for holding articles printed in periodical publications falls on the editor of the publication, as well as on the chief offender.

5 Violations of decrees concerning the press which are subject to prosecution (pending the enactment of the Court Decrees of November 20, 1864) are handled in the special Sessions of the Criminal Chamber which act as a lower court and which are organized for this purpose in St Petersburg and Moscow; these sentences can be appealed to the Governing Senate.

6 The special Sessions consist of the Chairman of the Criminal Chamber, two Colleagues of the Chairmen of the Criminal and Civil Chambers, and four Assessors of those chambers [all of whom] take turns according to a system determined among themselves in order that the Session should be a complement of two Assessors of the Criminal Chamber and one from each Department of the Civil Chamber.

7 The institution of judicial prosecution for violations, in accordance with the regulations governing the press, must commence within a year from the date of the perpetration of the violation.

8 In handing down punishment for offenses and misdemeanors of the press as fixed by vol. 15, part 1, the court is granted the right, depending on the circumstances, to reduce the severity of the punishment by one or several degrees, and even to reduce the verdict to the highest degree of the next lowest category of punishment.

9 Independent of the felonies and misdemeanors in matters of the press which are prosecuted under vol. 15, part 1, the following are also subject to judicial prosecution and punishment.

(1) Whoever prints insulting references to the laws operating in the Empire with the aim of undermining public confidence, or to established governmental or judicial decrees and orders, or who permits himself to call into question in the press the compulsory force of the laws and to approve or justify the acts forbidden by them with the aim of arousing disrespect for the laws is liable to imprisonment for the term indicated in vol. 15, part 1, article 42, or to detention from 4 days to 3 months or, finally, to a fine not exceeding 500 rubles.

(2) Whoever makes an appeal in the press which incites one segment of the population of the state to animosity against another, or one class against another is subject to incarceration in a detention center or in a prison for the term defined in vol. 15, part 1, articles 40–42, or to detention from 4 days to 3 months, or to a fine not exceeding 500 rubles.

(3) If someone is guilty of directly calling into question or censuring the principles of property or the family unit in printed publications with the intention of undermining or weakening their foundations, even though there is no incitement to commit a crime, he will be liable to a fine not exceeding 300 rubles and to detention of not more than 6 weeks, or to only one of these punishments according to the discretion of the court.

(4) Those guilty of publishing and promulgating resolutions of assemblies of the gentry and urban and zemstvo assemblies without the permission of the Governors-General in the capitals and of the provincial governors in other cities are liable to a fine not exceeding 300 rubles and to detention of not more than 3 weeks, or to one of these punishments according to the discretion of the court.

10 If someone publishes about a private individual or official or society or institution in the press such circumstances which may damage their honor, reputation, or good name [i.e., defaming circumstances], he is liable to a fine not exceeding 500 rubles and to imprisonment for the term defined in vol. 15, part 1, article 42, or to one of these punishments according to the discretion of the court.

11 If someone is guilty of an insulting reference in the press to a private individual or official or to a society or establishment, and if this reference expresses or implies abuse or insult without indication of specific defaming circumstances, he is liable to a fine not exceeding 300 rubles and to detention for a period defined in vol. 15, part 1, article 43, for first and second degree offenses, or to imprisonment of not more than 6 months.

12 Anyone who prints insults of one kind or another against private individuals is not, under any circumstances, granted the right to furnish evidence of their validity.

13 If the insult points to any defaming circumstances, and if it concerns the official or public activities of an individual holding a post by appointment of the Government or through election, then anyone who prints the insult is granted the right to present any written proofs he may have in his possession as confirmation

of the truth of his testimony. Testimony of witnesses is not admissible in this case.

14 For his part, anyone who undertakes an action against a charge of defaming circumstances imputed to him in the press has the right to use any means, both to refute the validity of the proofs presented by the accused on the basis of the preceding article, and to present witnesses to confirm his moral qualities; however, the accused is forbidden to present witnesses to dispute the moral qualities of the plaintiff.

15 Anyone who proves the truth of a defaming circumstance on the basis of article 13 is free from punishment as understood in article 10; however, he may be liable to a fine under article 11 if the court discovers an obvious intention to insult an official or establishment in the form of the work being prosecuted or in the method of its distribution and other circumstances.

16 A discussion of individual laws and general legislation or of the publication of governmental decrees is not liable to criminal charge and is not subject to punishments provided that the published article does not contain an incitement to disobey the laws, does not dispute their obligatory force, and is not insulting to constituted authority.

17 In meting out punishment for offenses and misdemeanors of the press, the court may decide on the obliteration of a drawing, book, etc., or of only those sections of a work which contain a criminal trend of thought; the court may also decide to close down printing houses, lithographic works, or etching works.

18 In meting out punishment for offenses discovered in a periodical publication, the court is allowed:
    (1) to order the suppression of such a periodical publication for a period it considers necessary, or its complete suppression;
    (2) having decided to suspend or discontinue a periodical publication, at the same time to forbid the publisher and editor, or one of them if they have been proved guilty, to accept the title of publisher or editor of any periodical publication whatever for a certain period of time which, however, shall not exceed 5 years.

19 In handing down a verdict concerning a periodical publication, the court may decide that the next number of the publication should carry a notice of the aforesaid verdict provided that the publication has not been discontinued; it is forbidden to print an objection or refutation along with the notice. [. . .]

Vissarion Belinsky, "A Letter to Gogol"
Literary critic Belinsky wrote this letter in 1847. Addressed to Russian author Nikolai Gogol, the letter references characters from Gogol's Dead Souls *and the content of his* Selected Passages from Correspondence with Friends. *Although Belinsky once held Gogol in high esteem for his artistry, he is disillusioned by Gogol's portrayal of Russian intellectual life in his recent publication. Belinksy's letter was censored for its critique of the Russian Orthodox Church but was nonetheless read widely in liberal circles. Members of the Petrashevsky Circle, including Dostoevsky, were arrested for reading this piece.*

Source: V. G. Belinsky, "Pis'mo Gogolyu," Biblioteka Maksima Moshkova, accessed July 15, 2024, http://az.lib.ru/b/belinskij_w_g/text_3890.shtml. Translated by Linda M. Mayhew, summer 2024.

You are only partially right if you recognize anger in my article: This epithet is too weak and tender to express my state of mind after reading your book. But you are not entirely right in ascribing this to your comments, which were not entirely flattering, about the admirers of your talent. No, there was a more important reason here. Offended vanity can be tolerated, and I would have enough sense to keep quiet on this topic, if only this whole affair would conclude just with this, but it is impossible to tolerate these offenses; the sense of truth, of human worth. It is impossible to keep silent when under the mantle of religion and the defense of flagellation, lies and depravity are professed in place of truth and virtue.

Yes, I loved you with my whole heart, as a person bound by blood to their country can love its hope, honor, glory, one of its great leaders on the path to consciousness, development, progress. And you had good reason, although just for a minute, to leave the peaceful state of mind after losing the right to this type of love. I say this not because I considered my love a reward for great talent but because of this relationship: I represent not one person but many people, the exact number of whom neither you nor I can see and who, in turn, have never seen you.

I am not in the state of mind to give you even the slightest idea of the indignation that your book incited in all virtuous hearts or the screams of wild joy that your enemies—both fictional ones (the Chichikovs, the Nozdrevs, Gorodnichies, and so on) and nonfictional ones, whose names are well-known to you—let out upon its publication. You yourself see that even people who apparently are of the same mind have backed away from your book. If it had been written on account of deep-rooted, sincere convictions, then it should have made that impression on the public. If everyone (with the exception of a few people, who you need to see and know to be displeased with their approval) had taken it for a clever, but over the top, unceremonious prank intended to achieve purely earthly goals through divine means—only you would be guilty. And this is not at all surprising, but it is surprising that you find this surprising! I think this is because you have intimate knowledge of Russia as an artist but not as a thinker, a role which you unsuccessfully took upon yourself in your fantastical book. And this is not because you are not an intellectual but because for so many years already you have become accustomed to looking at Russia from your beautiful far-away; and of course there is nothing easier than seeing things how you want to see them; because in this beautiful far-away, you live as a foreigner, alone, within yourself, or in a like-minded circle, similarly inclined and powerless to oppose your influence. Because of this, you didn't realize that Russia sees its salvation not in mysticism, not in asceticism, not in pietism, but in the successes of civilization, enlightenment, and humanity. We do not need sermons (we've heard enough!) or prayers (we've repeated them enough!), but we do need the masses to awaken their sense of human worth, enough for all the years lost in filth and grime—we need justice and laws, created not with the teachings of the church, but with common sense and justice and with the strictest possible implementation. And instead of this, the book portrays a terrifying vision of a country, where people traffic people, not having the means for this; and of the justification that is cleverly used by American plantation owners, who insist that slaves are not human beings; and of a country where people are called not by their first names but by their nicknames: Vankas, Vaskas, Steshkas, Palashkas; of a country, where, finally, there are neither safeguards of any kind for individuals, honor, and property, nor even civil order; there is only a large network of various state thieves and robbers! The most relevant and current national questions in Russia now are: the abolition of serfdom, the elimination of corporal punishment, the strictest possible enforcement of existing laws. The government itself (which knows very well what the landowning classes do with their serfs, and how many of the latter annually kill the former) is aware that these questions are substantiated by its fainthearted and fruitless half measures for the benefit of white slaves and its comical replacement of a one-tailed whip with a three-tailed lash.

These are the questions that worry all of Russia in its apathetic sleep! And at the same time, a great writer, who has nurtured Russia's self-awareness with his wonderfully artistic, deeply insightful work, allowing the country to look at itself as if into a mirror, publishes a book that in the name of Christ and religion instructs the barbarian landowning gentry to capitalize even more on the serfs, instructs them to thrash the serfs more . . . and this shouldn't fill me with indignation? . . . If you had made an attempt on my life, then I could not despise you any more than I do for these shameful lines. . . . And after this, you want us to believe your sincerity: the purpose of your book! No. If you would have actually been filled with the truth of Christ and not the devil's teachings—you certainly would not have written that in your new book. You would have said to the landowning gentry that because his serfs are his brothers in Christ, and as a brother cannot be the slave of his own brother, then he should give them their freedom or, at least, make use of their labor in a way that is advantageous for them, recognizing, from the depths of his heart, that he is in an improper relationship to them.

And the expression: "Oh, you unwashed mug!" From which Nozdrev, from which Sobakevich, did you overhear this and share it with the world like a great discovery for the benefit and education of the peasant men, who don't wash themselves anyway and who, having trusted their landlords, don't consider themselves people? Your understanding of Russian national justice and punishment, the ideal which you found in the stupid old woman in Pushkin's tale and, according to which, both the guilty and the innocent should be flogged? Well, that is how it is often done here, although even more often they flog only the innocent, if they don't have anything to bribe their way out, and another proverb then said is: The guilty are without blame! And that is the kind of book that can result from a difficult internal process and lofty spiritual enlightenment! It's not possible! Either you are ill—and you need treatment, or—I don't dare to finish my thoughts. A prophet of the whip, apostle of ignorance, devotee of obfuscation and bigotry, eulogist of Tatar morals—what are you doing! Look under your feet—you are standing over an abyss. . . . Why you base thinking like this on the Orthodox Church, this I understand: The church has always supported flogging and has flattered tyrants. But why did you involve Christ here? What did you find in common between Him and anything, especially the Orthodox Church? He first proclaimed to people the teachings of freedom, equality, and brotherhood and was sealed with martyrdom, affirming the truth of his teachings. And they were the salvation of people, up until the time until they were organized into the church and accepted as the foundation for Orthodox principles. The church was a hierarchy, and it follows, is an advocate for inequality, a sycophant of power, an enemy and persecutor of brotherhood among people—and continues this even now. But the philosophical movement of the last century revealed the meaning of Christ's words. And this is why some Voltaire, who used mockery as a weapon to extinguish the flames of fanaticism and ignorance in Europe, is, of course, more a son of Christ, flesh of his flesh and bone of his bone than all your priests, bishops, metropolitans, patriarchs! Do you really not know this? This is not really even news for any high school student. . . . And that is why, even you, author of *The Inspector General* and *Dead Souls*, even you sincerely, from your heart, sang this hymn to the vile Russian clergy, placing them immeasurably higher than the Catholic clergy? Let's suppose that you don't know that the second thing once was something, while the first thing was never anything except a servant and slave to secular power; but you really actually don't know that clergy are universally held in contempt by Russian society and Russian people? About whom do you think the Russian people tell obscene stories? About the priest, the priest's wife, the priest's daughter, and the priest's worker. Who do you think the Russian people call "stupid breed" or "knocked up stallion"? Priests . . . But isn't every priest in Rus' for all Russians a representative of gluttony, greed, obsequiousness, impudence? As if you don't know this? How strange! According to you, the Russian people are the most religious in the world: a lie! The foundation of religiousness is piety, reverence, and fear of God. A Russian, scratching himself, utters God's name. . . . He says of the icon: It's useful for praying, but it's not useful for covering the chamber pots.

Look a little closer and you will see that by nature, this is a deeply atheistic people. They have many superstitions but not a trace of religiousness. Superstitions fade as civilization succeeds, but religion often coexists with it; France is a contemporary example, where there are many devout Catholics among enlightened and educated people, where many, after setting aside Christianity, still stubbornly stand up for some kind of god. The Russian people are not that kind; mystical worship is not in their nature; they have too much good sense for that, too much clarity and determination in their minds, and in this here, perhaps, is the magnitude of their monumental destiny in the future. Religiosity has not caught on, not even among the clergy, as several isolated unusual individuals, distinguished by their cold ascetic awareness, don't prove anything. The majority of our clergy are always distinguished by their thick bellies, pedantic nit-picking and wild ignorance. It is a sin to accuse them of religious intolerance and fanaticism; they are more likely to be praised for exemplary indifference in the matter of faith. Religiosity appeared in this country only in the schismatic sects, so divergent in their spirituality from the masses and so insignificant in terms of numbers.

I will not expound on your dithyramb of the love relationship between the Russian people and their sovereigns. I'll say it directly: This dithyramb did not find sympathy in anyone and discredited you in the eyes even of people whose opinions on other topics were similar to yours. As for me personally, I'll allow your conscience to revel in the examination of the godlike beauty of autocracy (it is resting easy, yes, and advantageous). Just continue to thoughtfully examine it from your beautiful far-away. From up close it is not so beautiful and not so safe. . . . I will note just one thing: When the Europeans, especially Catholics, acquired a religious spirit, they denounced unjust power, like the Jewish prophets, who condemned the iniquity of the powerful on earth. In our country it is the opposite: A person (even an upstanding one) falls ill with a disease known by the psychiatrists as religiosa mania, he immediately begins to praise the earthly god more than the heavenly one, and that is so much that he would like to reward him for his slavish fervor, but he sees that he would be discredited by this in the eyes of society. . . . Our brother, the Russian man, is a brute! . . .

I also recall that in your book, you assert as a profound and undeniable truth that literacy for common people is not just useless but positively harmful. How to respond to that? Yes, your Byzantine god will forgive you for this Byzantian thinking, if only, after handing over the paper, you didn't know what was said. . . . But maybe you would say: "Let's suppose that I made a mistake, and all my thinking was wrong, but why has my right to make mistakes been taken away and why won't anyone believe that I made an honest mistake?" Because, I would answer, topics like this in Russia are no longer news. Not even that long ago Burachok and his brother wore this topic completely thin. Of course, in your book there is more intelligence and even talent (although neither is very abundant) than in their essays, but they developed it more broadly; with you the teaching has great energy and great consistency, but they bravely reached the conclusive results. They gave everything to their Byzantine god and left nothing for Satan; then you, wishing to light a candle for both, began to make contradictions, defending, for example, Pushkin, literature, and theater, from your point of view; if only you had the integrity to be consistent. Not many can work to save their souls, but many can work toward its destruction. . . . Who could stomach the thought of similarities between Gogol and Burachok? You placed yourself too highly in the opinion of the Russian public for it to believe in you and the sincerity of such convictions. What seems natural among fools does not seem so among clever people. Some paused at the thought that your book is the fruit of an intellectual breakdown, akin to obvious mental illness. But they quickly backed off such a conclusion—clearly, this book was written not in a day, not in a week, not in a month, but, maybe, in a year, or two, or three; it is cohesive; the deliberateness shows through the careless narration, and the hymn to the powers that be nicely frame the earthly position of the devout author. This is why in Petersburg, the rumor was spread that you wrote this book with the goal of earning a tutor position for the heir to the throne's son. Even before your letter to Uvarov became public knowledge in Petersburg, where you express regret that your essays about Russia are misunderstood, then you find dissatisfaction with your previous work, and then announce that you will be satisfied with your essays when the tsar is satisfied with them. Now decide yourself whether or not to be surprised that your book damaged the public's opinion of you, as a writer and even more so as a person?

As far as I can tell, you do not understand the Russian public very well. The situation of Russian society, where fresh forces simmer and flood out, determine its nature. These forces, compressed under a heavy weight, don't have any outlet and produce only melancholy, loneliness, apathy. Only a single literature, despite the barbaric censorship, has life and forward movement. This is why the name of a writer is so well regarded in our country, because here literary success is so easy, even for someone with minimal talent. The title of poet, the name for a literary figure, overshadowed the glitter of epaulets and multicolored uniforms long ago. And that is why anyone of the so-called liberal movement is rewarded with public recognition, even if they lack talent, and why the popularity of great talents, sincerely or insincerely submitting themselves into the service of orthodoxy, autocracy, and nationalism, drops so quickly. A striking example is Pushkin, who had to write only two or three loyalist poems and put on a cadet's livery, to suddenly lose the people's love! And you are greatly mistaken if you think, joking aside, that your book fell into decline not because of its vile direction but because of its harsh truths, as each and everyone told you. Let's suppose you could think this of your brothers in writing, but how could the public fall into this category? Did you really express anything in *The Inspector General* or *Dead Souls* less harshly, with less reason and talent and less bitter truth? And the old school, naturally, was driven into a fury, but *The Inspector General* and *Dead Souls* did not fall into decline because of this; then your most recent book dropped through the earth. And the public was right here: They see Russian writers as the only leaders, defenders, and saviors from Russian autocracy, orthodoxy, and nationalism, and because they are always ready to forgive a writer for a bad book, they will never forgive a malicious book. This shows the raw, healthy instinct that lives in our society, although it is still a seed, and it shows that our country has a future. If you love Russia, join me in taking pleasure at the fall of your book.

I will tell you, with some sense of satisfaction, it seems to me that I know the Russian public a little. Your book frightened me with the possibility of a malicious influence on the government, on censorship, but not on the public. When the rumor spread in St. Peterburg that the government wants to print a run of several thousand copies of your book and see them for the lowest possible price—my friends lost heart; but then I told them that no matter what, your book will not have any success and will soon be forgotten. And actually, the book is more memorable now for all the articles about it than the text itself. Yes, the Russian people have a deep, although still developing, instinct for the truth.

Your conversion, maybe, could have been sincere, but the thinking—and bringing it to the public's attention—was very unfortunate. The time for naïve piety has already passed for our society. They already understand that praying doesn't make any difference, that in Jerusalem the only people searching for Christ are those who have never carried him in their hearts or who have lost him. Whoever is able to suffer when seeing another's suffering, whoever is distressed at the sight of other people's oppression—that person carries Christ in their heart, and for that person there is no reason to walk in Jerusalem. The humility that you preached about is, first of all, not new, and secondly, it smacks, on one hand, of terrifying pride but, on the other hand, of the most shameful humiliation of your own human value. The idea of achieving some kind of abstract perfection, to become better than everyone else through humility, may be the fruit of either pride or dementia, and in both cases it unavoidably leads to hypocrisy, bigotry, apathy. And at the same time, in your book, you allowed yourself to talk cynically and sordidly not only about others (that would have just been impolite!) but about yourself as well—this is despicable; because if a person who hits his neighbor on his face arouses indignation, then a person who hits himself arouses suspicion. No, you are just tarnished, not enlightened; you understand neither the spirit nor the form of Christianity of our times. Your book does not breathe the truth of Christian teachings but a sickly fear of death, the devil, and hell! What is this language, what are these phrases?—"Now everyone turns into dirt and rags"—did you really mean to say "every" instead of "each" person and to write in a biblical style? What is this great truth that when a person completely gives himself over to lies, his mind and talent abandon him? If your name had not been on your book, who would have thought that this bombastic and sloppy frenzy of words and phrases was the work of the author of *The Inspector General* and *Dead Souls*.

As to what is relevant to me personally, I repeat: You were mistaken in considering my article an expression of annoyance with your review of me, as one of your critics. If this had only angered me, I would have only responded with annoyance, and I would have expressed everything else calmly and impartially. And it's true that your review about your followers is doubly bad. I understand the need to sometimes thwap an idiot whose praise, whose admiration for me only amuses me, but this need is difficult because human nature makes it awkward to repay even false love with hostility. But you had in mind people, who even if they don't have excellent minds, are not idiots. In their surprise at your creation, these people made, perhaps, a great deal more fuss than the amount of things said about them; but all their enthusiasm for you stems from such a pure and noble source that you should not completely hand over all their heads to your common enemies and in addition blame their intention to give some kind of distorted interpretation of your writings. You, of course, did this through enthusiasm for the main idea of your book and through indiscretion, while Vyazemsky, a prince in aristocracy and a serf in literature, developed your idea and published a flawless denunciation of your admirers (and therefore, most of all, me). He did this, probably, out of gratitude to you for making him, a terrible rhymester, into a great poet, which apparently, as much as I remember, is "dull verse, dragging along the ground." None of this is good. And that you expected only a time when you could do justice to the admirers of your talent (having done this with proud resignation to your enemies) I didn't and couldn't know, and, I admit, I didn't want to know. Your book, but not your intentions, were in front of me: I read it and reread it 100 times and still did not find in it anything other than what was in it, and that deeply outraged and offended my soul.

If I gave free rein to my feelings, this letter would have quickly turned into a thick notebook. I never thought that I would write you about this issue, although I was tormented with the desire to do so, and although you gave each and every person in print the right to write to you without ceremony, having one truth in mind. Living in Russia, I could not do this, as the local "Postmaster Spekins" open other people's letters not out of their own personal satisfaction but out of a sense of duty, in order to make reports to the authorities.[2] This summer, the early stages of consumption sent me overseas, and Nekrasov forwarded your letter to me in Salzbrun, which Annenkov and I are leaving today for Paris, traveling through Frankfurt. Your letter, which was unexpected, gave me the opportunity to tell you everything I have in my heart against you and your book. I am not able to hold my tongue, not able to equivocate: This isn't in my nature. Let you or time itself show that I was mistaken in my conclusions about you. I will be the first to rejoice in this, but I will not regret what I said to you. The issue here is not about me or you personally but about a topic which is much greater not only than me, but even than you; the issue here is about truth, about Russian society, about Russia. And here is my last concluding word: If you had misfortune with proud humility from disavowing your truly great work, then now you should with sincere humility disavow your last book and should atone for the grievous sin of its publication in the world through new creations that will remind us of your previous ones.

Salzbrun,
3 July (15 July according to the old calendar) 1847

Selections from Nikolai Dobrolyubov, "What Is Oblomovism?"

Nikolai Dobrolyubov (1836–61) was a literary critic. He coined the term Oblomovshchina *in this popular essay on Ivan Goncharov's novel* Oblomov. *Goncharov's work was published in* Notes from the Fatherland *in 1859, while Dobrolyubov's essay was published in 1861 in* The Contemporary. *Through the commentary on Goncharov's novel, Dobrolyubov explains how the main character's attitude and lifestyle embody all of Russia's social ills. This text has been abbreviated from its original version. Italic ellipses in brackets indicate the author's omissions.*

Source: N. A. [Nikolai Aleksandrovich] Dobrolyubov, *Selected Philosophical Essays*, trans J. Fineberg (Moscow: Foreign Languages Publishing House, 1948), 174–217.

Where is the one who in the native language of the Russian soul could pronounce for us the mighty word "forward"? Century after century passes, and a half a million stay-at-homes, lubbers, and blockheads are immersed in deep slumber, but rarely is a man born in Rūs who is able to pronounce this mighty word . . . GOGOL. [. . .]³

How was Goncharov's talent expressed, what was it spent on? This question can be answered by an analysis of the content of the novel.

Apparently, Goncharov did not choose a wide field for his delineations. The story of how good-natured and indolent Oblomov lies and sleeps, and how neither friendship nor love can awaken and make him get up, is, after all, not such an important one. But it reflects Russian life; in it there appears before us the living contemporary Russian type presented with relentless severity and truth; it reflects the new word of our social development, pronounced clearly and firmly without despair and without puerile hopes, but in full consciousness of the truth. This word is *Oblomovshchina*; it is the key to the riddle of many of the phenomena of Russian life, and it lends Goncharov's novel far greater social significance than all our exposure novels possess. In the Oblomov type and, in all this *Oblomovshchina*, we see something more than a successful production by the hand of a strong talent; we see a production of Russian life, a sign of the times.

Oblomov is not altogether a new personage in our literature, but never has he been presented to us so simply and naturally as he is in Goncharov's novel. Not to go too far back into the past, we shall say that we find the generic features of the Oblomov type already in Onegin; and then we find them repeated several times in the best of our literary productions.⁴ The point is that this is our native, national type, which not one of our serious artists could brush aside. But in the course of time, as social consciousness developed, this type changed its shape, established a different relationship with life and acquired a new significance. To note these new phases of its existence, to determine the substance of its new significance, has always been an enormous task, and the talent who succeeded in doing it always did a great deal for the advancement of our literature. This is what Goncharov has done with his *Oblomov*. We shall examine the main features of the Oblomov type, and then we shall try to draw a slight parallel between it and several types of the same kind which have appeared in our literature at different times.

What are the main features of the Oblomov character? Utter inertness resulting from apathy towards everything that goes on in the world. The cause of this apathy lies partly in Oblomov's external position and partly in the manner of his mental and moral development. The external position is that he is a gentleman: "he has a Zakhar, and another three hundred Zakhars," as the author puts it.⁵ Ilya Ilyich (Oblomov) explains the advantages of his position to Zakhar in the following way:

"Do I fuss and worry? Do I work? Don't I have enough to eat? Do I look thin and haggard? Am I in want of anything? Have I not people to fetch and carry for me, to do the things I want done? Thank God, I have never in my life had to draw a pair of stockings on. Do you think I would go to any trouble? Why should I? . . . But I need not tell you all this. Haven't you served me since childhood? You know all about it. You have seen how tenderly I was brought up. You know that I have never suffered cold or hunger, that I have never known want, that I don't have to earn my bread and, in general, have never done any work."

Oblomov is speaking the absolute truth. The entire history of his upbringing confirms what he says. He became accustomed to lolling about at a very early age because he had people to fetch and carry for him, to do things for him. Under these circumstances he lived the idle life of a sybarite even when he did not want to. And tell me, pray, what can you expect of a man who grew up under the following circumstances:

Zakhar—as his [Oblomov's] nurse did in the old days draws on his stockings and puts on his shoes while Ilyk, already a boy of fourteen, does nothing but lie on his back and put up one foot and then the other; and if it seems to him that Zakhar has done something not in the right way, he kicks him in the nose. If the disgruntled Zakhar takes it into his head to complain, he gets his ears boxed by the adults. After that Zakhar combs Ilya Ilyich's hair, helps him on with his coat, carefully putting his arms into the sleeves so as not to incommode him too much, and reminds him that he must do so and so and so and so: on waking up in the morning—to wash himself, etc.

If Ilya Ilyich wants anything he has only to make a sign—and at once three or four servants rush to carry out his wishes; if he drops anything, if he reaches for something he needs and cannot get at it, if something has to be brought in, or it is necessary to run on some errand—he sometimes, like the active boy he is, is just eager to run and do it himself, but suddenly his mother and his father and his three aunts shout in a quintet:

"—Where are you going? What for? What are Vaska and Vanka and Zakharka here for? Hey! Vaska, Vanka, Zakharka! What are you all dawdling there for? I'll let you have it! . . ."

And so Ilya Ilyich is simply not allowed to do anything for himself. Later on he found that this was much more convenient and he learned to shout himself: "Hey, Vaska, Vanka, bring me this, bring me that! I don't want this, I want that! Go and bring it!" [. . .]

An important factor here is the mental development of the Oblomovs, which, of course, is also molded by their external position. From their earliest years they see life turned inside out, as it were, and until the end of their days they are unable to understand what their relation to the world and to people should reasonably be. Later on much is explained to them and they begin to understand something; but the views that were inculcated in them in their childhood remain somewhere in a corner and constantly peep out from there, hindering all new conceptions and preventing them from sinking deep into their hearts. . . . As a result, chaos reigns in their heads: sometimes a man makes up his mind to do something, but he does not know how to begin, where to turn. . . . This is not surprising: a normal man always wants to do only what he can do; that is why he immediately does all that he wants to do. . . . But Oblomov . . . is not accustomed to do anything; consequently, he cannot really determine what he can do and what he cannot do— and consequently, he cannot seriously, *actively*, want anything. . . . His wishes always assume the form: "how good it would be if this were done," but how this can be done he does not know. That is why he is so fond of dreaming and dreads the moment when his dreams may come in contact with reality. When they do, he tries to shift the burden to another's shoulders; if there are no other shoulders, why then, perhaps it will get done *somehow*. . . .

[. . .] Sometimes he liked to picture himself an invincible general, compared with whom not only Napoleon but even Yeruslan Lazarevich was a nonentity; he would picture a war and its cause: for example, Africans would come pouring into Europe, or he would organize new crusades and would fight, decide the fate of nations, sack towns, show mercy, execute, perform acts of kindness and generosity.

Sometimes he would picture himself as a great thinker or artist who is followed by admiring crowds. . . . Clearly, Oblomov is not a dull, apathetic type, destitute of ambition and feeling; he too seeks something in life, thinks about something. But the disgusting habit of getting his wishes satisfied not by his own efforts but by the efforts of others developed in him an apathetic inertness and plunged him into the wretched state of moral slavery. This slavery is so closely interwoven with Oblomov's aristocratic habits that they mutually permeate and determine each other, so that it becomes totally impossible to draw any line of demarcation between them. This moral slavery of Oblomov's is, perhaps, the most interesting side of his personality, and of his whole life. . . . But how could a man enjoying the independent position of Ilya Ilyich sink into slavery? If anybody can enjoy freedom, surely he can! He is not in the civil service, he does not go into society, and he has an assured income. . . . He himself boasts that he does not have to bow and scrape and humiliate himself, that he is not like "others" who work tirelessly, fuss and run about, and if they do not work they do not eat. . . . He inspires the good widow Pshenitsyna with reverent love for himself precisely because he is a *gentleman*, because he shines and glitters, because he walks and talks so freely and independently, because "he is not constantly copying papers, does not tremble with fear that he might be late at the office, because he does not look at everybody as if asking to be saddled and ridden on, but looks at everybody and everything boldly and freely, as if demanding obedience." And yet, the whole life of this gentleman is wrecked because he always remains the slave of another's will and never rises to the level of displaying the least bit of independence. He is the slave of every woman, of every newcomer; the slave of every rascal who wishes to get him under his thumb. He is the slave of his serf Zakhar, and it is hard to say which of them submits more to the power of the other. At all events, if Zakhar does not wish to do a thing Ilya Ilyich cannot make him do it; and if Zakhar wants to do anything he will do it, even if his master is opposed to it—and his master submits. . . . This is quite natural: Zakhar, after all, can at least do something; Oblomov cannot do anything at all. It is needless to speak of Tarantyev and Ivan Matveyich, who do everything they like with Oblomov in spite of the fact that they are far inferior to him both in intellectual development and in moral qualities. . . . Why is this? Again the answer is, because Oblomov, being a gentleman, does not wish to work, nor could he even if he wanted to; and he cannot understand his own relation to everything around him. He is not averse to activity as long as it is in the form of a vision and is far removed from reality: thus, he draws up a plan for the improvement of his estate and zealously applies himself to this task—only "details, estimates, and figures" frighten him, and he constantly brushes them aside, for how can he bother with them! . . . He is a gentleman, as he himself explains to Ivan Matveyich:

"Who am I? What am I? you will ask. . . . Go and ask Zakhar, he will tell you. 'A gentleman' he will say! Yes, I am a gentleman, and I can't do anything! You do it, if you know how, and help if you can, and for your trouble take what you like—that's what knowledge is for!"

Do you think that in this way he is only shirking work, trying to cover up his own indolence with the plea of ignorance? No, he really does not know how to do anything and cannot do anything; he is really unable to undertake any useful task. As regards his estate (for the reorganization of which he had already drawn up a plan), he confesses his ignorance to Ivan Matveyich in the following way:

I don't know what *barshchina* is.[6] I know nothing about husbandry. I don't know the difference between a poor *muzhik* and a rich one. I don't know what a quarter of rye, or oats is, what its price is, in which months different crops are sown and reaped, or how and when they are sold. I don't know whether I am poor or rich, whether I will have enough to eat next year, or whether I shall be a beggar—I don't know anything! . . . Therefore, speak and advise me as if I were a child . . .

In other words: be my master, do what you like with my property and leave what share of it you think best. . . . And that is what happened: Ivan Matveyich nearly grabbed Oblomov's entire estate, but unfortunately Stolz prevented him.

But Oblomov was not only ignorant of agricultural matter, he not only failed to understand the state of his own affairs: that would only have been half the trouble! . . . The main trouble was that he could see no meaning in life in general. In the Oblomov world nobody asked himself: why life, what is life, what is its meaning and purpose? The Oblomovs had a very simple conception of life.

"They conceived it as an ideal of repose and inaction, disturbed at times by various unpleasant accidents such as: sickness, losses, quarrels and, incidentally work. They tolerated work as a punishment imposed on our ancestors, but they could not love it, and they always shirked it whenever possible, deeming this permissible and right."

This is exactly how Ilya Ilyich looked upon life. The ideal happiness that he described to Stolz consisted in nothing more than a life of plenty, with conservatories, hothouses, picnics in the woods with a samovar, etc.—a dressing gown, sound sleep by way of a rest in between—idyllic walks with a meek but plump wife, gazing at the peasants at work. Oblomov's mind was so moulded from childhood that he was able, even in the most abstract arguments, in the most utopian theories, to halt in the present and never leave this *status quo* in spite of all the arguments. In depicting his conception of ideal bliss Ilya Ilyich never thought of asking himself what its inherent meaning was, he never thought of asserting its lawfulness or truth, he never asked himself where these conservatories and hothouses were to come from, who was to maintain them, and on what grounds he was to enjoy them. . . . Failing to put such questions to himself, failing to clear up his own relation to the world and to society, Oblomov, of course, could not grasp the meaning of his own life and, therefore, found everything he had to do irksome and tedious.

When he was in the civil service he could not for the life of him understand why all those documents were being written; and failing to understand, he could think of nothing better than to resign and do no more writing. He went to school, but he could not understand the purpose of this instruction; and failing to understand, he piled his books up in a corner and indifferently watched the dust accumulating on them. He went into society, but he could not understand why people visited each other; and failing to understand, he gave up all his acquaintances and lolled on his couch for days on end. He tried to become intimate with women, but he began to ask himself what could be expected of them, what one should expect of them; and after pondering this matter, and failing to find an answer, he began to avoid women. . . . Everything bored and wearied him, and he lolled on his couch filled with utter contempt for the "human ant heap," where people worried and fussed, God knows what about . . .

Having reached this point in explaining Oblomov's character we deem it appropriate to turn to the literary parallel we drew above. The foregoing reflections have brought us to the conclusion that Oblomov is not a being whom nature has completely deprived of the ability to move by his own volition. His indolence and apathy are the result of upbringing and environment. The main thing here is not Oblomov, but Oblomovshchina. Perhaps Oblomov would even have started work had he found an occupation to his liking; but for that he would have had to develop under somewhat different conditions. In his present position he cannot find an occupation to his liking because he sees no meaning in life in general and cannot rationally define his own relations to others. This is where he provides us with the occasion for comparing him with previous types, which the best of our writers have depicted. It was observed long ago that all the heroes in the finest Russian stories and novels suffer from their failure to see any purpose in life and their inability to find a decent occupation for themselves. As a consequence, they find all occupations tedious and repugnant, and in this they reveal an astonishing resemblance to Oblomov. *[. . .]*

The feature common to all these men is that nothing in life is a vital necessity for them, a shrine in their hearts, a religion, organically merged with their whole being, so that to deprive them of it would mean depriving them of their lives. Everything about them is superficial, nothing is rooted in their natures. They, perhaps, do something when external necessity compels them to, just as Oblomov went visiting the places that Stolz dragged him to, he bought music and books for Olga and read what she compelled him to read; but their hearts do not lie in the things they do merely by force of circumstances. If each of them were offered gratis all the external advantages that they obtain by their work they would gladly give up working. By virtue of *Oblomovshchina*, an Oblomov government official would not go to his office every day if he could receive his salary and regular promotion without having to do so. A soldier would vow not to touch a weapon if he were offered the same terms and, in addition, were allowed to keep his splendid uniform, which can be very useful on certain occasions. The professor would stop delivering lectures, the student would give up his studies, the author would give up writing, the actor would never appear on the stage again and the artist would break his chisel and palette, to put it in high-flown style, if he found a way of obtaining gratis all that he now obtains by working. They only talk about lofty strivings, consciousness of moral duty and common interests; when put to the test, it all turns out to be words, mere words. Their most sincere and heartfelt striving is the striving for repose, for the dressing-gown, and their very activities are nothing more than an *honorable dressing-gown* (to use an expression that is not our own) with which they cover up their vapidity and apathy. Even the best educated people, people with lively natures and warm hearts, are prone in their practical lives to depart from their ideas and plans, very quickly resign themselves to the realities of life, which, however, they never cease to revile as vulgar and disgusting. This shows that all the things they talk and dream about are really alien to them, superficial; in the depth of their hearts they cherish only one dream, one ideal—undisturbed repose, quietism, *Oblomovshchina*. Many even reach such a stage that they cannot conceive of man working willingly, with enthusiasm. Read the argument in *Ekonomicheskii Ukazatel'* to the effect that everybody would die of starvation resulting from idleness if by the equal distribution of wealth people were robbed of the incentive to accumulate capital. . . .[7]

[. . .] That word is —*Oblomovshchina*.

Now, when I hear a country squire talking about the rights of man and urging the necessity of developing personality, I know from the first words he utters that he is an Oblomov.

When I hear a government official complaining that the system of administration is too complicated and cumbersome, I know that he is an Oblomov.

When I hear an army officer complaining that parades are exhausting, and boldly arguing that marching at a slow pace is useless, etc., I have not the slightest doubt that he is an Oblomov.

When, in the magazines, I read liberal denunciations of abuses and expressions of joy over the fact that at last something has been done that we have been waiting and hoping for so long, I think to myself that all this has been written from Oblomovka.

When I am in the company of educated people who ardently sympathize with the needs of mankind and who for many years have been relating with undiminished heat the same (and sometimes new) anecdotes about bribery, acts of tyranny and lawlessness of every kind, I, in spite of myself, feel that I have been transported to old Oblomovka. . . .

Who, then, will in the end shift them from the spot to which they are rooted by the mighty word "forward!" which Gogol dreamed of, and for which Rūs has been longing and waiting for so long? So far we find no answer to this question either in society or in literature. Goncharov, who understood and was able to reveal our *Oblomovshchina* to us, could not, however, avoid paying tribute to the common error which is prevalent in our society to this day: he set out to bury *Oblomovshchina* and deliver a panegyric over its grave. "Farewell, old Oblomovka, you have outlived your time," he says through the mouth of Stolz, but what he says is not true. All Russia which has read, or will read, Oblomov will disagree with him. No, Oblomovka is our own motherland, her owners are our teachers, her three hundred Zakhars are always at our service. There is a large portion of Oblomov within every one of us, and it is too early to write our obituary. [. . .]

In intellectual development, Olga is the highest ideal that a Russian artist can find in our present Russian life. That is why the extraordinary clarity and simplicity of her logic and the amazing harmony of heart and mind astonish us so much that we are ready to doubt even her imaginary existence and say: "There are no such young women." But following her through the whole novel we find that she is always true to herself and to her development, that she is not merely the creation of the author, but a living person, only one that we have not yet met. She more than Stolz gives us a glimpse of the new Russian life; from her we may expect to hear the word that will consume Oblomovshchina with fire and reduce it to ashes. . . . She begins by falling in love with Oblomov, by believing in him and in the possibility of his moral transformation. . . . She toils long and stubbornly, with loving devotion and tender solicitude, in an effort to fan the spark of life in this man and to stimulate him to activity. She refuses to believe that he is so incapable of doing good; cherishing her hopes in him, her future creation, she does everything for him. She even ignores conventional propriety, goes to see him alone without telling anybody, and, unlike him, is not afraid of losing her reputation. But with astonishing tact she at once discerns every false streak in his character, and she explains to him why it is false and not true in an extremely simple way. He, for example, writes her the letter we referred to above and later assures her that he had written it solely out of concern for her, completely forgetting himself, sacrificing himself, and so forth.

"No," she answers, "that is not true. If you had thought only of my happiness and had believed that for it was necessary that we should part, you would simply have gone away without sending any letters."

He says that he fears that she will be unhappy when she learns that she had been mistaken in him, ceases to love him, and loves another. In answer to this she asks him:

"Where do you see my unhappiness? I love you now and I feel good; later I will love another, hence, I will feel good with him. You need not worry about me."

This simplicity and clarity of thought are elements of the new life, not the one under the conditions of which present-day society grew up. . . . And then— how obedient Olga's will is to her heart! She continues her relations with Oblomov and persists in her love for him, in spite of unpleasantness, jeers, etc., from outside, until she is convinced of his utter worthlessness. Then she bluntly tells him that she had been mistaken in him and cannot combine her fate with his. She continues to praise and pet him while she rejects him, and even later, hurt by her action she annihilates him as no other Oblomov was ever annihilated by a woman. Tatyana says to Onegin at the end of the romance:

I love you (why conceal it?),
But to another my troth is plighted,
To him forever I'll be true.

And so, only formal moral duty saves her from this empty-headed fop; if she were free she would have flung her arms around his neck. Natalya leaves Rudin only because he himself was obdurate from the very outset, and on seeing him off she realizes that he does not love her and she grieves sorely over this. There is no need to speak of Pechorin, who managed only to earn the hatred of Princess Mary. No, Olga did not behave to Oblomov in that way. She said to him simply and gently:

"I learned only recently that I loved in you what I wanted you to have, what Stolz pointed out to me, and what he and I conjured up. I loved the future Oblomov! You are unassuming and honest, Ilya;

you are tender . . . like a dove; you hide your head under your wing—and you want nothing more; you want to coo in the loft all your life. . . . But I am not like that: that is not enough for me; I want something more, but what—I don't know!"

And so she leaves Oblomov and strives towards her something, although she does not quite know what it is. At last she finds it in Stolz, she joins him and is happy; but even here she does not halt, does not come to a dead stop. Certain vague problems and doubts disturb her, there are things she is trying to fathom. The author did not fully reveal her emotions to us and we may err in our assumptions concerning their nature. But it seems to us that her heart and mind were disturbed by the spirit of the new life, to which she was immeasurably nearer than Stolz. We think so because we find several hints of this in the following dialogue:

—"What shall I do? Yield and pine?" she asked.
—"No," he answered. "Arm yourself with firmness and serenity. We two are not Titans," he continued, embracing her. "We shall not follow the Manfreds and Fausts and challenge disturbing problems to mortal combat, nor shall we accept their challenge. We shall bow our heads and wait humbly until the hard times pass, and life, happiness, will smile again . . ."
—"But suppose they never leave us: suppose grief disturbs us more and more?" she asked.
—"Well, we'll accept it as a new element of life. . . . But no that cannot be, it cannot happen to us! It is not your grief alone, it is the common ailment of mankind. You have suffered only one drop. . . . All this is frightful when a man loses his grip on life, when he has no support. But in our case . . ."

He did not specify the our case, but it is evident that it is he who does not wish to "challenge disturbing problems to mortal combat," that it is *he* who wants to "humbly bow his head . . ." She is ready for this fight, she longs for it and is always afraid that her tranquil happiness with Stolz may grow into something that resembles the Oblomov apathy. Clearly, she does not wish to bow her head and wait humbly until the hard times pass, in the hope that life will smile again later. She left Oblomov when she ceased to believe in him; she will leave Stolz if she ceases to believe in him. And this will happen if she continues to be tormented by problems and doubts, and if he continues to advise her to accept them as a new element of life and bow her head. She is thoroughly familiar with Oblomovshchina, she will be able to discern it in all its different shapes, and under all masks, and will always be able to find strength enough to pronounce ruthless judgement on it. . . .

From Gleb Uspensky, "A Village Diary"

Gleb Uspensky (1843–1902) primarily wrote about living conditions in rural areas using a journalistic, almost ethnographic style for his sketches where he described the details of peasants' daily lives. He was closely connected with Notes from the Fatherland. *This essay provides a detailed description of the economic situation of peasants following emancipation from serfdom. This text has been abbreviated from its original version.*

Source: Gleb Uspensky, "A Village Diary," in *Readings in Russian Civilization*, vol. 2, *Imperial Russia, 1700–1917*, ed. Thomas Riha (Chicago: University of Chicago Press, 1969), 358–67.

While strolling about the country place where I spent the summer of 1878 I could see an old peasant walking toward me. He was carrying a little girl, about one-and-a-half years old. Another about twelve, was walking beside him. They were walking slowly, as beggars do who are always watching for someone who might give them alms, fixing their attention on every window, every door, looking over fences and into half-open doorways. They resembled beggars, too, in their outward appearance. Even for country folk they were poorly dressed. The man's trousers were ragged and torn, exposing his bare body beneath, and he was barefoot. The little girl was so thin and jaundiced that she seemed ill. Her blond hair was disheveled and hung in uneven dirty strands, with little cakes of dirt visible between them. The other girl's appearance also bespoke poverty and ineradicable untidiness....

When this little group came up I expected the man to beg; but he said nothing, only stopped and bowed.

"Are you begging?" I asked uncertainly.

"What!" said the peasant, looking at me with obvious astonishment. "I am the local watchman—Merciful heaven!—"

"Oh, well then, excuse me for—" "The watchman, the watchman, dear sir—God forbid I should be reduced to—These are my grandchildren come to visit, and we're just out for a walk—No! God preserve us from such a thing—"

I again begged his pardon, and said: "The little girls are so thin, that's why—"

"That they are, my friend, and how else when there's no food for them?"

"How is it they have no food?"

"There isn't any, that's all. We had a cow, but the Lord took her from us—she died—So, no milk."

"Then what do you feed this little one?" I asked.

"What do we feed her? Same things we eat—kvas, bread—"[8]

"To such a little child?!"

"And just what would you do?—God willing, this fall the heifer will be grown, and we'll sell her. And for the summer I have to be watchman for the master—Adding in what I make from that, God willing we'll buy a cow before winter. But in the meantime, we have to endure—can't be helped!—"

"You stand watch at night?"

"Just so, only at night. But if I had a horse, my days would not be wasted—" I should mention here that in the village where I was living there is a lot of construction work, and the peasants could earn good pay doing day labor in their free time.

"If you have a horse," continued the peasant, "they'll pay seventy kopecks a day; so I would really be all set at the end of the summer. That is something to grieve a body, my friend, for I haven't a horse, nor any way to get one—I haven't a wife any longer, she's been dead two years now. Their father," he said, pointing to the girls, "my daughter's husband, they took him into the army, so there I was, alone to feed them, and no way to manage—Ah, but if I only had some old horse—there were some for fifteen rubles at the fair—Then, no matter what, I'd be able to be on my feet again come winter."

"Well, there's a cooperative, a bank here—Why don't you get your fifteen rubles from the bank?"

"That bank gives nothing to us, mister—"

"What do you mean? Why not?"

"Because they don't, that's all. Besides, dear sir, you have to have someone sign for you, and where would I find anyone willing to do that? Now somebody with means, he can have all he wants from that bank. But somebody like me, who has nothing—who would back me up? If something were to happen, nobody would be willing to back me up."

The district where the unfortunate watchman lives is unquestionably the richest area that I myself have ever seen. The whole region is wealthy, and bountifully supplied with natural riches. It lies along the Volga, in the steppe of Samara province. This is the breadbasket of Russia, where five puds of grain sown commonly returns a hundred—often even more.[9] Besides the wonderful land, what lush meadows there are, what abundant feed for cattle, not to mention the beauty of the place! The wide Volga is a plentiful source of food. There are not many places like this, where fish can be had so cheaply. But besides the Volga, the many smaller rivers which flow through the region provide so much edible life that, as they say, "You'll never catch it all, you'll never eat it all." And how many different kinds of birds and wildfowl fly and sing in the meadow marshes and over the lakes of this steppe region, and hide in the fragrant high grasses. "Paradise!" So one might say, looking upon all this natural beauty, all this natural wealth....

This village I am talking about is provided with just as many of these natural blessings as other parts of the region. It is situated along a stream; and another, an even wider, deeper, and richer stream, flows not more than a third of a mile away. The lands and meadows which the peasants farm are wonderfully fertile and rich. Besides that, as a supplement to this natural wealth, monetary resources are available in the village as well—a savings and loan association, in which every one of the seventy village households is a member. Finally, so that the reader may be completely convinced of the prosperity of this village, I must say that although there is still no school here, and no doctor, still, since the Emancipation of February 19, 1861, there is not, has not been, and most probably will not be, a single kopeck of arrears in this village. I can back up this argument on behalf of the area's prosperity with the official survey. But my personal observations lead me to the conclusion that such faithfulness and regularity in meeting their obligations, which is generally such a difficult burden for the peasant, has been accomplished here without any special labor. For the quitrent income from the mill, the river, the tavern, etc., is enough to cover all taxes and dues. For instance, the tavern keeper alone pays 600 silver rubles yearly to the commune for his license to trade.

What else, then, is lacking, so that a man living here will have enough food, clothing, and shoes, and would be if not rich, then at least not a beggar?—And yet just imagine—among such blessings not a day passes that you do not run into some happening or scene or conversation that instantly shatters all your fantasies, spoils all your deductions and views about the people's life: in a word, leaves you completely unable to comprehend how the things you see could occur in the given conditions.

Here, alongside the home of a peasant who has 20,000 rubles in savings, lives an old woman and her granddaughters, with nothing to fall back on, and no fuel to cook her dinner, unless she can pick up some splinters of firewood somewhere—not to mention winter, when she will freeze from the cold.

"But aren't there communal forests?" you, the dilettante of rural customs, exclaim with astonishment.

"Oh yes, but they won't let us gather firewood there."

"Why not?"

"Well, some are allowed to, but not everyone." Or: "Alms, sir, for the sake of heaven!" "You,—do you live here?"

"Yes, I live here."

"Well then, how has it happened you have come to such a condition?"

"How did it happen? I'll tell you—We used to live well, mister. But one day my husband was working in the manor house, and fell from the roof—They said we should take him to the city, but I had no way to get him there—Now I am alone with the children—The commune took our land."

"How could the commune take your land? Why?"

"And just who was going to pay the poll tax for it? They first relieved us of the poll tax, but when they saw we weren't able to work the land, they took it too."

"What about hiring someone to help?"

"Where would we get the money?"

"What do you mean, where? You have your own money, money you and your husband have saved—you have cash, in the communal funds!—I know there are several hundred rubles there. You can hire someone, and buy food for yourselves too. Why do you go around begging? Ask for money from the communal funds—part of it is your own money!"

"Oh, is that so? And they will give it to us, I suppose—Alms, for the sake of heaven, God will bless your mercy."

Finally, consider the watchman I described above: here is a member of the commune who cannot obtain a loan of 15-20 rubles, although available resources include not only communal funds, but also a village bank run by the village assembly and supplied with credits of 15,000 rubles by the State Bank. This member of the commune sees no chance of recovering by doing the type yet it is clear to all that he could easily work off a 20 ruble debt. . . .

In such a prosperous region, where the land is held communally, in a place with a savings association and a bank, in a place where there are no arrears in land payments, can it be that a working man cannot support his family, and has nothing to eat!? . . .

Certainly this seems like the result of some sorcery! Admittedly, if in this village of seventy households you were to meet only that watchman, or the old woman I described earlier, you would be puzzled, and hard put to explain their situation. But what would you say should you come across such incomprehensible phenomena at each step, phenomena which convinced you that such personal disasters are taken lightly in this wealthy village where it would seem everything favors prosperity. . . .

The first thing one notices from observing the contemporary rural order is the almost complete absence of moral bonds among members of the village commune. During serfdom, the village people were united by the awareness of common misfortunes, for all were bound to obey every whim of the landlord. The master had a right to interfere with a family's affairs, and arbitrarily direct a man's private life: he could determine his profession, make him a scientist, a musician, a cook, or a tailor; he could arrange marriages regardless of a man's own wishes, and so forth. The continual possibility of such arbitrariness bound the commune through the same belittling of human dignity. . . . Nowadays no one interferes with the family life except the government, which conscripts soldiers. Nowadays everyone answers for himself, and runs his own affairs as he knows best. But the bond of the "moral yoke," that unity fostered by common resentments, has not been replaced by any positive appreciation of the necessity for general prosperity, and for a better life for all. In place of the old arbitrary rule has come neither knowledge, nor development, nor even a kind word between neighbors. Nothing has destroyed the old habit of trembling before authority, seeing oneself as a perpetual laborer, or the habit of making daily bread the goal of one's entire existence on earth. These habits hold the peasant in their power to this day.

Arbitrary authority is much less of a factor in the peasant family life now than during the days of serfdom. And yet little value is placed on another's existence, and no sympathy or concern for another's private interests. A sick child may cry all night and all day, or all week, while the parents worry and grieve for him—but the family knows nothing of medicine, and no one comes with help or skill, exactly as it was when they were all serfs. A doctor who earns 1,200 rubles yearly serving a population of 300,000, says: "But I can't be everywhere at once!" The doctor's assistant can't be everywhere at once, either. . . . And meanwhile, a child is dying—and his death impresses those who loved him with the weight of their cares and their ignorance. . . .

There is a school, but the teacher only cares about earning his bread; has little knowledge himself, and is poverty stricken. In the summer, he likes to keep to himself, or visit with his neighbor the priest. And when he is teaching, how can he cope with all his sixty students? Even teaching them the alphabet is a major task. As he himself told me, he shouted himself hoarse doing it. How could he have any time for cultivating social consciousness? What is needed is simply socially conscious and concerned villagers, and lots of them—but there are none.

There is no enlightenment which could come into the peasant family from the outside and give these people a better and a wider perspective on the world about them, which would let them breathe freely, and show them that man is destined for more than shedding sweat and blood. Without all this, each peasant household remains burdened with cares, which would disappear if only they were the subject of the common village concern. Each such household then is like an isolated island, where a stubborn struggle with life goes on from day to day, with a patience and frantic labor which is scarcely comprehensible to its inhabitants. The weight of those cares is so great that it seems impossible to exist in the face of them. It is this burden of cares which forces the peasant family to struggle so, and thus produces a deep fatalism in their way of thinking:

"It is God's will that thousands and millions of people struggle just as we do." This is how each peasant household explains its lot to itself, as the family rises at cock's crow to begin another day's work. . . .

There are a great many examples which may be given to demonstrate the complete isolation of the peasant family, and the alienation of the members of the commune from one another. For instance, merchants will use their influence with the rural authorities to persuade the commune to lease its fishing rights or vodka-selling rights to them. The more persuasive they are—that is, the more vodka they give to the elders and officers—the less they will have to pay to lease the commune's commercial rights. Ordinarily meetings called to deal with this kind of communal business include all the members of the commune; but this is because the merchants will provide a glass or two of vodka for everybody. The motivation for deciding to lease the village's commercial rights, then, generally has nothing to do with concern for the common interest. This is confirmed by the absolute unconcern which all the members show in the money which is thus earned. The members of the commune know that no one will get his share of the 600 rubles which is paid to the commune by the tavern. They leave this money, as it almost always happens, to the plunder of the people who have access to the village funds....

If only there were some mutual concern for one another's welfare among the villagers, the money taken in from the tavern could be used for a thousand useful things—if only those matters were considered worthy of common attention. Why could not that peasant who broke his leg be taken to a hospital at the commune's expense? Then he would soon be able to start working again—and his family would be saved from ruin. A doctor's assistant could be sent for; or that talented self-taught lad could be sent to a high school, later to return to be the communal clerk, perhaps. These things are not done, because in all these ventures there is no real monetary gain for any member of the commune, and monetary gains are the only kind they think about—they know nothing about any kind of profit other than personal.

Because of this complete absence of "social consciousness" in today's rural thinking the communal use of the land generally does not spare the villagers from death by starvation. Amazing cases of this type happen very simply. Here is a peasant family, for instance, which pays a poll tax for two, and farms a double allotment of land. A household like this will have one working man, though perhaps five or six mouths to feed. Now if this man has fallen from the roof and broken his leg, he stays at home unable to work. The money in the communal cash fund, to which he has contributed, and which would pay for a doctor and hospital care, has been squandered—perhaps by the village clerk or one of the elders. But the disabled man would anyway not expect to be helped through communal money. So he stays home, work stops on the family's land, and the family grows poor. They cannot pay the double poll tax, so they ask the commune to reduce their tax by half. The commune takes away half the tax obligation, but also takes the land which goes with it. Deprived of land and income, the family grows still poorer. Thus it may well be that the following year the second allotment will also have to be taken away from them, leaving the family completely without land, forced to wander about the world like beggars. Yet the man is a member of a commune well provided with lands, forests, and sums of money. Who will rescue him in such a plight? His family might help, his relations and friends might save him—blood ties and personal relationships to private persons can help—but there is no communal concern for him as an individual. The workings of the communal system can destroy him, but cannot help him stand on his feet. They give the land which was taken away from him to another, someone who has not been afflicted by misfortunes which have forced him to lose heart. But he has been ruined, must wander from place to place, hire himself out as a laborer to his neighbor, who too is a fully privileged member of the commune. Where is the much-praised "harmony" of the communal system??

I submit, in conclusion, still another incident which I investigated, to prove that contemporary rural institutions are not at all durable or harmonious. Adjoining this village's land is a large estate with 600 desiatins of land, including 100 desiatins of forest (which in this area is quite valuable).[10] The owner of this estate does not manage his own lands, but only visits the estate in the summer. Under the former owner, this land was readily leased by the local people and neighboring peasants. But the new owner proposed to sell it in one piece to the commune as a whole. To facilitate this purchase and let all the villagers participate in it, he proposed that the peasants pay him for this land—not with money—but with the very forest they would be buying as part of the estate! Under the terms he proposed, the peasants acting as a group would cut down four desiatins of this forest each year, and deliver the wood to the landlord, who would pay them at the going rates for the wood and the carting. The whole operation was to be completed in twenty-five years. Thus, at the end of the last year, although the old forest would have been cut down, the peasants would have a new one—the twenty-five-year growth. At the same time, they would have had the use of the other five-sixths of the estate since the day the agreement was signed. The whole affair was to be arranged through the commune, and guaranteed by the whole village. But it is already two years since the offer was made, and nothing is to be seen of this guarantee. The peasants continue to rent land for cash, either from neighboring landlords or from peasants who have fallen into difficulties and lost their allotments. They will pay each other 3–5 rubles per desiatina. At the same time the estate owner is overwhelmed by requests from some peasants who want to buy portions of the estate. One peasant even wanted to buy the entire estate, on the suggested terms, but the landlord does not want to sell the land in any other way but to the whole commune. But the whole *commune* does not agree, the members cannot get together, and so they remain passive while this good, cheap, needed land lies unused. What is the reason for such an incomprehensible phenomenon?

From my conversations with the peasants upon this subject I could be sure of only one thing: the mutual dissensions among members of this commune had reached an almost dangerous level. Should the whole commune buy the estate (several peasants explained to me), it would be necessary to choose one man who would deal with the landlord, make accounts of the required woodcutting operations each year, and keep track of working days for each villager. This would have to be a man the whole commune could trust. But there is no such man among the seventy households! Now the villagers choose elders and the tax collector, but these are official persons who deal with the government, and anyway the law says they must choose such officers. But to choose their own man, who would watch over the common interest as well as his own, seems impossible to these people. Each thinks that a man can look only to his own private interests, and that anyone in a position of special privilege must finally end up better off than all the others. Whomever I named, the village people said he could not be trusted.

"It doesn't matter what a man says, just see what he does if you give him a chance—" This is how the village people characterize each other. This lack of trust in an as yet unselected manager, lack of faith in the possibility that any person would not take advantage of others if he could, is just as prevalent among the wealthy peasants as among the poor ones. These two rather distinguishable rural groups are equally reluctant to conclude a deal which would be profitable to everyone. For the poor not to allow the strong to become still stronger is a real pleasure. And their confidence that if all participated equally in a purchase the strong would get more than the poor, that the poor would turn out to be only laborers for the richer, is so strong, and based on what seem to them such irrefutable facts, that the landlord's plan seems completely impracticable. . . .

It seems to me that one, small, generally unnoticed factor provides the clue to understanding the essence of the rural way of life. To this day you very frequently hear the word *barshchina*—the collective term for labor dues—in rural conversations. But since serfdom and labor dues are a past affair, you attach little significance to it. Yet it appears that although this word really belongs to the past, the remnants of this past are far from effaced today. And so, as you observe rural life you become convinced that in the contemporary village there is not a phenomenon, there is not a character trait, not even one habit, which the labor dues system alone will not explain.

Now what actually was this *barshchina*, the labor dues system? In general outline, this was work performed by the whole village for one manor house—this labor was an obligation the peasant had been burdened with from time immemorial, something they never questioned. The lord, to whom the village belonged, could change either for the better or for the worse. But for the village all these changes meant nothing: they had to work all the same, whether for conservatives or liberals or even radicals, whoever came to live in the manor house. A landlord demanded only one thing from the village—work; work which took up the greater part of the day, of the year, of one's lifetime, work for someone else. This fundamental principle of *barshchina* was strengthened in the people's mind by all possible means, and finally produced a completely defined ideal for the creature known as the muzhik (the peasant). The ideal required, first, unquestioning fulfilment of another's commands; second, that this fulfilment be deeply rooted in a conviction that a peasant's own life is a matter of little concern.

In this way, serfdom has left us a legacy of peasants who are, first, tireless workers who struggle and labor at their work, who sweat and toil from day to day; second, men who pay their dues in full—and for whom these dues and obligations are the first care before which all private cares must fade; third, men who do not argue, whatever happens—they only ask "What must I do?" "How much is my tax?" Tax assessments are almost the only subject discussed in the village assembly. Personal or private village matters never come up—such things have never been learned. Fourth, to work, and to struggle, is the goal of life, the thread joining days and years into a whole human life. Our peasant is at peace after tiring and exhausting himself at his work, because he has done exactly as demanded of him. He forces his son to marry "a good worker" disregarding all other considerations.

It is in the name of this ideal that the peasant continues to live as he did in the days of serfdom. Where the system of obligatory labor was dominant, the peasant has remained almost a serf. Just as in the past, he goes out to the fields before sunrise, he struggles to pay his dues, keeps silent with unthinking indifference, fulfills everything that the elders order him to do. In such villages the peasants have a completely worked-out view of themselves and of their place in God's world. Thanks to it, they know what it is they do, and why they must struggle. Here is why it seems that the peasants of a poor village, overloaded with work and taxes, without any supplementary income, with less land than their neighbors, still live better, keep up their payments better, are wiser and healthier than those in a village where the *barshchina* ideal was for some reason weaker.

But are there really, in this prosperous village, so few personal needs that no one voices them? How many children in the village grow up illiterate, not knowing how to count or read or write? How many do not know what the moon or the sun are, or where money comes from—in short, who know exactly nothing? How many poor people are there in the village, how many cripples, orphans, and homeless? How many have met accidental misfortunes and been left to the arbitrary whims of fate? Some thought ought to be given to these problems—some thought which is not taken up with other worries. But no one concerns themselves with these things, because no one knows that such things deserve concern or worry. The commune's affairs consist exclusively of land or tax distribution, and vodka drinking. If there is no distribution, the men get together and drink vodka—nothing else ever happens....

The peasant today still does not try to live for his own private interests, and is barely aware of them in his own daily life. How else would you explain, for instance, a scene like the following. A mill. There are several carts of grain awaiting their turn. Peasants of various ages are sitting on the ground or on the carts, waiting. On the hill nearby is the new house of the man who leases the mill, a merchant. He is sitting at an open window, drinking hot tea, cup after cup, and, constantly wiping his fat neck and red face with a towel.

"Look!" says one of the waiting men. "See the red-faced devil drinking tea!"

"Brother, is he drinking tea!"

"I've been counting and counting the cups, but I gave up. The housekeeper just keeps bringing him more."

"You'd think he would burst!"

"Are you kidding? He can take it all right."

"Sure, all he has to do is drink tea."

"That's all!—and there's nothing to it, you just sit and drink, that's all there is to it."

"That's how he does his business, too."

"You and I, my friend, break our backs to earn a kopeck. But there he is, doing nothing, not dirtying his pretty white hands, and raking in money while he drinks his tea—See there, how he fills his trousers!"

Many of the peasants lying about sigh in agreement.

"What cunning! He has set up a granary there, that's all, nothing more. But every year he pockets about 2,000 rubles from it—Ah, but you and I groan over every penny."

More comments on this theme could be heard all around. But let us go up to speaker and ask:

"Whose mill is that?"

"Ours!"

"Is this the communal mill?"

"Yes, That fellow over there (pointing to the hill)—the one drinking tea—we lease the mill to him."

And then a story followed, as if to prove the dishonesty of the miller who was drinking tea. You may judge for yourself as to that. Ever since anyone could remember, the peasant told me, a small shed had stood near the mill, which was rented from the peasants by grain merchants. These merchants bought up grain in small batches from all over the village. "That one there, drinking tea," that "scoundrel," had leased the mill and the old granary from the village, but then had built a large sturdy barn in place of the old rickety granary. Ever since, each winter he has earned no less than 2,000 rubles from this granary, literally without lifting a finger.

The tone with which this "cunning" is described is somewhat obsequious, and resentment is clearly audible in it. And actually it is offensive to see how this merchant sits and drinks tea, all the while getting rich. But no one so much as suggests that a member of the commune might have built the granary, that someone could have been appointed to watch over the mill and report its accounts to the commune. There are no customs or procedures for such common enterprises. This, too, is a result of the old labor dues system. Under that system, the peasant concerned himself only with his own little plot, only occasionally showing off at the tavern. Someone else took care of the real income and expenses. For, the muzhik it was all right if he was given the glass of vodka prescribed by the customary ritual; but the commune's income—this was not the peasant's affair. It was as if heaven had reserved this activity for outsiders.

Here is another brief illustration of the extent to which the peasant has divorced himself from really vital communal affairs. Public and appanage lands which are rented out everywhere at very low prices and in large quantities fall into the hands of these peasants only through a middleman. That is, these lands are first leased by a merchant, who rents the whole portion. Afterward the peasants lease land in small bits from him for three times the original rental price. Announcements of sales and rentals, of field and forest lands are constantly circulated among village clerks and village elders. But I saw no case where the commune itself resolved to lease land. The peasants know about available land, but they wait to see who will take the land.

"Who leased that meadow?"

"Some city fellow."

"Where is his agent?"

"Right over there."

And the peasants will go to the land agent, who leased the land yesterday for one ruble a desiatina, and lease it from him today for three, four or six rubles. The merchant takes in the money, and sits in the hot afternoon drinking tea. The people look at him from afar (never up close), and grumble with anger:

"Look at the scoundrel! See how he steams his tummy while he rakes in the cash—"

Selections from Alexander Herzen, *The Bell*

Alexander Herzen was a socialist Russian journalist who emigrated from Russia in 1847. He published The Bell *while living in London from 1857 to 1865 and from Switzerland from 1865 to 1867. Although banned in Russia, copies of the politically liberal journal were smuggled into the country and read widely. Despite the ban, Alexander II was rumored to read the journal. Because it was published abroad, this is considered the first journal published in the Russian language that was free of censorship. This text has been abbreviated from its original version.*

Source: Alexander Herzen, *A Herzen Reader*, trans. and ed. Kathleen Parthé (Evanston, IL: Northwestern University Press, 2012), 72–73, 73–78, 287–91, 292–97.

LOGOPHOBIA[11]
[1858]

The other day the *Kölnischer Zeitung* announced a new ban on *The Bell* in Prussia. In Saxony all our periodicals are banned. In Naples the embassy secretary is frightening the booksellers; commercial travelers of the Third Department in the uniforms of adjutant generals, and councilors of state who imagine themselves privy councilors, are floating all around the corrupted parts of Europe, nosing about the shops, making discoveries and denunciations, using German ministers as police detectives and truffle spotters and German princelings as bulldogs in pursuit of *The Polestar* and *The Bell*. What is all this about? What is the source of this crude impatience? It would be a pity if it comes from the sovereign: it is so unworthy of him. It would be a pity if it comes from Gorchakov: they tell us that he is a well-intentioned person, and we were prepared to believe this![12]

Or are these the pranks of people in "supporting roles," volunteer zealots and Nicholaevan gendarmes who are left without anything to do?

Can it be that every power, even one that wishes to do good, is fated to have no other means of hearing the truth than when it is wrapped in completely servile phrases, and sweetened with vulgar flattery? The language of a free man grates upon ears grown soft with the rhetoric of Byzantine eunuchs in guards uniform, old stewards in the livery of their late master. . . .

JULY 1, 1858[13]
[1858]

A year ago the first issue of *The Bell* appeared. We stop for a moment and glance back at the path we have traveled . . . and feel sadness and heaviness in our hearts.

Meanwhile, in the course of this year one of our most ardent hopes has been realized; one of the greatest revolutions in Russia has begun, the one that we have predicted, craved, and called for since childhood—the liberation of the serfs has begun.

But we don't feel any better, and this year we almost took a step backward. The reason is obvious, and we will state it directly and steadfastly: *Alexander II has not justified the hopes that Russia had at his coronation.* Last June he still stood, like the hero of our fairy tales, at the crossroads—whether he would turn to the right or to the left no one knew. It seemed that he would without fail follow the path of development, liberation, construction . . . taking one step, and then another—but suddenly he thought better of it and turned

From the left to the right.[14]

Maybe there is still time . . . but he is being hurried along by the palace coachmen, who are taking advantage of the fact that he does not know the road. And our *Bell* is ringing out to him that he has gone astray, ringing out Russia's distress and the danger that he faces.

But that is the problem—the powerful people of this world do not know how to either listen or remember. History lies before them, but it is not for them that it tells of the bitter experience of nations and of posterity's harsh judgment of tsars.

Not to make use of the remarkable position in which events in Europe and the previous reign left Alexander II is to such a degree absurd that it is difficult to find room in one's head for it.

Having the possibility of choosing one of two roles—Peter I or Pius IX—to choose Pius IX is the ultimate example of Christian meekness.

"But," they will tell us, "Peter I was a genius—geniuses aren't born every century, and not every tsar who wants to be Peter I can succeed." The thing is, to be Russia's Peter in our time one does not have to be a genius; it would be sufficient to love Russia, to respect and understand the human dignity in a Russian man, and to listen closely to his thoughts and his aspirations. A genius might do great harm, as Peter did; he would inject his own will instead of developing the new growth that has appeared, when one just has to avoid weeding it out, trampling it, or constraining it, removing any obstacles and allowing it to grow on its own. Peter I had to create and destroy—in one hand he had a spade, and in the other an axe. He made a clearing in the wilderness, and, of course, cut down the good along with the bad. But we have ceased to love terror, no matter what kind and for what purpose.

Terror is no more necessary in our time than genius. The active, thinking part of Russia is moving ahead rapidly, knowing what it wants and revealing it in the form of public opinion. At the end of the last reign, in spite of the danger and persecution, the thoughts fermenting in people's minds were so strong that they created an underground literature in manuscripts, which were passed from hand to hand. Subsequently, the same thought process led to expressions of delight with all the fine initiatives of the new government. Half of Peter's work—the most difficult half—is now being done by a chorus. Around Peter, everything was silent; waking earlier than everyone else, he had to rouse others, make guesses, and be inventive. Now many have woken up and gone ahead, waiting to be called to give advice.

Except for a very few, everyone opposed Peter's reforms; now the entire nation, except for the decayed part of the gentry and old men who have lost their faculties, is ready to further the reforms of Alexander II. As for the sham service oligarchy, all the parvenus from the barracks and the inkwells, the mental hospitals and prison battalions of Nicholaevan students —they have no opinion. Today they beat the serfs who want to be free, and tomorrow they will shoot the gentry who do not want to free them.

However, it could be that the reforms that Alexander II has talked about in his speeches, manifestoes, decrees, orders, and official journals do not coincide with the wishes of thinking Russia, thoughts which have manifested themselves in literature and public opinion.

Not at all—they are exactly the same.

This is the boundless, heart-rending irony and tragicomedy of our situation. A government is never so powerful as when it is in agreement with public opinion. . . .

The tsar tries very hard to extend a hand to the people, and the people try very hard to take hold of it but they can't get past Panin and company.[15] It's like a scene out of Aristophanes! Just when the sovereign is completely ready, one of those gray-haired children—Orlov or Zakrevsky—stands on tiptoe and touches his extended hand, shouting: "Your majesty, for God's sake! They will bite off your finger!"[16]

Let them just try! The sovereign was in the Caucasus during the troubles there and he loves bear hunting.[17] What are Circassians and bears to him? Doesn't he daily face dangers from these pillars of the fatherland, who shield him from Russia and create around him a pleasant garland of old men, who, if needed, by moving slightly can form themselves into a noose?

And K. I. Arseniev taught Alexander Nikolaevich the *criminal affair* that is Russian history from Peter I to Alexander I.[18]

We have nothing to hide, as we are always saying. Let every reader, with hand on heart, say where in *The Bell* are to be found impossible demands, political utopias, or calls for rebellion?

The existence of *The Bell* marks a boundary and a turning point. With the promulgation of the rescript on the liberation of the serfs our path had to change, not in its essence but in its type of activity.[19] We sacrificed in part our polemics and restricted even more the scope of our questions. We came closer to the government because the government came closer to us. We are concerned with the form of government—we've seen them all in action and none of them will do if they are reactionary, and all of them are suitable if they are contemporary and progressive. We sincerely and frankly believed that Alexander II would replace the bloody era of revolution and would serve as a peaceful and mild transition from antiquated despotism to a humanely free state of Russia.

We may have been mistaken in this, but thinking as we did, for the six months while the rescript was in the works we consistently and almost exclusively occupied ourselves with its realization.[20]

What did we demand, and what did we write about?

We demanded that the gentry not snatch emancipation away from the serfs, and that the wish—expressed timidly and with an upper-class lisp by the government—concerning estates and land not be interpreted to the benefit of the landowners. Were we correct? The proof can be found in the eloquent words of Bezobrazov and Blank, in the central committee, in the increased censorship, gentry opposition, and the forced resettlement of serfs on poor land.[21]

Besides, we said that the emancipation of the serfs was not sufficient, that alongside the landowner was a second scourge of the Russian people—the government official, that is, the police and the courts. We said that until the Japanese-style table of ranks fell—while we still had an inquisitorial court behind closed doors along with official secrecy, and while the police admonish people with birch rods and lash them without a trial—until that time the liberation of the serfs would not bring genuine benefit.

It could be that the sovereign is frightened that the entire civil service—those fraudulent handlers of official papers—do not share this opinion, but if Panin affirmed or favorably received his proposal, then maybe we would have defenders for the accused and jurors, and the court would operate in the light of day.

The sovereign wished to make changes, but he is in the dark and does not know where to begin; everyone deceives him, from the lowest clerk to the chancellor, and the voices of people outside government do not reach him. The public status of those who are not in service or who have not served long enough is such that only the gentry might be allowed to dance in the tsar's presence at a ball, and the merchants might on some sad or happy occasion greet him with bread and salt on a golden platter.

This leads logically to our third demand—*openness*.

Isn't it absurd that they put up the dam themselves, bar access to it, and then are surprised there's no water? Lift the censor's floodgate and then you will find out what the people think, what is hurting, pressing, tormenting, and ruining them . . . maybe all sorts of rubbish will at first float to the surface—what does it matter as long as the water carries away all those halfdead Vladimir cats and Andreevsky hares.

With openness, there can be publicity about legal cases that will throw a terrifying light on the subterranean misdeeds of the police and the courts, like that of our articles about Sechinsky, the Kochubey trial, Vrede, Elston-Sumarokov, Governor Novosiltsev, and others.[22]

If one removes the censorship restrictions, then the *Third Department* can be closed down; writers will denounce themselves, and finally this nest of spies will be destroyed in Russia. . . .

Have we demanded anything else?

Whatever our theoretical opinions, however "incorrigible" we were about them, we did not express them, we expunged them willingly while the massive government coach plodded its way forward, but when it began to go backward, crushing legs under its heavy wheels, then we proceeded along a different path.

This is the third phase into which *The Bell* has entered.

We established a motto—I summon the living!

Where are the live people in Russia? It seemed that there were live ones even at court and we addressed our words to them—we do not regret that. No matter what happens, the sovereign, having begun the process of liberating the serfs, has earned a great name in history and our gratitude is unchanged. But we have nothing to say to him. The live ones are those people of thought scattered all over Russia, good people of all castes, men and women, students and officers, who blush and weep when they think about serfdom, the arbitrariness in the courts, and the willfulness of the police; they are the people who ardently wish for openness and who read us with sympathy.

The Bell is their organ and their voice; on the barren, stony heights there is no one to listen to it, but in the valleys its pure sound rings out all the more powerfully.

PETERSBURG UNIVERSITY IS SHUT DOWN![23]
[1861]

. . . The new administration has taken a sharp turn: students will be admitted to lectures by ticket, and non-students are forbidden to attend lectures, student assemblies are forbidden, they wanted to eliminate the library, and so on. Students gathered in the auditorium despite the fact that the doors were locked, invited the vice-rector Sreznevsky, and expressed their dissatisfaction.[24] On September 24 (October 6) it was announced that the university would be closed until further notice. The next day all the students (up to 1,500 people) gathered on Vladimirskaya street in front of Filipson's apartment and demanded that he appear, but suddenly Ignatiev showed up with a platoon of guards.[25] Filipson emerged in full uniform and suggested to the students that they set off for the university, with him following on foot. A large crowd attached itself to them. Filipson, having gotten tired, rode ahead. When they arrived at the university, mounted gendarmes appeared, along with a fire brigade carrying axes, and the police. The students behaved with complete calm. An officer of the gendarmerie unsheathed his saber, and two gendarmes prepared to plunge into the crowd. Shuvalov and the brotherhood stopped them.[26] Student deputies approached them. At this moment Ignatiev showed up, saying: "Everything is ready, the operation may begin." Filipson answered that he knew from the Caucasus how with such means you can cause misfortune but you will not stop the young people. One of the students said: "There is no need for troops, I will be responsible for keeping order." Ignatiev insisted that Filipson had no right to negotiate with the students, but the latter took the responsibility on himself and promised that the library would open immediately, and that lectures would begin on October 2/14, and by that time new rules would be announced. The students promised to remain calm. The orderliness on the part of the students was remarkable, and the crowd showed them sympathy. There were a great number of officers and there was one person they wanted to arrest but they held back. One soldier in the guards unit shoved a student, who said: "Aren't you ashamed—you're armed and you shove someone who is unarmed?" . . . the soldier blushed. One field officer violently shook a policeman's arm: "Hey you, did you come to do battle?"—"What can I do, your honor, they gave an order!" answered the policeman. One peasant said to another: "The blue caps are rebelling!" and heard in answer: "What should they do when their institution is shut down?" There were almost no military forces in the capital, and the soldiers were dispersed to their regular duties; they had been summoned by telegraph.

Thus, the university is closed! The government opposes enlightenment and freedom and *doesn't know enough to yield in good time*. We prophesied its *downfall* during the second part of this transitional era; it seems we were mistaken—*it will happen much earlier*.

A LETTER TO EMPEROR ALEXANDER II[27]
[1866]

Sovereign,

There was a time when you read *The Bell*—now you do not read it. Which of the eras was better, the era of liberation and light, or the one of confinement and darkness? Your conscience will tell you. But whether or not you read us, *you must read* this sheet.

You are surrounded by deceit, and there is no honest person who would dare to tell you the truth. Torture is being carried out near you, despite your order, and you do not know this. You are assured that the unfortunate fellow who shot at you was the instrument of a vast conspiracy, but there was no conspiracy at all, large or small; what they call a conspiracy is the aroused thought and untied tongue of Russia, its intellectual movement, your good name along with the emancipation of the serfs. You are led from one injustice to another, you will be led to destruction, if not in this life then in the future light of history. You will, in fact, be led to destruction by conspirators—the ones who surround you—not because that is what they wished, but because it is advantageous to them. They will sacrifice you the same that they now sacrifice hundreds of innocent people of whose innocence, they are aware, the way they sacrifice the honor of families, handing out prostitute tickets to honest women. . . .[28]

That this cannot please you I am certain, and that is why I resolved to write to you. But this is not enough. Find out the truth *for yourself*, and carry out *your* will, as you did at the time of the emancipation.

For the fourth time I have set out along the path that you are traveling, and, have stopped on it, in order to turn your attention not to myself but to you.

"People expect from you mildness and a human heart," I wrote when you ascended the throne. "You are exceptionally lucky!" "And they are still waiting—faith in you has been maintained," I added two and a half years later.

Seven years went by, and how much happened during those seven years! I was in the south of France when your son expired. The first news that I heard in Geneva was news of his death. I did not hold back, and, although cursed by many, picked up my pen and wrote you a third letter, in which I said: "Fate has touched you inexorably, dreadfully; in human life there are moments of terrible solemnity. You are at such a moment, so seize it. Stop under the full weight of this blow and think, only without the Senate and the Synod, without ministers and the General Staff, think about what has happened and where you are heading. Decide now, do not await a second blow."

You did not make up your mind. Fate touched you a second time—let them call me crazy and weak, but I am writing to you because it is so difficult for me to abandon the idea that you have been drawn by others to this historical sin, to this terrible injustice that is going on around you.

You cannot wish evil for Russia in return for its love for you. That would be unnatural. Stand up for it at full height, it is exhausted under the weight of slander and frightened by the secret court of law and by obvious arbitrariness.

In all likelihood this is my last letter to you, Sovereign. Read it. Only endless and agonizing grief about the destruction of youthful, fresh strength under the impure feet of profane old men, having grown mean with their bribes, dirty tricks, and intrigues—only this pain could make me stop you once more on the road and once more raise my voice.

Pay attention, Sovereign, pay attention to matters at hand. Russia has the right to ask that of you.

ISKANDER

Geneva, May 31, 1866

FROM PETERSBURG[29]
[1866]

Finally, a letter from Petersburg. I relate its most important section:

The most outrageous and groundless arrests continue. No matter what the cost, they wish to frighten the sovereign and convince him that his meekness and placid nature have allowed a plot to mature that now encompasses all Russia, and that decisive measures are required. The evil caused by the denunciatory journals is boundless. At first the whole of society was ready to believe that if not today then tomorrow an immense conspiracy will be revealed; everyone was ready to aid the police, and at the forefront were the Guards officers. The secrecy with which the case is being handled, after Muravyovs' promise of openness, dampened the ardor of many, and they began to suspect some intrigue. But the deed is done and the push has been given. . . . Trepov expels everyone from the police who, according to his understanding, is incapable of maliciously persecuting all that is young and lively, and teachers are being expelled from schools if their students behave in an unduly familiar manner during lessons.[30] There are a huge number of spies here, many have been sent to Moscow and to the provinces and abroad, especially to Switzerland (*welcome!*). Muravyov has doubled their salaries.

Karakozov does not acknowledge himself to be Karakozov and does not recognize his cousin who acknowledged him. Muravyov demanded that Chernyshevsky be brought back from Siberia, *to which the Tsar did not agree.* Among well-known people who have been arrested: *Blagosvetlov, Eliseev, Evropeus* with his wife and brother, *Kovalevsky, Sleptsov*; many young ladies and women have been arrested (nihilists). Among the latter several have been released and given *a yellow ticket, which is given to prostitutes.*

"Have signs of any society been uncovered?" Muravyov was asked by an acquaintance. There is no society, but there will be if the harmful tendencies are not destroyed. Muravyov searches for these tendencies everywhere, even abroad. He wishes to drag into the business of April 4/16 not only the unmaskers, negators, and nihilists found here, but also those who are abroad. It is said that an auditor at the medical academy, *Belsky* (or *Belgin*), a healthy, handsome, young man, while under arrest became ill, and was sent to a secret section of the military hospital. Last Saturday, April 30 (May 12), at 9 in the morning, he hung himself in his cell. On the wall he had written: "On Muravyov's orders I was flogged."

They say that Karakozov has been tortured in many innovative ways. He answered firmly at the first session. At night the questioning began again and went on without a break for three days. They do not dare torture him by surgical means; *they claim that the sovereign had not ordered it,* and therefore they have resorted to new means *that do not leave a trace* and to science. At first they placed him in some kind of case, but Doctor *Edenkauer* said that he would either die or go completely out of his mind, and therefore the learned doctor advised them to replace the case with an electrical shock. (Edenkauer was elevated on April 16/28 to the rank of *privy* councillor!) The unfortunate patient became ill, stopped eating, and they say he is close to death. Many insist that he died May 2/14 (?). (What will Muravyov do, find a fresh Karakozov?) . . .

On the day the shot was fired, Countess Ridiger said to the empress that she had been hearing for some time there would be an attempt, that she had heard this from Pototsky and had told Annenkov, who did not believe it. Pototsky had been imprisoned and went out of his mind (this fact we read in *The Times*). Muravyov's party and *The Moscow Gazette* are trying on the sly to cast suspicion on Konstantin Nikolaevich. . . . Muravyov has already quarreled with Shuvalov.

P.S. The Kurochkins have been released.

In the presence of this letter we stopped in a kind of endless, burning pain. . . . Here is where this reign of *liberation* has arrived, and it is not the tsar's fault (from the letter it is clear how he is struggling in the darkness which has been created around him), but *society*, which has turned into the police, and the immoral *press*, which has been society's informer and accuser under Muravyov.

It is an unfortunate nation, in which such an insolent and distorted environment could arise and mature, teaching, applauding, and stirring up the executioners with impunity!

"We have yet to mature," said someone in Petersburg, and everyone was angry with him. "*But have already decayed*," we added, "*decayed terribly . . .*"

Our article was finished, but having read the letter we tore it up—it was weak and poor, words failed us, and we felt it deeply!

But one cannot simply fold one's arms in idle bitterness, and one cannot simply remain silent with a curse on the lips! No, that would be a betrayal of our entire life, and there isn't much left of it. We will use what remains of it to expose to the world the historic crime taking place in Russia, and to sustain and comfort the unhappy younger generation, being martyred for its sacred love for truth and its youthful faith in Russia. We, the old men, stand at the bedside of those being persecuted, wiping away the stains of slander and blessing the lost prophets of a *future Russia*.

They will not torture it away, and Edenkauer will not cure it with his electric shock.

. . . But it is good that electricity was used. Science and the press, fulfilling the function of the executioner and instrument of torture. . . . Humanity cannot decline much further than this.

What, then, can one add? Perhaps the *yellow tickets* that were given to young ladies and women because they cut their hair and dreamed that it was better to live by their own labor than on someone else's account, and the journal threw mud at them. . . .

We were recently criticized that we laugh as we speak about the vileness and brutality now taking place in Russia.

Our laughter has not been understood.

Never mind; we will speak seriously, and, first, will pose a question about the origin of the vastly increased impatience in society that circles, like a wreath, the investigative factory, in which Muravyov weaves a nonexistent conspiracy? Whence this new frenzy against *nihilism*, by which is now meant every kind of free, independent thought, every kind of learning that does not resemble the preaching of the neo-serf owners?

Can it simply be out of love for Alexander Nikolaevich, who freed the majority of the most furious unmaskers from half their income?[31] They are not that sentimental: here the roots go much deeper.

. . . Two years ago, for the first time at the summit of the nobility in Russia, a demand appeared for mature institutions, and a wish was expressed for civic freedom and private control of one's affairs. That took place in Moscow—what could be better?

But here's what is not so good. The *first* word spoken by the Moscow assembly of the nobility was hostile to the independent press, and, following the expression of gratitude to the journalist-denouncer there was the feeble speech of Orlov-Davydov, who demanded limitations to autocracy and to *book-publishing* (among us!), cursing the arbitrariness of bureaucrats and the translation of Buckle. . . .[32]

An environment that cannot bear free speech has chemically combined with inquisitors and executioners. As for Karakozov—or whatever he is called, the matter is not about him and he was immediately pushed into the background—with denunciations in their journals and blame for the assassination attempt placed on all *freethinking people in Russia*, dating from the nihilists to Chernyshevsky, and from Chernyshevsky to Petrashevsky, reaching Belinsky, and so on. Whether Karakozov lives or dies is all the same to them: that is the reason for such *secrecy* with the public and even doubly so with the sovereign, who must at all costs believe *in a universal conspiracy*.

What kind of *freedom* was necessary to these Asiatic slaves with their fear of freedom of thought and speech? What use is it to them? They are permitted to weep for serfdom—they themselves do not know how to go on without livery: they grew used to it and it will be awful and cold for them in the open air. . . . It's the same old landowners and the same old bureaucrats in a different form. Their weapons were taken from the jails and the criminal courts, and their literature is the investigative file; neither they nor their journals are interested in a serious debate. In a serious debate we were the first who were prepared to throw down the gauntlet; other locations could have been found if their objections did not carry a whiff of the Peter and Paul Fortress. They do not argue, but complain about the administration; they address themselves not to their adversaries, but denounce the disorders; they provoke not objections but executions, and wish not to convince but to *suppress*.

While the conservative-liberal gentry was united with its literary majordomos in weak-nerved opposition, it was ludicrous. Now that it is in unison with Russia's fears, with Muravyov, with three police forces, the army, and electric shocks—even Valuev consenting to be on their side—it is no laughing matter.

Together they represent that dark force which leads the weak sovereign from one crime to another and pushes Russia toward its former chaos.

. . . Why does the sovereign lack the energy to break free of these constraints? Why can he not do what Napoleon I and Sully managed, and question Karakozov himself, in order to learn the truth not only about the shot but with that the truth about how investigations are carried out in Russia in the second half of the XIX century?

Why? . . .

FROM THE SOVEREIGN TO P. P. GAGARIN[33]
[1866]

Prince Pavel Pavlovich,

The unanimous expression of loyal devotion by the people whose rule was entrusted to me by divine plan is a pledge of the sentiments in which I find the greatest reward for my efforts toward the good of Russia.

The more comforting is this realization for me, the more I fulfill my obligation to preserve the Russian people from those kernels of false teaching, which in time could shake the smooth functioning of society, if no obstacle was made to their development.

The event that summoned from all corners of Russia declarations of loyalty also served as an occasion for a more precise examination of those paths by which these pernicious false teachings were promoted and spread. The investigation being carried out by the special commission I have ordered is already pointing to the root of the evil. In that way Providence was pleased to open the eyes of Russia to the consequences that one can expect from the aspirations and philosophizing of those who would brazenly encroach on all that has been sacred to it from time immemorial, on religious beliefs, on the principles of family life, on property rights, on obedience to the law, and on respect for the powers that be.

My attention is *already* directed to the upbringing of young people. I have given instructions to the effect that it be organized in the spirit of religious truths, respect for property rights, and observance of the fundamental principles of the social order, and that in educational institutions of all types no overt or clandestine preaching will be allowed of those destructive concepts which are equally harmful to all aspects of the moral and material well-being of the people. But instruction which meets the true needs of youth would not bring the benefit expected from it if in private family life there was teaching not in accord with the rules of Christian piety and the obligations of loyalty. For this reason I have the firm hope that my views on this subject will be fervently acted upon in the sphere of domestic education.

No less important for the true benefit of the state in its totality and for every one of my subjects is the complete inviolability of the right to property in all its aspects, as determined by the general laws and by the Statutes of February 19, 1861. Independent of the legality of this right, one of the most fundamental principles of well-functioning civil societies, it is indissolubly tied to the development of private and national wealth, which are tightly linked to one another. Any doubts about these relationships could only be raised by enemies of the social order.

The affirmation and preservation of these principles should be the aspiration of all those invested with the rights and responsibilities of government service. In a proper state system the first duty of all those called to serve me and the fatherland consists of precise and active fulfillment of their responsibilities without any deviation in any branch of government. The authorities' excessive behavior and their lack of action are equally harmful. Only with the steadfast fulfillment of these responsibilities can the unity of government actions, which is necessary for the realization of its views and the achievement of its goals, be guaranteed.

I am aware that *some people in government service* have participated in the disclosure of harmful rumors or judgments about the actions or intentions of the state and even in the dissemination of those teachings, contrary to social order, whose development should not be permitted. The very rank of civil servant renders, in such cases, greater weight to their words and in the same way facilitates the distortion of the state's views. This type of confusion cannot be tolerated. All those in management positions *must keep track of the actions of their subordinates* and require of them the direct, exact, and unswerving fulfillment of their assigned responsibilities, without which harmonious governance is impossible, and by which they themselves must set an example of respect for authority.

Finally, for the decisive success of the measures being taken against the ruinous teachings which have developed in the social sphere and which seek to shake the most fundamental bases of faith, morality, and social order, all heads of the separate branches of government are required to *keep in mind those other healthy, conservative, and reliable forces* with which Russia has always been richly endowed, and which, to this day, thanks be to God, it has in abundance. These forces consist of all the classes in which property rights are valued, the right to landownership, guaranteed and defended in law, social rights founded in and determined by law, principles of social order and social security, principles of state unity and sound organization, the principles of morality and the sacred truths of our faith. In view of their important properties these strengths must be utilized and preserved when officials are appointed in all branches of government. In that way we will be saved from ill-intentioned reprimands in all levels of society concerning their confidence in the governing authorities. Toward this goal, in accordance with my customary wishes and my frequently expressed desire, it behooves all branches of government to pay complete attention to the preservation of the rights of property and entreaty, in relation to its use and need (the right of petition!) by various districts and various sections of the population. It is important to curtail the repeated attempts to stir up enmity between various classes and particularly the stirring up of enmity against the nobility and against landowners in general, in which enemies of social order naturally see their immediate opponents. A firm and unswerving observance of these general principles will place a limit on those criminal aspirations, which have now been uncovered with sufficient clarity and must be subject to the just retribution of the law. I direct you to announce my rescript to the appropriate leadership, to all ministers and all heads of all the divisions.

I remain, etc.
ALEXANDER
In Tsarskoe Selo, May 13/25, 1866

. . . There we have it, the final echo of the shot!

Fear in the face of something indeterminate, pious—but hardly new—thoughts, a poor style, nameless hints, a lesson learned by heart and a moral coup d'etat. . . .

We decided to reprint in its entirety this gloomily thought-out and gloomily written dissertation, because in it we see a kind of historic border post, a poorly made, poorly painted, clumsy boundary marker, but all the same a marker.[34]

If this were a rhetorical exercise about the corruption of minds and hearts, about false teachings and theories of property [. . .] we would not pay it the slightest attention. We have read such marvels in the journals that stand in the way of Russian development. But a royal diatribe, cast down from the heights upon which the throne stands, is a completely different matter. No matter how little genuine substance there is, it must fly down to our low-lying fields like a cannonball and either smash something or get smashed itself.

Looking closely at this royal document, which reminds us—with its worldly philosophy—of the spiritual icon painting with which Metropolitan

Filaret adorned the emancipation manifesto, we are struck most of all by *three things*.[35]

First, it is as clear as day that that there was no conspiracy linked to the shot on April 4/16 (as we have stated and repeated), to the extent that they could not draw one out no matter the shadows in which the investigation was carried out, nor the choice of an investigator, nor the methods which he employed. A conspiracy and Poles, the participation of nihilists and international revolution—all of this is intrigue, lies, and slander. They did not dare put this in the mouth of the sovereign. What remained was to exploit *moral participation*, i.e., immoral *complicité morale*, having intercepted correspondence between friends and family and having made note of certain thoughts, then confused them with all thinking people in the younger generation, all those who awoke to intellectual life and breathed freely after the death of Nicholas. It is impossible to make out to what guilty people the letter refers. In the Karakozov case, the only guilty ones are *those who participated with him*, and not all those people who think that the Russian government is not the ideal of all forms of governance and who debate property rights. [. . .]

A *single* adversary was pointed out and identified, not by name, but as a living force, a rival with whom it is necessary to contend, which is growing and will continue to grow unless it is suppressed now. [. . .] The giant in the cradle, which the government fears and in which it senses its future successor, is social thought, the ideas of a few inconsequential writers, young people, nihilists, and, I am ashamed to say, us. The character of this movement, which seeks to break down the old forms of Russian life that prevent its new forces from taking shape, is instinctively recognized as social[36] . . . and for that reason the government stands on the eternal peaks of conservatism and reaction, in favor of landed property; it wishes to defend it and be defended by it . . . to its aid it summons the catechism, domestic education, spying by department heads, and all of its forces, i.e., all its police.

This tsarist adornment we see as a *second victory*.

The third victory—"not unto us, not unto us," but also not unto *the Russian people*.[37] Apropos of the people: one of the most remarkable facts about the letter to Gagarin is the utter absence *of the people*, who were so recently being flattered . . . not one tender word, not one greeting, not even a thank you for saving his life! They are tired of the *paysans*. [. . .] The third victory goes to the tsar's old childhood friend—*the gentry landowner*. Like a weak little chick, the two-headed eagle takes it under both wings, and the government, like Mitrofanushka's mama, is prepared to scratch out anyone's eyes for the sake of the perpetual young oaf.[38] The letter *puts an end* to any open discussion of the great process involving landowners and peasants.

That's all.

Then the sovereign, through Gagarin, tells the people that he wants to lead Russia along a *different* path. Which one? It seems that he himself does not thoroughly understand but it is clear that it will be a nasty one. From this letter the irritation is obvious, the desire to govern more severely, to tighten the reins, to press harder, to trample more firmly. . . . With this go Prince Gagarin's sovereign correspondent proposes turning all department heads into spies over their subordinates, and then instructs them to "keep in mind *those other* healthy, conservative and reliable forces with which Russia is richly endowed." [. . .]

We imagine how the sovereign, bored by this lengthy missive from Gagarin to Gagarin, wiped the sweat from his powerful face and, throwing down the pen with which he had signed it, said: Well, thank God, throne, altar, nobility, property, morality, and order have been saved. [. . .]

The sovereign lets out a sigh.

And the nobility, who since the year 1860 have been trembling with fear and anger, also let out a sigh. [. . .]

Sleep, brothers, rest yourselves! [. . .]

And you, poor exiles, held in captivity, surviving in chains, toiling in the mines, persecuted friends—take heart. Together we lived to see a great age. You do not suffer in vain, and we have not worked a lifetime in vain. *This is the dawn of the harvest, a day which we have long awaited.*

... When the Emperor Trajan sent Pliny to investigate the false teaching of the Nazarines, when the Roman senate pondered the spread of the absurd and immoral sect of the executed Judean, while Tertullian defended it from the vile accusation of *murders*, when earlier Nero had heaped blame upon them as arsonists for a fire, and other caesars tormented them *openly and publicly*, like naive Muravyovs let out of a menagerie—the case of the Christians was won.

And we march forward holding caesar's most recent missive. The tsar's countersignature is there and we will not forget May 13/25, 1866.

It is the beginning of the battle . . . it is the beginning of the war.

We shall not see its end . . . it is unlikely that even the very youngest will see it. History develops slowly, and what is passing away defends itself stubbornly, and what is establishing itself comes into being slowly and dimly . . . but the process itself, the very drama of historical gestation, is full of poetry. Every generation has its own experience, and we do not grumble over our share, we have lived not only to see a red patch of light in the east, but also long enough for our enemy to see it. What more can one expect from life, especially when a man, with his hand on his heart, can say with a clear conscience: "And I took part in this massive struggle, and I did my bit. . . ."

. . . And you, Pavel Pavlovich, write another letter to yourself, some sort of commentary on the Tsarskoe Selo missive, or like Pliny the Younger, write to Caesar himself about bringing down the new Christians, about their insignificance, about your contempt for them . . . just keep writing!

Selections from Nikolai Chernyshevsky, "The Aesthetic Relations of Art to Reality"

Nikolai Chernyshevsky was a Russian literary scholar and philosopher, best known for his novel What Is to Be Done? *(1863). Arrested in 1862 for involvement with revolutionary circles, he was exiled to Siberia. His work, however, continued to circulate among Populist groups and influence their thinking. In the essay below, Chernyshevsky shares his philosophy of art and realism. This text has been abbreviated from its original version. Italic ellipses in brackets indicate the author's omissions.*

Source: Nikolai Chernyshevsky, "The Aesthetic Relations of Art to Reality," in *Russian Philosophy*, vol. 2, *The Nihilist, the Populists: Critics of Religion and Culture*, eds. James M. Edie, James P. Scanlan, and Mary-Barbara Zeldin, with collaboration of George L. Kline (Knoxville: University of Tennessee Press, 1976), 16–28.

The sea is beautiful; looking at it, we never think of being dissatisfied with it, aesthetically. But not everyone lives near the sea; many people never in their lives get a chance to see it. Yet they would very much like to see it, and consequently seascapes please and interest them. Of course, it would be much better to see the sea itself rather than pictures of it; but when a good thing is not available, a man is satisfied with an inferior one. When the genuine article is not present, a substitute will do. Even the people who can admire the real sea cannot always do so when they want to, and so they call up memories of it. But man's imagination is weak; it needs support and prompting. So to revive their memories of the sea, to see it more vividly in their imagination, they look at seascapes. This is the sole aim and object of very many (the majority of) works of art: to give those people who have not been able to enjoy beauty in reality the opportunity to acquaint themselves with it at least to some degree; to serve as a reminder, to prompt and revive memories of beauty in reality in the minds of those people who are acquainted with it by experience and love to recall it. . . .

Thus, the first purpose of art is to reproduce nature and life, and this applies to all works of art without exception. Their relation to the corresponding aspects and phenomena of reality is the same as the relation of an engraving to the picture from which it was copied, or the relation of a portrait to the person it represents. An engraving is made of a picture not because the latter is bad, but because it is good. Similarly, reality is reproduced in art not in order to eliminate flaws, not because reality as such is not sufficiently beautiful, but precisely because it is beautiful. Artistically an engraving is not superior to the picture from which it is copied, but much inferior to it; similarly, works of art never attain the beauty and grandeur of reality. But the picture is unique; it can be admired only by those who go to the picture gallery which it adorns. The engraving, however, is sold in hundreds of copies all over the world; everyone can admire it whenever he pleases without leaving his room, without getting up from his couch, without throwing off his dressing gown. Similarly, a beautiful object in reality is not always accessible to everyone; reproductions of it (feeble, crude, pale, it is true, but reproductions all the same) in works of art make it always accessible to everybody. A portrait is made of a person we love and cherish not in order to eliminate the flaws in his features—what do we care about these flaws? We do not notice them, or if we do we like them—but in order to give us the opportunity to admire that face even when it is not actually in front of us. Such also is the aim and object of works of art; they do not correct reality, do not embellish it, but reproduce it, serve as a substitute for it. . . .

While not claiming in the least that these words express something entirely new in the history of aesthetic ideas, we think nonetheless that the pseudo-classical "imitation of nature" theory that prevailed in the seventeenth and eighteenth centuries demanded of art something different from the formal principle implied by the definition: "Art is the reproduction of reality." In support of our statement that there is an essential difference between our view of art and that contained in the imitation of nature theory, we shall quote here a criticism of that theory taken from the best textbook on the now prevailing system of aesthetics. This criticism will, on the one hand, show the difference between the conceptions it refutes and our view, and, on the other, will reveal what is lacking in our initial definition of art as reproducing reality, and will thus enable us to proceed to a more exact development of concepts of art.

The definition of art as imitation of nature reveals only its formal object; according to this definition art should strive as far as possible to repeat what already exists in the external world. Such repetition must be regarded as superfluous, for nature and life already present us with what, according to this conception, art should present to us. What is more, the imitation of nature is a vain effort which falls far short of its object because in imitating nature, art, owing to its restricted means, gives us only deception instead of truth and only a lifeless mask instead of a really living being.

Here we shall observe, first of all, that the words, "Art is the reproduction of reality," as well as the sentence, "Art is the imitation of nature," define only the formal principle of art; to define the content of art we must supplement the first conclusion we have drawn concerning its aim, and this we shall do subsequently. The other objection does not in the least apply to the view we have expounded; from the preceding exposition it is evident that the reproduction or "repetition" of the objects and phenomena of nature by art is by no means superfluous; on the contrary, it is necessary. Turning to the observation that repetition is a vain effort which falls far short of its object, it must be said that this argument is valid only when it is assumed that art wishes to compete with reality and not simply serve as a substitute for it. We, however, assert that art cannot stand comparison with living reality and completely lacks the vitality that reality possesses; we regard this as beyond doubt. . . .

Let us see whether further objections to the imitation theory apply to our view:

Since it is impossible to achieve complete success in imitating nature, all that remains is to take smug pleasure in the relative success of this hocus-pocus; but the more the copy bears an external resemblance to the original, the colder this pleasure becomes, and it even grows into satiety or revulsion. There are portraits which, as the saying goes, are awfully like the originals. An excellent imitation of the song of the nightingale begins to bore and disgust us as soon as we learn that it is not a real nightingale singing, but some skillful imitator of the nightingale's trilling; this is because we have a right to expect different music from a human being. Such tricks in the extremely skillful imitation of nature may be compared with the art of the conjurer who without a miss threw lentils through an aperture no bigger than a lentil, and whom Alexander the Great rewarded with a medimnos of lentils.[39]

These observations are perfectly just, but they apply to the useless and senseless copying of what does not deserve attention, or to the depiction of mere externals devoid of content. (How many vaunted works of art earn this biting, but deserved, ridicule!) Content worthy of the attention of a thinking person is alone able to shield art from the reproach that it is merely a pastime, which it all too often is. Artistic form does not save a work of art from contempt or from a pitying smile if, by the importance of its idea, the work cannot answer the question: Was it worth the trouble? A useless thing has no right to respect. "Man is an end in himself"; but the things man makes must have their end in the satisfaction of man's needs and not in themselves. That is precisely why the more perfectly a useless imitation bears external resemblance to the original, the more disgust it arouses. "Why were so much time and labor wasted on it?" we ask ourselves when looking at it. "And what a pity that such lack of content can go hand in hand with such perfection of workmanship!" The boredom and disgust aroused by the conjurer who imitates the song of the nightingale are explained by the very remarks contained in the above criticism: a man who fails to understand that he ought to sing human songs and not make the trills that have meaning only in the song of the nightingale is deserving only of pity.

As regards portraits which are awfully like the originals, this must be understood as follows: to be faithful, every copy must convey the essential features of its original. A portrait that fails to convey the chief, the most expressive, features of a face is not a faithful portrait; and when, at the same time, the petty details of the face are distinctly shown, the portrait is rendered ugly, senseless, lifeless—how can it be anything but awful? Objection is often raised to what is called the "photographic copying" of reality; would it not be better to say that copying, like everything man does, calls for understanding, for the ability to distinguish essential from inessential features? "Lifeless copying"—such is the usual phrase; but a man cannot make a faithful copy if the lifeless mechanism is not guided by living meaning. It is not even possible to make a faithful facsimile of an ordinary manuscript if the meaning of the letters that are being copied is not understood. . . .

[. . .] But we have said above that art has another purpose besides reproduction, namely, to explain life. This can be done to some degree by all the arts: often it is sufficient to call attention to an object (which art always does) in order to explain its significance, or to enable people to understand life better. In this sense, art differs in no way from a discourse about an object; the only difference here is that art achieves its purpose much better than a discourse, particularly a learned discourse; it is much easier for us to acquaint ourselves with an object, we begin to take an interest in it much more quickly when it is presented to us in living form than when we get a dry reference to it. Fenimore Cooper's novels have done more to acquaint society with the life of savages than ethnographic narratives and arguments on the importance of studying this subject.

But while all the arts can point to new and interesting objects, poetry always of necessity points sharply and clearly to the essential features of an object. Painting reproduces an object in all its details; so does sculpture. But poetry cannot take in an excessive amount of detail; of necessity leaving a great deal out of the picture, it focuses our attention on the features retained. This is viewed as an advantage that poetic scenes have over reality; but every single word does the same to the object it denotes. In the word (concept), too, everything incidental is left out and only the essential features of the object are retained. For the inexperienced mind the word denoting the object may be clearer than the object itself, but this clarity is only an impoverishment. . . . An object or event may be more intelligible in a poetical work than in reality, but the only merit we recognize in that is the clear and vivid allusion to reality; we do not attach independent significance to it as something that could compete with the fullness of real life. We cannot refrain from adding that every prose narrative does the same thing poetry does. The concentration of attention upon the essential features of an object is not the distinguishing feature of poetry, but the common feature of all rational speech.

The essential purpose of art is to reproduce what is of interest to man in real life. But, being interested in the phenomena of life, man cannot but pronounce judgment on them, consciously or unconsciously. The poet or artist cannot cease to be a man and thus he cannot, even if he wants to, refrain from pronouncing judgment on the phenomena he depicts. This judgment is expressed in his work—this is another purpose of art, which places it among the moral activities of man.

There are men whose judgment on the phenomena of life consists almost exclusively in that they betray an inclination for some aspects of reality and avoid others: these are men whose mental activity is weak. The work of such a man-poet or artist has no other purpose than that of reproducing his favorite side of life. But if a man whose mental activity is powerfully stimulated by questions engendered by observing life is gifted with artistic talent, he will, in his works, consciously or unconsciously strive to pronounce a living judgment on the phenomena that interest him (and interest his contemporaries, for a thinking man cannot think about insignificant problems that interest nobody but himself). His painting or his novels, poems, and plays will present or solve problems that arise out of life for the thinking man; his works will be, as it were, essays on subjects presented by life. This trend may find expression in all the arts (in painting, for example, we can point to pictures of social life and historical scenes), but it is developing chiefly in poetry, which provides the fullest opportunity to express a definite idea. In such a case the artist becomes a thinker, and works of art, while remaining in the sphere of art, acquire scientific significance. It goes without saying that in this respect there is nothing corresponding to the work of art in reality—but this applies only to its form. As regards content, as regards the problems presented or solved by art, they are all to be found in real life, only without premeditation, without *arrière-pensée*.

Let us suppose that a work of art develops the idea that straying temporarily from the true path will not doom a strong nature, or that one extreme leads to another; or that it depicts a man in conflict with himself; or depicts, if you will, the conflict between passions and lofty aspirations (we are pointing to different fundamental ideas we have discerned in *Faust*)—does not real life provide cases where the same situations develop? Is not high wisdom obtained from the observation of life? Is not science simply an abstraction from life, the placing of life within a formula? Everything science and art express is to be found in life, and found in its fullest and most perfect form, with all its living details—the details which usually contain the true meaning of the matter, and which are often not understood by science and art, and still more often cannot be embraced by them. In the events of real life everything is true, nothing is overlooked, there is not that one-sided, narrow view from which all the works of man suffer. As instruction, as learning, life is fuller, truer, and even more artistic than all the works of scholars and poets. But life does not think of explaining its phenomena to us; it is not concerned with deducing axioms. This is done in works of science and art. True, the deductions are incomplete, the ideas are one-sided compared with what life presents; but they have been made for us by geniuses; without their aid our deductions would be still more one-sided and meager.

Science and art (poetry) are manuals for those beginning the study of life; their purpose is to prepare the student to read the original sources, and later to serve as reference books from time to time. It never occurs to science to conceal this; nor does it occur to poets to conceal it in their offhand remarks about the point of their works. Aesthetics alone persists in asserting that art is superior to life and reality.

Connecting everything that has been said, we get the following view of art: the essential purpose of art is to reproduce everything in life that is of interest to man. Very often, especially in poetical works, the explanation of life, judgment of its phenomena, also comes to the fore.

The relation of art to life is the same as that of history; the only difference in content is that history, in its account of the life of mankind, is concerned mainly with factual truth, whereas art gives us stories about the lives of men in which the place of factual truth is taken by faithfulness to psychological and moral truth. The first function of history is to reproduce life; the second, which is not performed by all historians, is to explain it.

By failing to perform the second function the historian remains a mere chronicler and his work serves merely as material for the true historian, or as reading matter to satisfy curiosity. By performing this second function the historian becomes a thinker, and as a consequence his work acquires scientific merit. Exactly the same must be said about art. History does not set out to compete with real historical life; it admits that the pictures it paints are pale, incomplete, more or less incorrect, or at all events one-sided. Aesthetics must admit that art, too, and for the same reasons, must not even think of comparing itself with reality, much less of surpassing it in beauty....

Defense of reality as against fantasy, the attempt to prove that works of art cannot possibly stand comparison with living reality—such is the essence of this essay. But does not what the author says degrade art? Yes, if showing that art stands lower than real life in the artistic perfection of its works means degrading art. But protesting against panegyrics does not mean disparagement. Science does not claim to stand higher than reality, but that gives it nothing to be ashamed of. Art, too, must not claim to stand higher than reality; that would not degrade it. Science is not ashamed to say that its aim is to understand and explain reality, and then to use its explanation for man's benefit. Let not art be ashamed to admit that its aim is to compensate man, in case he lacks the opportunity to enjoy the full aesthetic pleasure afforded by reality, by reproducing this precious reality as far as possible, and by explaining it for his benefit.

Let art be content with its fine and lofty mission of being a substitute for reality in the event of its absence, and of being a manual of life for man.

Reality stands higher than dreams, and essential purpose stands higher than fantastic claims.

Selections from Elena Andreevna Shtakenshneider, *Diary and Memoirs* (1854–1886)

As the hostess of a popular literary salon, Elena Shtakenshneider became well acquainted with many writers and publishers. Privy to confidential information and opinions from both editors and writers, her memoirs document the politics and risks of writing and publishing in an authoritarian state. These selections also include her recollections on women's efforts to gain access to higher education. Italic ellipses in brackets indicate the author's omissions.

Source: Elena Andreevna Shtakenshneider, "1868–1870 gody Dnevnik" and "Iz istorii zhenskogo dvizheniia," in *Dnevnik i zapiski (1854–1886)*, RoyalLib.com Electronic Library, accessed May 24, 2023, https://royallib.com/read /shtakenshneyder_elena/dnevnik_i_zapiski_18541886 .html#0. Translated by Linda M. Mayhew, summer 2023.

1868

ST. PETERSBURG, 1 OCTOBER

A holiday, the bells are ringing. It's quiet in the house.

"How did you get it into your head to live alone?" I am asked. "Isn't it expensive, and don't you miss everything?"

I explain that there, at home, there wasn't room for us.

The real reason that I ran away, bringing with me the fear of confusing our affairs and the faint hope of putting things right with some difficulty—that, I am not telling anyone.

I felt bad that I left, believe me, bad. For someone as educated as me, I had to be tortured to give in to the current, and for the current to wash me ashore.

And there is the shore! That is the real life of an old maid.

Yesterday evening I went to Polonsky to give him, as promised, English language lessons. I didn't give him any sort of lessons; we discussed my previous hatred of him.

2 OCTOBER

Yesterday evening Alya and Malevski came over. Alya said, by the way, that Goncharov censored Lazhechnikov's *Oprichnik* because of the stage design.

When this censorship was still a bureaucratic secret, Alya secretly shared it with someone in the theater. That person also gossiped, and it went all the way to the director, then to Born. They started to make noise about taking him away to the Main Directorate.

They raised a commotion but didn't find him at fault, and they made such a fuss that they fussed their way to permission to stage *Oprichnik*.

THURSDAY, 3 OCTOBER

The newspapers are completely dedicated to the revolution in Italy, and it, for lack of anything closer, provides a topic of conversation.

For me personally, far away Italy holds little interest. I don't know well the details of this uprising and the names of its heroes and victims.

I am struck and deeply surprised by the spirit of the Italian people. This is something fabled, unprecedented, unexpected.

Lavrov is already in Vologda; this is a great joy. There new places, new people will restore his frayed nerves. Judging by the postcard, which he did in Vologda, he has not recuperated and has not grown younger.

Not long ago I showed this postcard to Benediktov; he started to cry, looking at it, *c'est tout dire*.[40]

4 OCTOBER

Women's work is so much work! I took an exam to start up a school or teach in a state institution. I still can't open a school because I don't have enough money, I can't teach in a state institution because I didn't finish the classes in the Pedagogy Department, and I'm not up to chasing after private tutoring—what should I do? This is breaking my heart. Precisely now, when we need to shrink down and work on this, as on evil, we have gotten close to the "Koshins," to the idle, rich, and completely carefree people.

When I saw Natasha Vasilyevna Stasova, and once more fell into this world of charity and work, I became terribly sad and ashamed of the years I survived and the winters I experienced.

TUESDAY, 8 OCTOBER

Yesterday I was at Stasov's. Alexandra Romanovna came over for dinner, Mama, in the evening Masha and Olya visited.[41] My life is so empty: I was there, someone else was there. I have no energy for this because I have no faith in my strength. "The broken wings just hang!"[42]

And Nadezhda Vasilievna? In a fever, with burning cheeks, and with hands like ice: so weak she can barely move her legs, and practically can't speak from fatigue. The entire day she labors, works, and fusses. Yesterday I found her attending Belozersky's lessons and mending old napkins at the same time.

While sitting with me, she was mending the entire time. She has a mountain of books on her table, which she reads or looks over for translations. Tomorrow she's going to a committee meeting.

Yesterday she was in the house she managed in Vyborg. She and Trubinsky are publishing books, fiddling with a million difficulties, failures, unpleasantries, and see hundreds of people. I am surprised by her, envy her, and cannot find the faith to emulate her.

1869
MARCH

Shcherbin is dead.[43] That Shcherbin who appeared fifteen years ago in St. Petersburg like a social scourge, flogging society's prophets. I say like a scourge, because at work he was not a scourge, he just seemed that way. Aksakov said of him:

> Half-Uke and half-Greek,[44]
> A Nizhinian Greek, not a Milesian Greek.[45]
> Why do you shorten your time
> With empty childlike malice?[46]

But there wasn't ever any real malice. There was the delicacy of petty ambition, sentimental disgust with things that didn't fall into his hands. True malice wouldn't have agreed with the Main Department on printing, and true disgust wouldn't have been allowed to clothe itself in that uniform or in those ranks which they fiercely scoffed at.

FRIDAY, 17 OCTOBER

Negreskul told me several disturbing things.[47]

Several days, about two weeks ago, a young man that he knew walked out from a home in our region, Liteyny that is, at about 9 o'clock at night.

A carriage sat by the entrance, some sort of military officer got out of the carriage and invited the young man to sit inside.

The surprised young man refused, of course, this invitation. Then the officer showed him a paper, the warrant for his arrest. The young man surrendered, they went to some big house, entered it, and there the officer told the young man, "You saw the warrant for your arrest, now sign this promissory note for six thousand, otherwise you won't leave here alive, and all these individuals here will be brought in"—and showed him a list of names of young men and women that he knew.

The dumbstruck young man signed and was released. The first thing he did, of course, was to notify his friends about the officer's threat. They all decided right away to let the police know what happened, but, before they managed to do this, an anonymous letter appeared, which said that if they publicized the situation, then they would be brought in.

They were convinced and kept silent.

When Negreskul told me this story, I started to convince him to ignore the anonymous letter and tell the police everything, but my reasoning did not persuade him. He firmly believed in solidarity with the Third Department for these events and reasoned it like this:

"Let's suppose that they bring me in, they'll see that I am innocent, and they'll release me in a month. In that month, I will lose my employment and my health, of which I don't have much (that, alas, is entirely true), and, finally, I have a pregnant wife, from whom I am hiding half this story."

I only succeeded in convincing him to seek counsel with a lawyer; I gave him Arseniev's address.

This story is disturbing in many ways: First, it shows the extent of our intellectual youth's agitation and the distrust of their own safety, if they were prepared to see the arm of the government in such blatant extortion, and second, concealing this blatant extortion can enable its repetition, and, finally, it actually gives an entire circle of youth the appearance of guilt. They are not entirely out of danger.

As much as this story worried me, yesterday I headed to the Negreskuls' home on the 14th Line to find out more but did not learn anything.[48]

Manya's presence, in her delicate condition, was bothersome, and I did not have time to wait for her to leave the room; now I am waiting for Negreskul to come see me at home.[49]

When will there be an end to these Third Departments and arrests, these bogeymen and, at the same time, amusements, these romances of our youth? Because, I must confess, these strange toys that our crazy government has habituated us to have a romantic side. People, casting aside any luxuries, anything unnecessary, that a person can manage without, and even things that one can't manage without, simplifying to an impossible level their relationships, their lives, not flaunting anything, now flaunt their relationship with the government. Indeed, they show off, without even noticing, their criminal mindset, their own dangerous behavior.

In Solvychegodsky and Tsarevokoksjaicky, they go quench their thirst for adventure, their inherent youth, which no sort of intellectual labor can change or remove until the years extinguish it.

And all these are steps, all steps, that no one has walked along for a very long time. How can they go? Where is their strength when they don't have their health?

Does our childhood, our adolescence, our youth really give us health? And what are we without health?

SATURDAY, 3 NOVEMBER

Negreskul did not show up—probably nothing happened after the youth's adventures.

All the better! Now, some unpleasant rumors about Negreskul himself have reached my ears.

The Russian book trade is publishing the journal *Bibliograph*; Negreskul is the head of this journal. But because of this the businesses either didn't permit or wouldn't permit him to do the publication, so they found a fake editor, who was none other than our old friend, who's taken leave of his senses, Strugovshchikov.[50]

I say this because, not knowing him in his youth, I think he was more insightful then. I think this, although those who knew him then insist that he could never survive as there's no way that he could. By the way, this is not the problem, but rather that the translator Gete, the current head of the Novgorod zemstvo and Strugovshchikov's secret advisor, was invited to be the responsible editor.

When Lavrov was forbidden from being the editor of *Messenger Abroad*, Afanasyev-Chuzhbinsky had the tact to avoid arguing about anything with Lavrov, being satisfied with an honorarium, as if the honor of underwriting a book, composed by Lavrov, did not compensate him for his passive role.

Strugovshchikov could not fill the same role in a relationship with Negreskul that Afanasyev-Chuzhbinsky filled with Lavrov.

Whoever seized upon the sensible idea of complying with Lavrov, then to the same extent it occurred to them to not comply with Negreskul and his group.

But Negreskul and his group did not expect this at all. They had badly miscalculated. They thought, an old-timer, an advisor behind the scenes, ingenuous and kind, and they lost sight of the fact that the old-timer was a man of letters.

This oversight in and of itself shows what kind of men they were.

Once a month, Afanasyev-Chuzhbinsky was shown the last page of the book he was editing, the same one that he needed to sign.

The primary editor Strugovshchikov was saved by the contract. The editor de jure, the editor de facto arranged with the group to have a committee select the articles.

The editor de jure's article came up for review; the editor de facto rejected it, deciding that it was unlearned.

The author himself and his group rose up in support of the article. The old-timers wanted to resolve deliberations, but the one old-timer showed them the contract and asked them to distance themselves.

An even greater dispute occurred, and the tribunal disbanded, carrying away their resentment, bewilderment, and articles, and in addition to this, Strugovshchikov took his contract and placed it on his desk.

Suddenly on the next day, while Strugovshchikov was out, Negreskul shows up at his house, went into his office under some sort of pretext, took the contract off his desk, and left.

Strugovshchikov returns, finds out what happened, and quickly goes to Trepov's to complain.

Trepov gives him a clerk to help.

More details on this act of a dark comedy I don't know, but the result is this. Strugovshchikov was reinstated in his role as the responsible editor, and Negreskul was removed from the editorial staff.

All this would have been funny if it had not been so sad. Where would Negreskul and his family now live?

Now even Lavrov did not stay on as an employee of *Bibliograph*. Yes, finally, how preposterously were the nihilists acting again?

I heard this story from several people, but not a single one of them said a word in defense of Negreskul. Everyone, all in agreement, laughed at him, but Strugovshchikov didn't seem funny to anyone, except us, his old friends. I still haven't seen *Bibliograph*, although it's said that it was published elegantly, but it didn't meet its goal as it wasn't thick enough and overintellectualized everything.

My prayers went unheard. I prayed that the generation of nihilists went extinct—go extinct, or it's better to say, decay.

Yesterday I saw them.

At Nadezhda Vasilyevna Stasova's home there was a meeting, which took place every first Friday of the month, on women's issues, that is, on arranging higher education courses for women. The inadequacy, the one-sidedness of views, the lack of comprehension, even—*tranchons le mot*—dishonesty![51]

All this, it seems to me, comes from one source—from ignorance.

Pokrovsky defines a nihilist in particular as having a way of thinking that belongs just to him, that is, to a nihilist. He says that a nihilist never exhausts a theme, taking it at face value—in extreme prose, a nihilist has no business with anything behind him; he denies the existence of anything beyond his horizon, but his horizon is not large; a nihilist doesn't have any sensitivity.

At its extreme, Pokovsky's sensitive nature is something intolerable; he throws himself at the nihilists with fervent anger.

I think this habit of denial and fear of greatness gave birth to this way of thinking.

Nihilists search for one thing only—the truth. They know the truth is naked, and they accept everything naked as truth and uncover everything in search of it. From this point, there is extreme poverty of thought.

MONDAY, 10 NOVEMBER

Sitting alone in our little apartment, having in front of me a block of free time, which I know that no one will interrupt, right now is my most invigorating pleasure, and even my only one.

It gives me that sense of consciousness when one is immersed in one's own thoughts, concentrating on things. And here I am, at the present moment, alone, and will be alone in the hours ahead of me, until evening, until night, and cannot concentrate.

The conversation we had here an hour ago didn't give me any peace. I sense thunder in the air, and moreover, I see how it is developing, and fear and hope put me on edge. Will thunder destroy us or will it be fruitful?

A person's life, maybe that of several people, is on the line—it's all or nothing.

People, strangers to each other, came together by chance at my house and began to have such strange relations with each other. That terrible thing, which was revealed to me a year ago, and the perpetration of which I can't discuss with anyone, or know the time or the place of the perpetration, is underway right now.

WEDNESDAY, 19 NOVEMBER

Negreskul was here just now; this is how he tells the story of Strugovshchikov.

The committee was dissatisfied with the layout of the first edition of *Bibliograph*. Strugovshchikov, who had compiled it, placed a series of news stories related to literature, but, truthfully, did not relate to bibliographies and did not fit into the plan for the journal; at the same time, he did accommodate the bibliographical news and the catalog of new books, which was very noticeable, by the way.

Despite the committee's disagreement about releasing the book with this layout, Strugovshchikov ordered it to be released. Negreskul and someone else, whose name I don't remember, went to the editorial staff and after realizing that the book had been released, asked them to postpone the publication or return all their articles. Negreskul appointed a special committee then went to Strugovshchikov's and, not finding him at home, asked for Yan, but he wasn't there either, so he asked the servant to take him to the office, and there, he wrote Strugovshchikov a note, requesting that he come to the committee meeting whenever it was convenient for him, either in the morning on in the evening, the next day. After writing the note, he saw on the table a printed table of contents for the articles in the next book.

Here Negreskul did one thing, which, he said, he had the right to do—he took the table of contents. He said that there was a provision allowing any member of the commission to take everything related to the publication from a colleague's desk. In any case, what Negreskul took was not a contract, as Zhokhov confirmed. And he did not take it secretly but with the servant's knowledge. Strugovshchikov, after finding out what occurred, went to Trepov's but didn't see him, so he related the entire affair to Kolyshkin. The next morning, Kolyshkin sent a telegram to summon Negreskul to him and then told him that Strugovschik complained about him and the group like they were rebels, revolutionaries, who bluntly carry out ideas.

Later, Negreskul, it seems, met Strugovschik at the editorial staff meeting and berated him to his face as he had found out beforehand from Vodovozov that Strugovshchikov had said that his son Mikhail had advised him to go to Trepov, and so he berated the son as well.

The next day, the son came to challenge him to a duel; he challenged him in front of his own sick wife. Negreskul answered that he did not fight with swindlers, and moreover, he was certain that he, that is Mikhail Strugovshchikov, would immediately go inform the police if he accepted the challenge.

That is the story in Negreskul's words. An arbitration court was assigned.[52] On Strugovshchikov's side were Kraevsky and Gaevsky. On Negreskul's side were N. Kurochkin and Lesevich. The super arbitrators were N. Neklyudov and Arseniev. I'll try to visit this tribunal and hope with all my heart that Negreskul and his group are found in the right.

Today was Rossi's third lesson; there were fourteen people. Pokrovsky and Antropov had lunch.[53] We argued greatly about Samarin's "The Periphery of Russia."[54] They are both followers of Katkov.[55]

How few have remained faithful to the legends of our youth.[56] But, perhaps, having entered life, after plunging, so to speak, into it, they cannot remain completely, absolutely faithful, and only people like me, standing outside of life, can do this.

I forgot to write that Strugovshchikov insists that, at the arbitration court, no one mention he went to Trepov's.

The problem with the young man and the six thousand ruble bill was worked out. Arseniev taught him how to get the bill sent back and cancel it. It turned out that it was just a fraud.

One of the students, by the way, was a certain Mme. Veber. She arrived early, and I chatted with her about the women's courses. We completely agreed on the split that had occurred, that is Solodnikova and company. She found faults and reason to initiate a split in Nadezhda Vasilyevna Stasova's behavior, although she did not doubt her sincere intentions related to the woman question. At the same time, she judged Solodnikova harshly. She did, by the way, use as an example her and Tkachova's behavior at one of the meetings at Trubinkova's. When the elderly Naranovich walked in and all the professors stood up to greet him, they both continued to sit and only whispered and giggled.[57]

Veber found this revolting, and she, by the way, in my eyes, is a nihilist.[58]

All the same, Nadezhda Vasilyevna again announced a meeting on Saturday, not heeding my advice or Belozersky's advice.[59] She wants to drag this out until a catastrophe that destroys the Women's Labor Society.

The last time Tkachova lost her temper, just one word was needed on her part, or on the part of Nadezhda Vasilyevna herself, and that broken machine called the woman question, which is so poorly built, but so necessary and important, would stop again on account of that cog that Tkachova or Stasova would like to break.

I would like to say this to them. . . . No, I don't want to say anything to them, but throw a reprimand in their face, that they don't love the work that they have undertaken.

MONDAY, 11 DECEMBER
Cherkesov was taken.[60]

Sometimes on a clear day, under a cloud free sky, thunder unexpectedly sounds from a barely noticeable storm cloud that snuck up, and you involuntarily jump.

We involuntarily jumped in the same way from the unexpected news that was spread: Justice of the Peace Cherkesov was taken. Why? Why? No one knew! The people closest to him, his wife, his friends, didn't know. They thought this arrest didn't have anything in common with Ushakova's escape.

What happened with Ushakova is also unclear.[61] While circulating in nihilist circles for a long time, I never heard such a name. Maybe, perhaps, she was not a nihilist.

Here is what they say about her: she fled abroad; her father filed a complaint with the Third Department. They started to make inquiries, and it turned out Cherkesov helped her escape, while others said that his shop assistant, Evdokimov, was the one, and gave her fifty rubles for the road.

There is not much believable in this story.

Others talked about the appearance of some sort of political leaflet.

In our circle, we got the news that in the county town Vyesegonsk, Tver province (3,000 residents), a political leaflet has made an appearance. At the advice of the minister of justice Palen, two officials from the first department of the Senate were sent that year to file a complaint or open an investigation. They didn't find anything except for nonsense and informed the authorities that such nonsense was not worth their attention.

Suddenly, it was found out that the political leaflet had not been circulated at all from Vesyegonsk but had been sent from Petersburg. The government officials and authorities were reprimanded and persecuted anew. They thought that Cherkesov's arrest, maybe, had something in common with this occurrence. We will see what he says tomorrow.

They first searched Cherkesov's store, then his apartment. But when they wanted to search the office, he put on his magistrate chain and didn't want to allow the search.[62] However, they visited Shuvalov, and in the end, Cherkesov consented.

Neklyudov, the chairman of the Congress, and the entire Congress, were outraged by this, and protested. They filed a lawsuit in district court, others put together a complaint for the minister of justice. Moreover, *Legal Messenger* published a story about the search and the arrest and received a warning.

They said it was all for nothing that *Legal Messenger* wrote about this; they were discredited by this completely lawfully, but the daring announcement about the international conference damaged publications. A special commission existed, created to review publication laws, and they found that literature does best if it keeps as quiet as possible and inspires as few reasons as possible for new oppressive laws.

They are expecting a scandal. Goldgoyer, the best of the senators, suggested, "Shuvalov wants a scandal; he has expected violation of the laws."

We'll see what he says tomorrow.

They say at Cherkesov's they found a note from Ushakova where she thanks him for the money. But seeing as how she transferred money for Cherkesov's library, she therefore, probably, also received money. They found the same thing from Herzen at his house. [. . .]

From the History of the Women's Movement[63]

In December 1867,[64] Evgenia Ivanovna Konrady submitted a letter to the Congress of Naturalists, in which, based on women's aspiration for higher education, she requested permission to attend the university.[65]

They didn't respond with a direct refusal but skeptically wondered if women actually had such aspirations.

Konrady then turned to M. V. Trubinkova as a

person who traveled among circles of women seeking intellectual work and education and asked her to tell them about her, Konrady's, endeavors, and to circulate her idea and, if they were sympathetic to her, urge them to unite in supporting its fulfillment.

Trubinkova responded passionately, and the first thing she did was rush to her friend—N. V. Stasova. And so, the three of them—Stasova, Trubinkova, and Konrady, began drafting a new letter or, more precisely, a request to the university president, Keslar—he was also a member of the Congress of Naturalists—on behalf of all women desiring a higher education in which they sought permission to attend university lectures. The letter was supposed to be signed by as many women as possible, and in about nine days 400 people signed it.

The signed papers were disseminated to every fiber of society, to the so-called nihilists, as well as to the aristocrats, and they were quickly covered with names, their embroidery reminding me, at least, of the ordeals for the creation of the Society for Women's Labor in 1863–65 and its untimely end; even more so, the familiar names that I came across from this time brought back memories. But there were new ones, for example, the name of the daughter of the minister of war, Milyutin, a very nice girl who collected many signatures from her circle, and whom we really counted on. And counting was necessary.

Meanwhile, spring arrived. On April 2, at our home, a clean copy of the petition was written out, and Trubinkova brought it to President Keslar and received a reply addressed to her.

He announced the following.

The academic council at the university read the letter, was sympathetic to women's ambition for education and their willingness to take upon themselves the work of organizing higher education courses for women, if the ministers gave permission for this.

The doors of the university, for coeducational lectures, were not opened.

To review and discuss this response, Trubinkova invited everyone who had signed the petition to her house—of course not everyone showed up, and they didn't decide on anything relating to the academic council's proposal. They decided to hold off on further discussions until fall, organize only circles, consisting of 400 people, who would send representatives, deputies to future meetings and would not show up in full force, as it would not be possible for that number to show up at the meeting.

They also decided to prepare in summer a preliminary schedule of courses with the help of university professors, and in fall, to discuss the program at the general meeting and then present it to the minister of public education along with the petition to open courses.

Fall arrived. The general meeting approved the schedule and the petition, and it only remained to decide who would bring it to the minister.

If only fate, not people—people, that is the masses, are always hindered by personal interest or other issues and don't act reasonably—if only fate, I repeat, put forward Trubinkova and Stasova to handle the matter, then they would have quickly and successfully gotten to the point of the matter and they would have opened the courses in that very fall.

But, alas, things worked out differently.

Trubinkova and Stasova were passionately devoted to the issue of women's education, and they possessed great tact and what is called knowing how to live "*savoir vivre.*"

Never abandoning their sense of self-worth or their convictions, they also employed the gentleness and graciousness of society women, which achieves more than harsh words and audacity, stopping at nothing.

Marya Vasilyevna Trubinkova, aside from being an excellent chairwoman, had a natural talent for debating. It was astonishing how she was able to listen, seize upon the main idea, respond intelligently, and anticipate both evasions and entrapments. If she was shrewder, then Nadezhda Vasilyevna was more thoughtful, passionate, and self-confident. She did not spare or begrudge her strength or her health for the common goal.

At the general meeting, it was decided to send Stasova, A. P. Filosofova, and Voronina, born Bykova.

The main person who initiated this, Konrady, remained behind the line of action; she was pushed aside.

This was the first difficulty that was reminiscent of the downfall of the Society for Women's Labor.

But it was impossible to take any other action. Konrady was too impatient and had a nasty quality.

Up until now, she was not well known in any circles, but in the period between spring and fall, she managed to make herself visible and managed to attract not just ill will—that would be nothing— but instilled the fear that because of her impatient nature, the whole thing would fall apart.

To make it less insulting, Trubinkova distanced herself and didn't go see the minister.

Konrady was offended, continued with her nastiness, but didn't step down from the deputy position, and essentially, her behavior did not have any serious consequences.

But then, the injured pride of another deputy had very serious consequences—Solodovnikovaya.

And if during this the whole didn't completely fall apart, then it was thanks to the energy, determination, and dedication of Nadezhda Vasilyevna.

It somehow came to light that Solodovnikovaya's apartment had been searched and that she even was arrested.

Not for long, and apparently, this arrest did not present anything important, as she was quickly released and once more was completely free, but at the meeting they began to say that she could not be a deputy now, that another situation like this with her could cast a negative light on the work we were starting and could harm it, so we protected and nourished it.

Solodovnikovaya heard these conversations, lost her temper, and relinquished the title deputy, and, thus, she ended up out of the movement, free to act as she wished, and took advantage of her ability to act freely.[66]

The minister received the women more than ungraciously, almost impolitely. Their petition was flat out refused.[67]

After Tolstoy's response, all of us quieted down but did not lose heart, thanks in part to Nadezhda Vasilyevna's energy. We decided one way or another that we would not let go of the work we'd started. Publicly—well, public lectures, then we'll see what comes after that. Once again, we invited professors to create a new schedule of public lectures. Meanwhile, internal turmoil ran its course, and the two parties whose coming together destroyed the Society for Women's Labor, once again opposed each other and ratted each other out. "The nihilists will ruin everything for us"—said the aristocrats. "We don't need philanthropists and patrons"—said the nihilists.

3 NOVEMBER 1878

Yesterday I was at A. P. Filosofova's. The former committee that founded higher education courses for women got together. The day after tomorrow, a new "Society for Funding Higher Education for Women," approved by the minister of foreign affairs, is being opened. Not many of us former members got together, but we discussed much. Our pillars— Stasova, Filosofova, Tarnovskaya, Mordinova, will of course remain in the new committee; Belozerskaya, Trubinkova, and I stepped down from the committee but remained members.[68] They said there were some kind of rumors spreading about the classes. The way they were talking, it was as if one of the students stood on the table and preached socialism; or as if Prince Oldenburgskij noticed how many cigarette butts were laying there on the floor when visiting the classes. Tarnovskaya, Stasova, and Mordinova assured us that this was all nonsense. They know, they are on duty there every day, and the one thing they complain about it how exuberantly students burst through the doors when the auditorium opens; in all other respects they behave with unusual propriety.

14 NOVEMBER 1878

Professor Tsitovich from Novorosiisky University published a brochure, "A Response to Scholars," where he not only passionately but furiously attacked the "journalistic science" being taught to the young scholarly generation.[69] The brochure had the truth at times, but the truth was presented not only sharply but ferociously. It alarmed the young generation. The young people are weak enough to take all the attacks personally and give a response. At our courses for young women, K. N. Bestuzhev—Ryumin forcibly stopped a demonstration, that is, a collective message to Tsitovich, and even then, not everyone paid attention to his warnings.

Pyotr Lavrovich Lavrov, "Foreword to the First Edition" and "Letter One: Natural Science and History " in *Historical Letters*

Lavrov, a Populist philosopher, served as editor for several journals including Forward! *(1873–76). Although he was involved with The People's Will, he considered himself a scholar above all else. He is best known for his essay collection* Historical Letters, *which was widely read among the intelligentsia. In this collection, he outlines the steps necessary to create a more just and equal society. Originally published in a serial format in the journal* The Weekly, *these letters were collected into a single volume in 1869.*

Source: Pyotr Lavrovich Lavrov, "Foreword to First Edition" and "Letter One," in *Historical Letters (1868–1869)*, Biblioteka Maksima Moshkova, accessed July 1, 2024, http://az.lib.ru/l/lawrow_p_l/text_1869_istoricheskie_pisma.shtml. Translated by Linda M. Mayhew, summer 2024.

Foreword to First Edition

I consider it necessary to preface this edition with a brief explanation, having presented readers with a new format and the whole series of letters, previously placed in *The Weekly*.

When I began to send these letters, I was not entirely sure whether or not the editors would find it suitable to place on their journal pages a systematic series of études on the questions examined here. The distance from the capital did not allow me to follow the development of matters and see to what extent I had managed to interest readers. A periodic publication should constantly have a goal in sight—to be read. Several times in the process of composing these letters, I could have thought that I needed to stop, and I realized only with the final printing that the letters comprised some sort of cohesive whole for the readers of the journal. Besides this, I know well that readers of journals rarely have the patience to track the development of abstract thought; if the start of this development is compiled in one issue, the continuation drags into several issues, and the conclusion is separated from the beginning by an entire year. All of this prompted me to compose each letter in a more polished format than would have been necessary for a cohesive set of études, and because of this the entire series would suffer in both cohesiveness and integrity. And stepping away from work and returning to it later, my own thoughts lent too much of a fragmentary quality. Therefore, when reviewing these letters, I had to point out the connections in certain instances, clarify the correlation between separate études, develop certain points, reorganize some things so the reader could absorb the entirety of the letters more easily. The primary difference between this edition and the original version of *Historical Letters* lies in this purely formal revision. I permit myself to hope that this new version with its more connected sections and clarification of fundamental thought will make my work a bit more worthwhile for the reader.

I would have liked to make more substantive corrections, but in this regard our critics did not help me at all. Neither the thick journals, nor the daily newspapers, nor the serious historical journals, nor the various partisan journals—at least as much as I succeeded in seeing them—showed the analysis, evidence, corrections, or admonishments that led me to think that it required more precision and development; perhaps I overlooked an important perspective in one place or mistook in another place a nebulous idea for an essentially important one. Maybe I wasn't able to sufficiently interest readers and critics with these letters. Maybe the critics considered the thoughts expressed here too rudimentary to receive any attention; it is possible though, finally, that precisely those publications that I would have needed never reached me. However, in this regard I was at the mercy of myself and some fragmented, subjective reviews that reached me. The last ones were particularly focused on one flaw: abstract, dry, difficult to read.... Unfortunately, this flaw lies in part in the topic itself. Nonetheless, I confess that it belongs to my writing style. In a separate publication I tried to correct this in some places, entering examples, but I did not intend to write a new essay and wanted only to present the reader with the previous work in an improved format. An excessive array of examples could, it seemed to me, somewhat damage the cohesive development of thought. The last was left completely unchanged and only in some places were the previous expressions replaced with more precise ones.

Not wanting to change the overall title of my work, I considered it, however, unnecessary to keep some form of the epistolary phrases in it that I had used before.

I am completely unaware to what extent the readers of *The Weekly* read my letters or ignore them. Maybe, now the critics will find they are not worth their attention. I stated in the last letter that I myself recognize the many flaws in this work, especially given the importance of the subject. I am giving to the readers what I can, as I can.

Kadnikov, 1869

Letter One: Natural Science and History

If movements in contemporary thought interest the reader, then two areas will quickly assert their rights for your attention: natural science and history. Which of these is more relevant for contemporary life?

At first glance, it is not as easy to answer this question as it would seem. I know that natural scientists and the majority of thoughtful readers will not think of responding in favor of natural science. Actually, it is very easy to prove that questions of natural science lie in a person's life every minute, as one cannot turn, look, breathe, think without employing the complete range of the laws of mechanics, physics, chemistry, physiology, and psychology! In comparison to this, what is history? Diversion for idle curiosity. The most influential figures in the private or public spheres can live or die without ever having any need to know that once upon a time, Hellenism along with Alexander the Great's troops swept through Asiatic tribes; that Codexes, Pandekts, novellas, and so on that lay the foundation for contemporary legal procedures in Europe shaped the era of the world's most despotic rulers—that was the age of feudalism and knighthood, when the crudest and animalistic impulses coexisted with euphoric mysticism. Transitioning to the homeland's history, we ask ourselves whether or not knowledge of the bogatyr's byliny, Russian Truth, Ivan the Terrible's wild *oprichina*, or even Peter the Great's battle with ancient Moscow over European forms is useful in the lives of many contemporary people? All of this occurred in the past, and the new subsequent questions, requiring all the care and all the thought of the modern person, keep from the past only an interest more or less of dramatic pictures, more or less clear embodiment of ideas common to all of humanity.... And so, obviously, there cannot be any comparison between the knowledge that defines every element of our life and other knowledge that elucidates aspects that are simply interesting—between the essential bread of thought and a pleasing dessert.

Natural science is the basis of intellectual thought—that is indisputable. Without clearly understanding its requirements and basic laws, a person is blind and deaf to their most ordinary needs and to their most sublime ideas. In a strict sense, a person who is completely unfamiliar with natural science does not have even the slightest entitlement to the knowledge of a contemporary educated person. But once he takes that point of view, the question arises, what is more relevant to their real-life interests than anything else? Are there questions on multiplying cells, evolving forms, spectral analysis, binary stars? Or are they on the laws of development of human knowledge, the conflict between the start of common good and the beginning of justice, the battle between national unity and human solidarity, the relationship between the economic interests of the starving masses and the intellectual interests of the more well-off minority, the connection between social development and the formation of a system of government? If the question is posed in this way, then hardly anyone, except the philistines of knowledge (of which there are more than a few), will admit that the latter questions are closer at hand, more important, and more tightly intertwined with their daily life than the former.

Even, specifically, one of them is closer at hand and one of them is more important. The first ones are only as important and close to it as much as they provide better understanding of the easiest resolution of the *second* ones. No one argues about the use of grammatical correctness, about its obvious necessity for human development, but it hardly has any defenders so dumb that they suggest it possesses some kind of independent, magical strength. There is hardly anyone who will say that the *process* itself of reading and letter writing is important for a person. This process is important for a person only as a *means* of mastering those ideas that a person can acquire by way of reading and share by way of letter writing. A person who gets nothing out of reading is not much better than an illiterate person. The phrase "illiterate person" is a negation of the fundamental requirement of education, but literacy in and of itself is not the entire purpose—it is only a *means*. Natural science just barely plays this role in the general system of human education. It is just a *literacy of thought*; but this literacy uses developed thought to resolve purely human questions, and these questions comprise the *essence* of human development. It isn't enough to read a book; it's necessary to understand it. In this same way, it's not enough for a developed person to understand the fundamental laws of physics and physiology, or to be interested in experiments on proteins or Kepler's laws. For the developed person, protein is not only a chemical compound but is an integral part of food for millions of people. Kepler's laws are not only formulas for the abstract movement of planets but are one of the things gained by the human spirit on the way to acquiring general philosophical understanding of the constancy of the laws of nature and their independence from any divine abuse of power.

We note here even the direct contradiction to what was said above about the comparative importance of the basis of natural science and history for daily life. Chemistry experiments on proteins and mathematical equations for Kepler's laws are *only curiosities*. The economic value of proteins and the philosophical meaning of the invariability of astronomical laws is extremely vital. Knowledge of the external world provides completely essential material, which is necessary to consider when resolving all the questions that occupy a person. But the questions, for which we are exploring this material, are essentially questions not of the external world but of the internal world, questions of human *consciousness*. Food is important not as an object of the process of nourishment but as the product for eliminating the conscious suffering from hunger. Philosophical ideas are important not as a display of the process of developing the soul in its logical abstraction but as a logical form of *consciousness* with a person higher or lower than their worth, broader or more focused ideas of their existence; they are important as a form of protest against the present in the name of wanting better and more just social classes or as forms of satisfaction with the present. Many thinkers have noted the progress in ideas about humanity, having concluded that humans, who first positioned themselves at the center of all existence, subsequently became aware of themselves as just one of numerous products resulting from the application of the invariable laws of the external world; that humanity had transitioned from a subjective view of themselves and nature to an objective one. True, this was very important progress. Without it, science was impossible, the development of humanity unthinkable. But this progress was only the first step, after which the second was unavoidable: the research of the external world's invariable laws in their *objectivity* to achieve the state of humanity that would subjectively be recognized as the best and most fair. And here the supreme law was confirmed, divined by Hegel and justified in many spheres of human consciousness; the third step was the observable proximity to the first but the *actual* allowance for contradiction between the first and second steps. Humanity once again became the center of the entire world, but not for the world, as it existed in and of itself, but for the world as understood by humanity, submitting to his thoughts and directing them to his goals.

But this is precisely history's point of view. Natural science reveals to humanity the laws of the world, for which humanity itself has only a barely perceptible part; it recasts the products of mechanical, physical, chemical, physiological, and psychological processes; among the products of the latter processes in the entire animal kingdom, it locates the awareness of suffering and pleasure; in part of this kingdom, closest to humanity, is the awareness of the possibility of defining goals for oneself and striving to achieve them. This fact of natural science comprises the essential basis of the lives of separate beings in the animal kingdom and the history of separate groups in the world. History as a science accepts this fact as given and draws out for the reader the way that history as a process of human life arose from striving to eliminate what humans perceived as suffering and from striving to obtain what humans perceived as pleasure. What variations arose because of this in understanding as related to the words *pleasure* and *suffering*, in the classification and hierarchies of pleasure and suffering; what philosophical forms of ideas and practical forms of social layers were produced from these variations; through which logical processes did striving for something better and more fair produce protests and conservatism, response and progress; what connection existed in each era among human perception in the form of religious faith, knowledge, philosophical representation, and practical theories on improvements and justice, which were embodied in the actions of the individual, in the forms of society, in the state of the peoples' lives.

Therefore, the labors of a historian do not negate the labors of a naturalist but provide an essential supplement. The historian who holds disdain for the naturalist does not understand history; he wants to build a house without a foundation, to talk about the advantage of education, while negating the need for literacy. The naturalist, holding disdain for the historian, only shows his thoughts are narrow and underdeveloped; he either doesn't want or can't see that setting goals and striving for them is as unavoidable as is natural for any fact in human nature, like breathing, circulation of the blood, or the metabolic process; these goals may be shallow or lofty, may strive for pity or respect, take actions irrational or beneficial, but having goals, and striving for them, and taking action have always existed and will always exist; as a result, they are naturally the appropriate topic for study, like the spectral colors, like elements of chemical analysis, like species and subcategories of the plant and animal kingdom. The natural scientist, restricted to the external world, doesn't want or can't see that the entire external world is for humanity *only* material pleasure, suffering, desire, action; that the most specialized naturalist researches the external world not as anything external but as something perceptible and imparting *pleasure* to *him*, a scholar, in the process of perception, awakening *his* actions, entering into *his* life process. A natural scientist, who disregards history, imagines that whoever lays the foundation doesn't have in mind to build a home on it; he assumes that all human development should be limited to literacy.

Some will contradict, probably, my idea that natural scientists have two undeniable advantages in history, which allow the natural scientist to somewhat condescendingly regard the academic merit of a historian's work. The natural sciences developed precise methods, receiving uncontestable results and showing the capital of immutable laws, which were perpetually proven and which allowed the prediction of factual information. As it relates to history, it is doubtful whether or not even one law even belongs to it; it developed only elegant *pictures*, and the accuracy of its predictions is on the same level as weather forecasters. That is the first thing. The second thing and the most important is that contemporary goals for improvements and justice, as in a clear understanding of the goal, in a faithful selection of the method, in the intended direction of activity, draw their material almost exclusively from natural science data, while history provides incredibly little useful material due to the ambiguity of thought from past events, providing similarly beautiful arguments for directly contradictory theories of life and to the completely changed events at present that make applying the results to the present extremely difficult, drawing on several events that were unusual, even when the results were precise. Being inferior in both *theoretical science* and in its *practical application* to the work of a natural scientist, can the work of a historian be placed alongside it?

In order to clarify the question posed here, it is necessary to specify what meaning we assign to the word *natural* science. I don't mean here a strict classification of the sciences with all the controversial questions that it raises. It goes without saying that history, as a natural process, could be placed under the domain of natural sciences, and then the complete opposite, discussed above, would not have any place. In everything that follows, I will include in the term *natural* science two types of science: *phenomenological* sciences, which research the laws of repeating phenomena and processes, and *morphological* sciences, which study the allocation of objects and shapes that underlie the observed processes and phenomena, as the goal of these sciences is the consolidation of all observable forms and allocations at moments of genetic processes. Setting aside the group of morphological sciences, I draw your attention to the group of phenomenological sciences that I will mention: geometry, mechanics, physics-chemistry sciences, biology, psychology, ethics, and sociology. Having assigned the term *natural* science the meaning just indicated, I will turn to the question posed above.

The scientific rigor and competence of research methods are not discredited in studies that relate to mechanics, physics, chemistry, physiology, and to psychological theories of the senses. But even the theory of ideas, concepts in individuals, and personal ethics use very few methods of the previously mentioned natural sciences. Regarding social sciences (sociology), that is the theory of processes and products of social development, here almost all the tools of physics, chemistry, and physiology are inapplicable. This important part of natural science, closest to humanity, refers to the laws of the previously mentioned disciplines as if to already prepared data, but its own laws seek another path. Which? Where do the phenomenology of the spirit and sociology draw their own materials from? From biographies of individuals and from history. As much as there is nonscientific work of historians and biographers, there are nonscientific conclusions from a psychologist in the broad realm of their discipline, from the work of an ethicist, and from a sociologist in their scientific spheres. That is to say, natural science should be acknowledged as unscientific in the parts which are closest to human nature. Here the success of science is produced by a common manual for both areas of knowledge. Superficial observations of biographical and historical facts give the approximate truths of psychology, ethics, and sociology; this approximate truth allows more thoughtful observation of facts in biographies and history; this, in turn, leads to a more precise truth, which allows further refinement of historical observation and so on; an improved tool gives a better product, and a better product allows further refinement of the tool, which in turn influences even more refinement of the product. History, when used correctly, provides completely essential material for natural science, and only when referring to historical works can a natural scientist clarify the processes and products of the intellectual, moral, and social life of humanity. A chemist may consider their specialization more scientific than history and ignore its material. A person embracing the word *natural* science for all natural processes and products doesn't have the right to place this science above history and should recognize their tightly knit mutual dependence.

The aforementioned resolves the question of practical usefulness. If psychology and sociology are subject to uninterrupted advancement due to improved understanding of historical facts, then the study of history becomes unavoidably necessary for clarifying laws of life for the individual and society. These laws are based as much on data from mechanics, physiology, as on data from history. The decreased precision of the latter should not result in its elimination from study but, on the contrary, its expansion, as specialist-historians have not risen above the masses of readers on the basis of the precision of their conclusions, as much as chemists and physiologists have risen above the readers. Questions from contemporary life about what is the best and the most just require the readers to clarify for themselves the results of phenomenology of spirit and sociology, but this clarification is achieved not by accepting *on faith* the opinion of one or another school of economists, politicians, or ethicists. When debating these schools, a conscientious reader must turn to the study of the evidence itself on which these schools have built their conclusions; they must turn as well to the genesis of these schools to clarify their teaching of both the family tree of dogmas and the state of affairs at the time when one school or another came into existence; finally, they must turn to the events influencing its development. But all of this, except for these basic sciences, belongs to history. Anyone who doesn't bother to study it, that person shows their indifference to the relationship of the most important interests of the individual or society or their readiness to believe the word of practical theories, which incidentally first catches one's eye. Thus, the question posed at the beginning, which is more relevant for contemporary life—natural science or history, can be decided, in my opinion, in the following way: The fundamental parts of natural science comprise a completely essential support system for contemporary life but present a more abstract benefit. In terms of the higher parts of natural science, that is, a comprehensive study of the processes and products for the life cycle of an individual and society, this type of study is completely on the same level as history in terms of both theoretical science and practical usefulness; it can't be argued that these parts of natural science are connected with questions more relevant for humanity than history, but a serious study of them is completely impossible without the study of history, and they only hold meaning for the reader to the extent that history makes sense of them.

Therefore, it is in the interest of contemporary thought to rework questions of history, particularly ones closely connected with sociological issues. In these letters, I examine broad historical questions; those elements which shape society's progress; that value, which has the word *progress* for various sides of social life. Here, sociological questions unavoidably intertwine with the historical one, all the more so because, as we have seen, these two fields of knowledge are very closely interdependent. Of course, this gives the present thinking a more general, somewhat abstract character. In front of the reader are not pictures of development but conclusions and similarities from developments during different periods. There are not just a few stories from history, and, maybe, I'll manage to share them at a later time. But historical facts will remain, although understanding changes their significance, and when attempting to illuminate the past, every period brings its own contemporary concerns, its own contemporary development. Thus, historical questions become in every age a means for connecting the present with the past. I'm not forcing my views on the reader but explaining things as I understand them—this is how for me the past is reflected in the present, and the present—in the past.

Nikolai Nikolaevich Strakhov, "Comments on Contemporary Literature"

In this essay, originally published in The Citizen, *no. 20 (1873), Slavophile author Nikolai Strakhov critiques Westernizer journals for their steadfast admiration of European ideals. He acknowledges that there were once reasons to model Russian society after Europe but argues that journalists now blindly mimic Western culture instead of producing their own innovative work.*

Source: Nikolai Nikolaevich Strakhov, "Comments on Contemporary Literature," *Grazhdanin* 20 (1873), Biblioteka Maksima Moshkova, accessed June 13, 2021, http://az.lib.ru/s/strahow_n_n/text_0420oldorfo.shtml. Translated by Linda M. Mayhew, summer 2021.

X.

Messenger of Europe and *St. Petersburg News* could be called the genuine protectors of the Russian journalistic tradition. They are free of extreme views but, as many have noticed, are no different in the following ways: They idolize Europe, but it is unclear exactly why; they predominantly, as P. V. expressed, "continue the best traditions of the forties" but, of course, not with idolization and contradictions.

We'll stop here to discuss several opinions on Europe, which were found in the latest edition of *Messenger of Europe*. In an article on Belinsky, Gospodin Pypin shows that ideas about the corruption of the West, which the Slavophiles put forward and which Belinsky wrote against, are ridiculous.[70] He analyzes them as follows:

> Even if you believe the Western pessimists, then destruction was threatened in Europe only by well-known social structures, in which there actually was and is much decay, not through civilization itself, not through its collected wealth of science and art. The Socialists' pessimism of the West came from a sense of social justice, which was the offspring of that civilization and becomes more and more widespread. Our prophets of decay in the West didn't even understand or didn't want to understand the true significance of the Western opponents of contemporary European life, and in vain they made reference to the Western opponents—like how now they've gotten it into their heads to refer to Hartmann—because Western opponents, of course, were not satisfied with the resolution of the question that our philosophers proposed. Western dissatisfaction with European life was a mature person's discontent, the result of which was still very good for a little boy or youth, and our prophet of European decay made all the more of a strong impression, seeing that our very own education was truly impoverished. (*Messenger of Europe*, May 1873, p. 255)

These words clearly relate to the authors' thought regarding contemporary Europe as much as they did to Europe during the time of the first Slavophiles. The author admits that there is much decay in Europe now; however, he does take heart that the sense of social justice is becoming more and more widespread, and he thinks that, in general, opponents of contemporary European life, such as Hartmann, show a "mature person's dissatisfaction with the result" and so on. In a word, the author now views Europe just as Belinsky viewed it in his time, and therefore he delivers his words with exultation: "Europe is ill—this is true, but don't worry, it isn't dead; its illness is from an abundance of health, from an abundance of life force; this illness is temporary, this crisis is an internal fight of the old with the new below the surface: This—exertion renounces the social foundation of the middle ages and replaces this foundation with humanity's reason and nature as a base" on so on (p. 256).

What a strange intermingling of times! Does this line of reasoning really benefit us? Has nothing really been done or clarified since 1846, when Belinsky wrote and thought this? Then it was still possible to think that way, but now it is impossible; then was a time of rosy hope for Europe, now is a time of despair; then Slavophiles needed inspiring sympathy and courage in order to discuss the decay of the West; now—this decay has become a common, hackneyed place; then people read the golden dreams of Fourier; now they read the vulgar, coldhearted, and sorrowful Hartmann, complaining that there are only two true pleasures on earth—women and good food—and they are too quickly satisfied.

There is an extreme difference between these two times. Europe from 1815 and especially from 1830 to 1848 was so luminous and full of life that it could captivate and dazzle anyone. A surprising inspiration guided philosophy, science, art, and political and Socialist agendas. Everything seemed possible and attainable; it seemed that humanity could reserve all the rewards that it managed to attain throughout history, and in front lay an endless future of unparalleled happiness. These beliefs and hopes were betrayed, in our eyes, in the cruelest way. Since 1848, there has been disappointment after disappointment.

The Socialists' agenda turned out to be unrealizable, perpetuating chaos and misery, and little by little the study of peace and happiness grew into a sermon on hatred and destruction. And the inheritance of previous generations—philosophy, religion in conjunction with reason, resurrected romantic poetry—vanished and were replaced with unadorned materialism, continual doubt, and the absence of any sort of poetry. The age of true pessimism had dawned, which, in comparison, was the opposite of Belinsky's time, which was an age of happy hopes, a true time of optimism. Then they said: Europe is ill, but this illness will lead only to improved health and splendor; now they say: Europe is ill, and there is no hope for recovery, and ahead lies disaster from which there is no way out.

There was an enormous change that occurred in Europe but which was almost entirely unnoticed by our journalists. Not all Russian literature, however, remained blind. There was a very significant writer, specifically Herzen, who understood and expressed especially clearly the fracture in European life. He wholeheartedly and perceptively followed this life and, along with the sons of Europe, felt its despair, its hopelessness. He insistently, eloquently, and insightfully explained to us that Europe doesn't have the strength to save itself from the destruction that threatens it; he preached to us "distrust in words and banners, in the canonization of humanity, and a universal church for the salvation of Western civilization" (*My Past and Thoughts*, 4:53).

Here was a true Westernizer, not an Old Believer repeating once memorized lessons, but a person who in truth understood and loved the lessons taken from the West; therefore, he understood its failures when they were discovered and thereby mourned the destruction of hope in Europe. Our journals are far from a similar understanding; they bravely hold on to a once accepted symbol of faith and close their eyes from the consequences that result, to the facts of historical life that reveal where to lay the foundation. This is why it is fair to say that our journals, as a result of their admonitions, are wrong to introduce us to life in Europe of which we know only select facts, while a broader, thoughtful picture can't be found anywhere, as every journal has its reasons to keep one element or another of this picture in the dark.

Most interesting in these enlightened journalists is the belief that it's as if we don't need to know the life of contemporary Europe in detail. It's misgivings, despair, fear—all this is harmful to tell Russian readers, so as to avoid engendering their freethinking and doubt. If Europe is ailing, then this, Gospodin Pypin says, is "dissatisfaction of a mature person with the result, which was still very very good for boys and youths"; why, in view of this, would one want to disappoint a little boy ahead of time? Probably the boy will cease to study and to learn manners when he sees that studying and manners lead to a single "dissatisfaction." Europe's authority must be protected no matter what—such is the rule of our journals. Poor little boys!—they perpetually disappoint us—and the dear fathers, and the family tutors, and the journalists. Clever people will come out of you! You will produce geniuses, scholars, and politicians. Only don't look at what is happening in Europe; refrain from freethinking criticism of your teacher, and you will be thanked.

It's clear now how any thought about signs of ailing in European life caused such hatred in our journalists. In that little book *Messenger of Europe*, in an article by Gospodin Evg. Markov, there is the following hot-tempered conclusion:

People who are Bulgarian patriots, bombarding everyone with banners, of course attribute the fall of France (here of course is the defeat inflicted by the Germans) to the usual "decay of Europe," the immoral "new Babylon," a "Hydra of internal discontent," the raging on Socialist parties, and so on. I will not deny or dismantle any of this. I will allow it. But these heckler-chauvinists don't want to admit that if a rigid and exact analysis is applied to our society, then it probably appears in the eyes of an outside observer as a society of all types of uneducated, impoverished, and indolent citizens. (*Messenger of Europe*, May 1873, p. 349)

This means: How dare we judge and debate such equal rights in France and throughout Europe! Let the West decay, as it is not for us to sort out and analyze; we are ignorant, poor, and indolent, so if the West is rotten wood, then we are not even worth a piece broken off the rotten wood.

We will acknowledge the fairness of the author's feelings; as is apparent from the article, he's a hot-tempered patriot; he berates our society because he wishes for a rebirth; and a rebirth is necessary because it "is for us a question of state security, state power, and glory" (p. 349).

But despite all this, or, it's better to say, precisely because of this, he is prepared to lay out several paths for Russian thinking. Similar forethought for Russian intellectual life, similar decrees, deciding about what we should write and think, and about what strict silence is required—we are very habitual. Let's not propose a censorship agency that alone manages the correct course of our thoughts; there are many zealots who devote themselves to exactly the same activity. Such is our unhappy situation that we have no place for free thought, free art, or free science to exist. According to Gospodin Evg. Markov, movements on the decay of Europe are harmful because they can align with the heckler-chauvinists, people with Bulgarian tendencies, sour patriots who think that we will bombard everyone with banners. But because of the consequences of similar ideas, movements on many other topics are considered harmful. You write about one thing—you please the nihilists; you write about another—you please the conservatives; you praise something—the superstitious folk believers and the oppressors celebrate; you express outrage—spiteful Europeans pick up on it. Accordingly, one must eternally maneuver between Scylla and Charybdis—a disastrous situation that doesn't give us intellectual space and suppresses active thought.[71]

Every journal has its own politics; in advance, it's decided about what to keep silent, about what to talk, whom to praise, whom to berate, whom to ignore completely. There are journal writers who consider these politics as the highest wisdom of their business, who walk these shackles with enthusiasm and even think up sophisticated additions for them. Altogether, in essence, this is internal censorship, this incessant deceit—they should be agonizing over each one that has their own thoughts and their own feelings. All this is done for the sake of external ideas, not in the interest of truth and art, all for the sake of goals of a foreign literature. It follows, all this is harmful, much more harmful than any sort of external pressure. In order to make our boys obey us and honor the things we want, we leave things unsaid, blow things out of proportion, hold back; in a word, we nourish all their dishonesty. How good will the literature and how good will society be, raised with the help of such wise pedagogical practices!

No—full honesty and seriousness, completely free from any preconceived goals and any external precautions—that is the single condition under which anything truly good, truly useful, and engaging can be written. Our journalism forgot this rule; moreover, everything that extends beyond the instructional policies is considered harmful. And so an inevitable punishment has befallen our journalism: Boys lose faith in the journals, and not only the readers but also the authors are bored and fed up with journal articles.

Selections from Fyodor Dostoevsky, *The Diary of a Writer*

Source: Fyodor Dostoyevsky, *The Diary of a Writer*, vol. 2, trans. and ed. Kenneth Lantz, with an introductory study by Gary Saul Morson (Evanston, IL: Northwestern University Press, 1993), 889–95, 1063–67.

March 1877
1. ONCE MORE ON THE SUBJECT THAT, SOONER OR LATER, CONSTANTINOPLE MUST BE OURS

In June of last year, in the June issue of my Diary, I said that Constantinople "sooner or later, must be ours." It was an impassioned and a glorious time then: all of Russia had risen up in heart and spirit, and the People were going "of their own accord" to serve Christ and Orthodoxy against the unbelievers for the sake of our brethren in faith and blood, the Slavs. The article I wrote then may have been called "The Utopian Conception of History," but I myself believed strongly in my own words and did not consider them utopian; indeed, even now I am prepared to confirm them literally. This is what I wrote about Constantinople then: "Yes, the Golden Horn and Constantinople—all that will be ours and in the first place, it will happen of its own accord precisely because the time has come, and if the time has not yet arrived just now, then it is truly at hand, as all the signs indicate. This is a natural result; this is something decreed by Nature herself, as it were. If this has not happened before, it was simply because the time was not yet ripe."

Thereafter I explained my thought as to why the time was not yet ripe and could not have been ripe formerly. "Had Peter then hit upon the notion of seizing Constantinople rather than founding Petersburg," I wrote,

> then it seems to me that he would have abandoned the idea after some thought, even if he had had sufficient strength to crush the Sultan, precisely because the matter was still inopportune and might have even led to Russia's ruination.
>
> If in Finnish Petersburg we couldn't avoid the influence of neighboring Germans (who, despite their usefulness, paralyzed Russian development before its true path had been clearly revealed), then how, in the huge and distinctive city of Constantinople with its remnants of a mighty and ancient civilization—how could we have avoided the influence of the Greeks, a nation far more subtle than the coarse Germans, a nation with whom we have much more in common than the Germans, who are utterly unlike us? The Throne would have at once been surrounded by crowds of courtiers; they would have become educated and learned sooner than the Russians; they would have enchanted Peter himself, not to mention his immediate successors, exploiting his weak point by demonstrating their knowledge and skill in seamanship. In short, they would have gained political power in Russia; they would have at once dragged her off on some new Asiatic road, into another sort of seclusion, and of course Russia of that time would not have survived it. The development of Russia's strength and her sense of nationhood would have been halted in their course. The mighty Great Russian would have remained in isolation in his gloomy and snowy North, serving as no more than raw material for the renewal of Tsargrad and ultimately, perhaps, the Russian would have found it unnecessary even to follow Constantinople.[72] The South of Russia would have fallen entirely into the clutches of the Greeks. Orthodoxy itself might even have divided into two entirely separate worlds: one in a renewed Tsargrad, the other in old Russia. In short, the matter would have been most untimely. Now, however, things are quite different.

Now (I wrote), now Russia can take possession of Constantinople and do so without transferring her capital there, something that would have been impossible to avoid in Peter's time and even long after him. Now Tsargrad could be ours, and not as the capital of Russia but (I added) also not as the capital as Slavdom as a whole, as some people envisage: "Slavdom as a whole, without Russia, would exhaust itself there in struggling with the Greeks, even if it could manage to create some sort of political unity from its various entities. But to leave Constantinople as a legacy to the Greeks alone is now utterly impossible: we must not give them such a critical point on the globe; this would be altogether too generous a gift to them."

But in the name of what, in the name of what moral right could Russia make a claim on Constantinople? What lofty purpose could we use as a basis to demand it from Europe?

On just this lofty purpose: as leader of Orthodoxy, as its protector and guardian, a role set out for Russia since Ivan III, who placed as an emblem the double-headed eagle of Tsargrad above the ancient coat of arms of Russia, but a role revealed clearly only after Peter the Great, when Russia realized that she had the power to fulfill this mission and in fact became the actual and only guardian both of Orthodoxy and of the nations who profess it. This is the reason and the right to ancient Tsargrad, one that would be clear and inoffensive even to the Slavs who guard their independence most jealously, or even to the Greeks themselves. This would be the means to reveal the essence of the political relationships that must inevitably ensue in Russia toward all the other Orthodox nationalities, Slavic and Greek alike: Russia is their protector and even, perhaps, their leader, but not their ruler; she is their mother, but not their mistress. And if she should become their sovereign at some time, then it would only be because they would have proclaimed her so, allowing themselves to keep all those things by which they would define their own independence and individuality.

Of course, I conceived all these considerations in my June article last year as by no means bound to immediate fulfillment, but only as things that certainly must come to pass when their historical moment and destined time arrive and whose proximity or remoteness, though impossible to predict, may nonetheless be sensed. Nine months have passed since then. There is no need, I think, to recall those nine months: we all are aware of this exuberant period, initially full of hopes and then strange and disturbing, a period that has by no means yet come to an end, so that God alone knows (I think this the only way one can express it) what its resolution will be: will we draw our sword, or will the matter once more be dragged out endlessly by some compromise? But whatever may happen, I felt that at this particular moment, somehow, I must say a few supplementary and explanatory words to my June musings on the fate of Tsargrad. Whatever may happen there now—whether it be peace or concessions once again from Russia—sooner or later Tsargrad will be ours. That is what I want to reaffirm at this particular time, but now from a rather different point of view.

Yes, the city must be ours, not only because it is an illustrious port, because of the straits, because it is "the focus of the universe," "the earth's navel"; not because of the long-acknowledged need for such an enormous giant as Russia to emerge at last from his locked room in which he has already grown to reach the ceiling—to emerge into open spaces where he can breathe the free air of the seas and oceans. I want to set before you only one factor, also of the very greatest importance, that makes it impossible for Russia to avoid Constantinople. I set this factor before the others because, as it seems to me, no one now is taking it into account or, at least, they have long forgotten to take it into account, whereas it may be among the very most important ones.

2. THE RUSSIAN PEOPLE HAVE COMPLETELY MATURED TO A SANE CONCEPTION OF THE EASTERN QUESTION FROM THEIR OWN STANDPOINT

It may seem ridiculous to say it, but the four centuries of Turkish oppression in the East was, on the one hand, even beneficial to Christianity and Orthodoxy there—in a negative sense, of course, yet it worked to strengthen them and, most important, to unite them and make them one, in just the same way that the two centuries of Tatar domination also once worked to strengthen the church here in Russia. The oppressed and harassed Christian population of the East saw Christ and belief in Him as their only consolation and the church as the single and final remnant of their national personality and particularity. This was their last and only hope, the last plank left from their wrecked ship; for still, the church preserved these populations as a nationality, while faith in Christ prevented them—or parts of them, at least—from merging entirely with their conquerors, forgetting their heritage and their past. The oppressed nations themselves sensed all this and understood it very clearly; and they huddled more tightly around the cross. On the other hand, from the very conquest of Constantinople, the peoples of the whole immense

Christian East involuntarily and suddenly turned their prayerful gaze toward distant Russia, which only then had emerged from enslavement to the Tatars, and seemed to foresee her future might and their future, all-uniting center of salvation. Russia quickly and unhesitatingly took up the banner of the East and placed the double-headed eagle of Tsargrad higher than her own ancient crest; and in so doing, as it were, she took up her obligations toward the whole of Orthodoxy: to preserve it and all the peoples who profess it from final destruction. At the same time, the entire Russian People as well completely endorsed the new mission of Russia and their tsar in the future fates of the entire Eastern world. Since that time the People have firmly and unwaveringly given as the principal, beloved appellation of their tsar the word "Orthodox," "Orthodox Tsar"—and so they still see him. Having thus named their tsar, the People thereby essentially acknowledged his mission as well—his mission as guardian and unifier and, when God's commandment thunders forth, as liberator of Orthodoxy and of all Christendom professing it, from Mohammedan barbarism and Western heresy. Two centuries ago, and beginning with Peter the Great particularly, the beliefs and the hopes of the peoples of the East began to be realized in fact: the sword of Russia had already shone forth more than once in defense of the East. It was evident that the peoples of the East as well could not fail to see the tsar of Russia as a liberator and also as their own future tsar. But in the course of these two centuries European education and European influence appeared among them as well. The upper, educated portion of the people, their intelligentsia, little by little grew more indifferent to the idea of Orthodoxy, as did the intelligentsia in Russia, and even began to deny that in this idea lay the renewal and resurrection into a new, grand life for both the East and Russia. In Russia, for instance, a huge portion of the educated class stopped regarding this idea as Russia's principal mission and the pledge of her future vital force; instead they began to find her mission in new areas. Many, in Western fashion, began to see in the church no more than dead formalism, peculiarity, ritualism, and, since the end of the last century, even prejudice and bigotry: the spirit, the idea, the living force was forgotten. There appeared economic ideas of Western character, there appeared new political doctrines, there appeared a new morality that strove to correct the old one and to stand above it. There appeared, at last, science, and it could not help but introduce unbelief in the former ideas. . . . Apart from that, and as a most important factor, ideas of nationality began to be born among the peoples of the East: the fear suddenly arose that once liberated from the Turkish yoke they would fall under the yoke of Russia. Yet in the minds of the many millions of our simple People and in their tsars the idea of the liberation of the East and the church of Christ never died. The movement that caught up the Russian People last summer proved that the People had forgotten none of their former hopes and beliefs; the movement even astonished the immense portion of our intelligentsia to the point where they plainly could not accept it, regarded it skeptically and mockingly, began assuring everyone—and themselves above all—that this movement had been invented and falsified by some disreputable people who wanted to push themselves ahead into prominent positions. In fact, in our time, who among our intelligentsia—apart from a small group that has separated itself from the general chorus—could admit that our People might be capable of *consciously* understanding their political, social, and moral mission? How could they have admitted that this coarse, dark mass, enserfed until only recently and now drinking itself to death, could know and be certain that its mission was the service of Christ, and that of its tsar was the guardianship of Christ's faith and the liberation of Orthodoxy? "Granted, this mass never called itself other than Christian, yet it had no concept either of religion or even of Christ; it doesn't know the commonest prayers." That is what usually is said of our People. Who says this? You may think it is the German pastor who cultivated our Stundism, or some visiting European, the correspondent of a political newspaper, or some educated Jew of the higher orders—one of those who does not believe in God and whose numbers have now suddenly multiplied in our midst—or, finally, one of those Russians who have settled abroad and whose image of Russia and her People is merely a drunken peasant woman holding a vodka bottle. Oh, no, this is how the enormous portion of our own Russian and very best society thinks; and they don't even suspect that although our People may not know their prayers, the essence of Christianity, its spirit and its truth, has been preserved and reinforced within them more firmly, perhaps, than within any of the other peoples of this world—and this despite all their flaws. However, the atheist or the Russian European indifferent to matters of religion sees religion only as formalism and bigotry. They find nothing like bigotry among the People, and so they conclude that the People comprehend nothing of religion; they pray, when they need to, to a wooden plank, but are essentially indifferent, and their spirit is crushed by formalism. They can find no Christian spirit in them at all, perhaps because they themselves have long since lost this spirit and do not even know where it is to be found and where it is wafting. These "depraved" and dark People of ours, however, love the humble man and "the fool in Christ": in all their traditions and their legends they preserve the belief that the weak and the oppressed, who suffer unjustly and wrongfully for the sake of Christ, will be raised above the exalted and the powerful when God's judgment and pronouncement are heard. Our People also love to tell the story of the grand and glorious life of their great, chaste, and humble Christian hero Ilya Muromets, fighter for truth, liberator of the poor and the weak, humble and unassuming, faithful and pure in heart. And having, honoring, and loving such a hero, can our People not believe in the triumph of the now oppressed nations, our brethren, in the East? Our People honor the memory of their great and humble religious hermits and saintly men; they love to tell their children stories of the great Christian martyrs. They know these stories and have learned them by heart; I myself first heard them from the People, told with perception and reverence, and they have remained in my heart. Aside from that, every year our People themselves provide from their midst great repentant "Vlases" who give away all they own and go with tender feeling to perform the humble and great feat of truth, work, and poverty. . . . However, I will speak of the Russian People later; someday they will manage to make others begin to understand them or, at least, to take them into account. Others will realize that the Russian People indeed do count for something. They will realize, at last, this important factor as well: that not even once in the great, or even in the barely important moments of Russian history, could Russia manage without her People; that Russia is of the People; that Russia is not Austria; that in every significant moment of our historical life, the matter was always resolved in the spirit of the People and from their viewpoint, by the tsars of the People acting in the greatest degree of unity with them. Our intelligentsia usually passes over this remarkably important historical factor with scarcely a glance, and it is always brought to mind suddenly, somehow, when some new fateful moment in history looms ahead. But I've strayed from the topic; I began speaking of Constantinople. . . .

July and August 1877
CONFESSIONS OF A SLAVOPHILE

But that's not it. At this point I really must express some of my own feelings, even though, when I began publishing my *Diary* last year, I resolved to make no place in it for literary criticism. But feelings are not criticism, though I may express them about a work of literature. I am writing my "diary," in fact: that's to say, I'm recording my impressions of everything that most strikes me about current events, and so why should I deliberately impose on myself some artificial obligation always to conceal what may even be the strongest impressions I have simply because they pertain to Russian literature? Of course, the idea behind this decision was correct enough, but carrying it out literally, I can see, isn't right, if only because it means being literal-minded. Furthermore, the literary work on which I have refrained from commenting until now is much more than a literary work for me; it is a whole *fact* having significance of a different sort. Perhaps I am expressing myself in too naive a fashion, yet I am determined to say the following: this *fact* of my impression from the novel, from the fiction, from the "poem" coincided in my heart this spring with the enormous fact of the declaration of the war now in progress; both facts, both impressions, connected in my mind, and I found their point of contact striking. So instead of laughing at me, why not listen more closely?

In many respects my convictions are purely Slavophile ones, although I am perhaps not a complete Slavophile. The Slavophiles are still being interpreted in different ways. For some, the Slavophile doctrine even now means only kvass and radishes as it did in the old days for Belinsky, to take an example. Belinsky *really* went no further than that in his understanding of the Slavophile doctrine. For others (and, I'll note, for very many others, and for almost the majority of even the Slavophiles themselves), the Slavophile doctrine means striving for the liberation and union of all Slavs under the supreme leadership of Russia, a leadership that might not even be strictly political. And finally, for a third group, the Slavophile doctrine means, apart from this union of Slavs under Russian leadership, a spiritual union of all who believe that our great Russia, at the head of the united Slavs, will pronounce to the whole world, to the whole of European humanity and civilization, its own new, healthy word, a word that the world has not yet heard. This word will be uttered for the sake of a blessed and genuine union of all humanity in a new, fraternal, universal alliance whose fundamental principles are already found in the animating spirit of the Slavs and above all in the spirit of the great Russian People, who have suffered for so long, who have been condemned to silence for so many centuries, but who have always possessed mighty powers for the future clarification and solution of many painful and fateful misapprehensions of Western European civilization. And it is to this latter group of the convinced and believing which I belong.

Here again there is no cause for mockery and laughter: these words are old and this faith is ancient; the very fact that this faith does not wither and these words do not cease to be uttered but, rather, grow ever more emphatic, expand their meaning, acquire new supporters and new stalwarts ready to advance them—this alone ought to make the opponents and mockers of this *doctrine* take it a bit more seriously, at last, and abandon their empty and ossified animosity toward it. But enough said of that for the moment. The fact is, in the spring our great war was launched for a great feat which, sooner or later, despite all the temporary setbacks that delay settlement of the issue, will nonetheless be brought to its conclusion, even though its complete and desired conclusion may not be reached in the present war. This feat is so great and the aim of the war so improbable from Europe's point of view that Europe, naturally, is bound to be indignant over our *cunning*; she is bound to disbelieve what we told her when we began the war; she is bound to try to harm us in every way, using every possible means; and by allying herself with our enemy—though not openly, in a formal, political alliance—Europe will be at odds with us and will struggle against us, behind the scenes, perhaps, in expectation of open war. And all this, of course, stems from our stated intentions and goals! "The great eagle of the East has soared up above the world, his two wings glittering on the summits of Christianity": he seeks neither to conquer nor to acquire or expand his boundaries, but to liberate and restore the oppressed and forgotten, to give them a new life, for their benefit and for humanity's. However you look at it, however skeptically you view this matter, that, in essence, is our very aim, that precisely; and that is precisely what Europe refuses to believe! Believe me, Europe is not frightened so much by the supposed growth of Russia's power as by the very fact of Russia's capacity to undertake such tasks and have such aims. Note that particularly. Undertaking something not for one's own direct benefit seems so bizarre to Europe, so at odds with international practice, that Europe naturally takes Russia's action not only as the barbarism of a "backward, bestial, and ignorant" nation capable, *through meanness and stupidity*, of embarking in our day on something like the crusades of the dark ages, but even as something immoral, dangerous to her, and supposedly a threat to her great civilization. Just take a look: who has any particular love for us in Europe these days? Even our *friends*, our bona fide, formally declared friends, so to say—even they openly announce that they are *happy at our setbacks*. A Russian defeat is dearer to them than some of their own victories; it delights and flatters them. When we do have a success, these friends of ours have long since agreed among themselves to use every power to derive more benefit from Russia's good fortune than Russia herself will. . . .

But I shall say more of this, as well, later on. I began speaking mainly of the impression that everyone who believes in Russia's great future and universal significance must have had this past spring after the declaration of war. This unprecedented war for the sake of the weak and oppressed, to give them life and liberty, not take it away—this is an aim of war that the world has not seen for a long time, and it appeared suddenly, for all our believers, as a fact that solemnly and significantly confirmed their faith. It was no longer a dream or simply the words of some soothsayer but a reality *that had begun to happen*. "If it has already begun to happen, then it will go on to the end, to that great new word that Russia, at the head of a Union of Slavs, will utter to Europe. And even the word itself has already begun to be uttered, although Europe is still far from understanding it and will refuse to believe it for a long time." That is how the "believers" thought. Indeed, the impression was solemn and significant, and of course the faith of believers ought to have been tempered and strengthened even more. However, what had begun was so grave that disturbing questions cropped up even in the minds of believers: "Russia and Europe! Russia draws her sword against the Turks, but who knows: she might yet come to blows with Europe. Isn't that premature? A clash with Europe isn't the same as one with the Turks, and it will surely take place with more than just the sword." That was how the believers always perceived it. But are we prepared for this other conflict? The word has already begun to be uttered, true enough, but never mind Europe—do we ourselves understand it? Here we are, the believers, who prophesy, for instance, that only Russia has within her the principles capable of solving the fateful all-European question of our smaller brethren, without battle and without blood, without hatred and malice; but we say that Russia will utter this word when Europe is already soaked in its own blood, because until then no one in Europe would hear our word, and even if they should hear it, they would utterly fail to understand it. Yes, we believers believe this, but what do our own Russians answer meanwhile? They answer that all this is nothing more than the frenzied talk of soothsayers, religious mania, mad dreams, fits; and they ask proof of us, solid evidence and established facts. And what shall we show them, meanwhile, to support our *prophecies*? Can it be the liberation of the peasants—a fact that is still so little understood among us as a measure of manifestation of Russian spiritual strength? Can it be the innateness and naturalness of our brotherhood, which in our time is emerging more and more distinctly from beneath everything that has been crushing it for ages despite the rubbish and filth that it now encounters, which besmirch and distort its features to the point of unrecognizability?

But suppose we do show them these things: they will again answer that these facts are another form of our religious mania, a crazy dream and not facts; that they can be interpreted variously and unsystematically and as yet are incapable of proving anything. That is what almost everyone will answer; and meanwhile we, who so poorly understand ourselves and have so little faith in ourselves, we are coming into conflict with Europe! Europe—why it's a terrible and a sacred thing, Europe is! Oh, gentlemen, do you know how dear Europe is to us Slavophile dreamers who, as far as you're concerned, should only hate it, Europe, this "land of holy miracles"! Do you know how dear these "miracles" are to us and how we love and revere, with more than brotherly love and reverence, those great tribes that populate it, together with all the grand and beautiful things they have accomplished? Do you know the many tears we shed and the pangs of heart we suffer at the fate of this dear and native country, and how frightened we are by the storm clouds that are ever gathering on her horizon? Gentlemen, never did you, as Europeans and Westernizers, love Europe so much as we, Slavophile dreamers who, as far as you are concerned, are her mortal enemies! No, this land is dear to us—dear is the future peaceful victory of the great Christian spirit that has been preserved in the East. . . . And in our dread of conflict with Europe in the current war we fear most of all that Europe will not understand us, and as before, as always, will meet us with arrogance, contempt, and her sword, as if we were still wild barbarians, unworthy of speaking in her presence. Yes, we have asked ourselves what we can tell her or show her so that she might understand us. Evidently we still have so little of anything that might be *intelligible* to her and earn us her respect. Our fundamental, main idea, our emerging "new word" she will not understand for a long, long time yet. She needs facts that are intelligible now, intelligible to her *present* point of view. She will ask us: "Where is your civilization? Is there any economic structure to be perceived amid that chaos we all see in Russia? Where is *your* science, *your* art, *your* literature?"

Selections from Prince Vladimir Petrovich Meshchersky, *Recollections*

In these selections from conservative Prince Meshchersky's memoirs, he recounts his impressions and working relationship with Fyodor Dostoevsky on the journal The Citizen *in Chapter 12. Later, in Chapter 27, he shares his knowledge, as a member of the tsar's inner circle, on the underlying politics and decision-making of the Russo-Turkic war.*

Sources: Kniaz' V. P. Meshcherskii, *Moi vospominaniia*, pt. 1 (St. Petersburg: Tipografiya kniazia V. P. Meshcherskago, 1897), 125–34, 329–40. Translated by Linda M. Mayhew, summer 2019.

Part Two
CHAPTER 12. 1872–1873: MY FRIENDSHIP WITH DOSTOEVSKY. ITS CHARACTERISTICS.

Toward the end of the first year of my publication *The Citizen*, I had to give up hope on my alter ego, Gradovsky. Or, more truthfully, I became convinced that he didn't share my approach, and after a few small confrontations, in order to avoid more serious disagreements, we came to realize that our affiliation should be dissolved by mutual agreement and that starting the next year, I should find myself another editor.

The situation was critical. . . . Where to find such a colleague?

In this difficult moment, one of several, when over a cup of tea, we spoke about this question, I will never forget, with what a kindhearted and at the same time inspirational face F. M. Dostoevsky turned to me and said: Do you want me to come as the editor?

At first we thought that he was joking, but then there was a minute of serious happiness, as it turned out that Dostoevsky made this decision because of his feeling for the publication's goals.

But that isn't enough. Dostoevsky's decisiveness had its own spiritual beauty. Dostoevsky was, regardless of the fact that he was Dostoevsky—convinced; he knew that my personal and publishing means were limited, and because of that he said to me that he desired for himself a stipend that was only absolutely necessary for living expenses, having allocated himself 3,000 rubles a year and a per-line wage.

The horizon of *The Citizen*, having grown dim at the end of the year, brightened with this comforting fact, and understandably, brought hope for the success of *The Citizen*, thanks to Dostoevsky.

But Dostoevsky turned out to be a prophet.

"No," he said. "Don't sell an illusion. My name won't bring you anything: hatred for *The Citizen* is stronger than my popularity; and what popularity do I have? I don't have any, they're on to me, they've found out that I go against the grain."

And it turned out that he was right.

Something cold, something evil, greeted Dostoevsky in all his publications from that time in his new role as the manager of *The Citizen*. He was seen as guilty of committing heinous acts and undeserving of any sort of leniency. Attacks on *The Citizen* became more spiteful and more intense, and as a result, subscriptions for 1873 were found to be a very insignificant amount, with an increase of approximately 200 subscribers.

This was an undoubtedly significant time. The first year, it was possible to explain *The Citizen*'s lack of success with my stupidity or ineptitude, I willingly allowed. But when in the second year Dostoevsky became the mind and heart of the publication and still there was no success, this directly indicated that the hatred for the conservative publication had been artificially implanted in that massive herd then known by the grandiose name of contemporary educated society.

At the beginning of the second year, a new young talent appeared in the manuscripts of *The Citizen*. One day, Dostoevsky came to me and excitedly informed me of the essays from the north by a certain Nemirovich-Danchenko. Correspondence with the talented author followed. He turned out to be a young exile in the Archangelsk Province. The confidence of his talent and the sentiments that filled his splendid letters at this moment of trial and tribulation compelled us to join forces and influence his fate. Count Pahlen, the minister of justice at the time, was sympathetic to our efforts, and the young talent was pardoned.

Dostoevsky's joyfulness when he happened upon any trace or sign of talent was touching and characteristic of him.

Once he came to me and, his face glowing, announced that he had found a second Gogol, buried in a pile of manuscripts. A huge comedic talent actually turned up in a brief short story "Boots." We contacted the author, a humble little official living in Okhta, and he began to fuss over him, but, by a strange series of events, his creative work didn't go any further. Everything he wrote after this story, much to his and to our sorrow, wasn't worth a half kopeck.

Dostoevsky was one of the most interesting and unique people that I've met in my life.

The story of his life involved a huge misunderstanding, a most unusual and peculiar one: a demotion in rank and his exile to Siberia for political disloyalty, moreover for participating in some sort of plot against Nicholas I! In my time, I never saw a more definitive conservative, never saw anyone more convinced of and committed to the royal banner of the monarchy, never saw a more fanatical supporter of autocracy than Dostoevsky. And this Dostoevsky ended up in Siberia in a camp for political crimes!

How this could happen, I never could understand. And from everything that I could find out from him about this tragic event in his life, when as a young engineer and officer, he got mixed up in and arrested as part of the so-called Petrashevsky group; I arrived at the conclusion that the main reason for such a dramatic episode in Dostoevsky's life was his proud and wholesome nature, making neither compromises nor concessions. Consequently, he wouldn't lift a finger to protect himself and, naturally, didn't say a word about any of those who had dragged him into this dramatic unpleasantness.

He was similarly proud during his troubles and in the camp. Even afterward, in the eighties, I happened to hear from Dostoevsky's comrades in the camp that there, in the place of his torture, among the convicts and the exiles, the author of "Notes from the House of the Dead" presented himself as the most fanatic apostle of the testament of loyalty to the Russian State and autocracy. His sermons made a strong and positive impression on the youth, who had faltered and wandered about in the darkness of their souls.

Because of the feelings of gratitude and friendship that I harbored toward Dostoevsky, there always arose in me the most sincere awe for this proud martyr of a fateful mistake, which gave the right if not to be spiteful, then to at least bitterly look upon life and people. Instead of feeling this bitterness from the undeserved punishment, which derailed his health for his entire life, his spirit endured, blazing with fiery loyalty for the Russian Sovereign Emperor and more determined than ever, tempered by all the strict principles of conservatism.

I never saw and never met someone so wholly and completely conservative.... We all were minutiae compared to his grandiose conservative figure.... An apostle of truth in everything, both large and small, Dostoevsky was, like an ascetic, strict, and, like a novice, fanatic in his conservatism.... And there was such a distinction when comparing who Dostoevsky was with his reputation among the Russian intelligentsia, who, thanks to his history, sought in him some sort of idol for the liberal revolutionary party.

Dostoevsky hated these followers of his. Dostoevsky was able to hate; that was part of his spiritual identity, which, in general, I rarely came across in people, much less so in conservatives.... Such an ability to hate with a political hatred, I encountered in only two people to a similar degree but with completely opposite types of ideas: Yu. F. Samarin and F. M. Dostoevsky. Samarin hated, for example, Russian nobility with every fiber of his being; Dostoevsky hated the Russian revolutionary with the exact same strength of spirit. But there was a great difference in the quality of spirit....
I rarely encountered such a rich soul that had at the same time love for the ideal and for humanity as Dostoevsky.... Samarin's abundance of hatred arose from a lack of love. Dostoevsky's hatred, like all apostles', was an unavoidable consequence of an abundance of love for ideals and for truth. From that, his soul breathed hate toward any type of untruth or lies.... Two factors drove Dostoevsky's hatred for revolutionaries: hatred for the harm they inflicted on the Russian people and hatred for the lies in their preaching.

There wasn't anyone kinder than Dostoevsky.... He was ready to give up everything, either his life or his last cent, to help another....[73] But how often I heard that no one seemed as nasty as he was. And actually, it happened, at my salons, as long as everyone who sat with him was a close friend, he would charm us with his stories, his wit, and his original, daring logic. But as soon as a guest arrived that he knew only slightly or not at all, Dostoevsky went like a snail into his shell and turned into a close-mouthed and malevolent dolt. This continued until the stranger succeeded in making a good impression on Dostoevsky.... If the stranger, not waiting to make this impression, decided to start conversation with Dostoevsky, there would be trouble: without fail, one had to expect from Dostoevsky a severe expression on his face and a rude retort.

Dostoevsky was an enemy of the contemporary woman question, then even more so than now, laughably personified by short-haired young ladies in blue glasses and similar outward appearances.... And meanwhile these short-haired and blue-glassed young women, not suspecting Dostoevsky's hatred of them, constantly sidled up to him as if he were *their* teacher.

More than once I happened to witness this comic quid pro quo. A contemporary woman enters. Not noticing Dostoevsky's severe expression and not paying attention to the sharp and harsh tone that he greets her with, saying: what do you want?—she, completely full of her contemporary motifs, immediately begins to choke on them to her heart's content, and with burning eyes and flaming cheeks, she blurts out her lament....

Dostoevsky listens to her attentively and skittishly, and I see by his face that each feature takes on some type of sharp quality, that inside a volcano is erupting. I sense that he is holding back, and that minute, having blurted out her series of contemporary motifs for the woman question, the unhappy short-haired woman expects approving words from *her* Dostoevsky. The unrelenting foe of the woman question turns to her with the question—"Are you finished? ..."

"I'm finished," the short-haired woman answers.

"Well then, listen to me, I will be briefer than you, you babbled a lot ... so I will tell you this: everything that you said is banal and stupid, you understand—stupid: Science can manage without you, but family, children, and the kitchen cannot manage without a woman.... A woman has one calling: to be a wife and a mother.... There is no other calling. There is not any sort of social calling and there cannot be; this is all stupidity, fantasies, nonsense.... Everything that you told me—nonsense, you hear, nonsense. I will not say anything more to you."

That is the conversation that I happened to hear and that I remembered.

Dostoevsky was this relentless and uncompromising regarding all modern liberal questions; he despised them because of their theatrics. . . .

And the power of conviction was so great and so deep that at the end of the year with my daily relationship with Dostoevsky, I understood that until meeting Dostoevsky, I was an adolescent in my conservatism, and I sensed how, thanks to him, I strengthened and grew in my conservatism. His influence on me was the deepest and most influential of my life.

CHAPTER 27: 1877, BEFORE THE WAR— DIPLOMATIC TIMIDITY—TURKISH MOOD— THE MISSION OF N. P. IGNATIEV— DECLARATION OF WAR

From the start of 1877 until the spring, the year was fairly strange due to its fluctuations and ambiguous nature.

The commander in chief in Chisinau was already called the commander in chief of the field army; the mobilization called nearly half a million troops to military service; substantial allotments for military spending were made, and meanwhile the political barometer in Petersburg gradually made powerful leaps in its forecast, moving from a combative disposition to a peace-loving one, sometimes in the course of one day. Old-timer Prince Gorchakov was at this time the most significant representation of this barometer. His attendants heard from him language such as: *mon cher, la paix avant tout, il faut eviter la guerre a tout prix*.[74] In the morning he spoke about *paix a tout prix*, but then, under the influence of Bismarck's letter that he received from Berlin, by the evening of that very day, he said: *mon cher, la guerre est imminente*.[75] But even in the most combative disposition, vacillation was the true barometer of the time. Prince Gorchakov spoke about needing to be done with the Eastern question and to back peace in Constantinople; that's what he said: yes, war is unavoidable, but our task is to restrict combat operations to the smallest area and to a limited number of military forces.

But most interesting and curious was that, while we lived in this time of vacillations and even abrupt transitions—from peace no matter what to war no matter what—in Constantinople the mood was far more definitive. In the beginning of January we found out that after ten meetings of the European Conference, Turkey categorically refused to accept Europe's proposed ultimatum and dumbfounded everyone with her energetic "*non possumus*." Then a large demonstration against the Porte took place.[76] All the ambassadors, with our ambassador Ignatiev at the head, shook off the dust from their shoes at Constantinople's doorstep and left, called back by their governments.

This demonstration had just taken place when the Porte seemed frightened by its own daring and sent a circular note with the notification that, although it had not agreed to accept the conditions as proposed by the European Conference, it nonetheless recognized its obligation to do not just everything for its Christian subjects that Europe required, but even much more.

The peace-loving currents once again grew stronger.

In Petersburg, the Porte's refusal strengthened the chances of war so significantly that they began to talk about starting the campaign quickly despite winter. . . . Such a decisive step seemed risky, but then there was reason to imagine that this idea of advancing the troops was the best, as Turkey, who was not preparing for war and would be caught unawares, would accept the most convenient conditions for peace with the warring states, and Russia's war with Turkey would be defused. They realized then that the Porte's refusal in the beginning of January was just one of its sly political tricks, which it employed exclusively to draw out matters and waste time so as to be able to prepare for war. This became evident in April, when the Porte responded to the new proposals made separately by Russia and separately by England with a categorical refusal only because it considered itself ready for war with Russia.

But Prince Bismarck was more cunning than the Porte, and in any case more devious. The Porte had to outmaneuver everyone because of its own luck, for the sake of its own hide, while Prince Bismarck was deceptive with the specific purpose of harming Russia under the pretense of sympathizing with their interests. . . . Prince Bismarck, as I already wrote, took our dignity, one could say, more passionately to heart than we did, but he did this because his primary goal with the Eastern question was to lure us into war no matter the cost. As soon as he received notice from Petersburg that the barometer was rising toward peace, he quickly wrote Prince Gorchakov announcing, naturally, his letter to the throne: Why are you vacillating; there has never been such a favorable moment to resolve the Eastern question in battle—don't pass it up; negotiations won't result in anything. Another time, he wrote to Petersburg that all efforts were required to force Austria to accept the most benevolent neutrality relevant to Russia, and then in the beginning of January when the Porte sent a refusal to the European Conference, Bismarck then wrote Prince Gorchakov: Would Russia really not decide to go to war now, when their honor has been directly affected? On top of that, in one of his messages to Petersburg, he wrote that Russia is submitting out of necessity to its Sovereign Emperor's peaceful resolution to avoid war and settle the affair peacefully. But Russia all the same will not forget this humiliation and must anticipate domestic displays of dissatisfaction with the government. In parliament Prince Bismarck again provoked Russia in a speech regarding the Eastern question. He spoke about Germany's neutrality, but at the same time, about his sympathy for Russia's noble goal to grant freedom for their brothers on the Balkan peninsula, even at the cost of war.

Nonetheless, a kind, peaceful disposition prevailed over the devious combative instincts that came from Berlin, and the Porte's notes served as a basis for stitching together new peaceful designs.

Ignatiev, finding himself free after our embassy's ceremonial departure from Constantinople, was sent to all the main capitals of European nations to secure, so to speak, sanctions from all of Europe for the Petersburg cabinet's new peacemaking step and to get the nations' moral commitment so that Russia could say that Europe had tied its hands from individually retaliating against Turkey in the event that Turkey refused the new proposal. Ignatiev's mission was crowned with such platonic success, which was all one could expect, that even the London cabinet announced it was prepared to promote Russia's peaceful aspirations by influencing the Turkish government. Two resolutions were even drawn up, one signed by our ambassador in London, Count Shuvalev, and the other signed by Lord Derby, the English minister of foreign affairs, to present to the Porte. Austria also took a peacemaking mission upon itself, but all these negotiations ended after dragging out for three whole months, as I said above, with the Porte flatly refusing in a cavalier way to accept England and Russia's proposal and consequently making it impossible for Russia to avoid declaring a war with them.

This occurred on April 12 (April 24), 1877—but it's necessary to point out that this occurred when the public's mood was completely different than the mood which, just like a flame, swept over all the strata of society just a year before this. Subsequently, in the Sovereign Emperor's presence, the Archbishop Pavel read the manifesto declaring war in Kishinev, at the field army's front. After declaring war, the Sovereign Emperor went to Moscow, where the Empress met him, and there, at the exit into the Kremlin, in front of everyone gathering in Moscow, he said the following words: "Six months ago within these very walls, in our country's venerable Kremlin, I expressed my hopes for a peaceful exit from Eastern political affairs. I wished against all hope to spare precious Russian blood, but my efforts were not rewarded with success. God wished to resolve this affair another way. My manifesto, signed April 12 (April 24) in Kishinev, proclaimed to Russia the moment, which I foresaw, that has come for you, and all of Russia, as I expected, will answer my call. Moscow first set this example and completely lived up to my hopes. Today I am happy that I, along with the Sovereign Empress, can thank all estates in Moscow from the bottom of my heart for their true patriotism, which they proved not only in word, but in deed.[77] I can honestly say that their contributions surpassed my expectations. May God help us fulfill our duty, and may He bless our glorious troops as they go to battle for faith, Sovereign Emperor, and Country."

It goes without saying that these truly wonderful words were met with an explosion of delight by all of Moscow.

The transaction that the Sovereign Emperor mentioned made him so happy, and even surprised him with its size, was a donation of 1 million rubles made by the city of Moscow. If you recall, in 1854, a certain Yakovlev donated a million, then you'll naturally think that Moscow could give even more; the problem is that ever since the donation was announced, I never could find out whether or not it was really made, and, quite the opposite, I heard more than once in Moscow that this million had long been in arrears. Whether or not this was true—I don't know. Having returned to Petersburg, the Sovereign Emperor took his speech from the city and the nobility regarding the donations and told the delegates approximately the same thing as in Moscow. Upon arriving in Petersburg, the Sovereign Emperor was greeted not with artificial but sincere enthusiasm.

All the European councils calmly accepted the declaration of war, except for two. One was the Berlin Council, represented by Bismarck, which was especially sympathetic to the situation and didn't spare any expressions of sympathy regarding the Russian state chancellor's address. The other came from the London Council, and, conversely, its message not only didn't sympathize with Russia but was overtly hostile and even impudent. . . . The first announcement, made by Lord Derby through our ambassador in London, Count Shuvalov, caused a sensation in Petersburg. In both its form and content, it had the tone of a defiant reprimand, the English government announcing to our government that they, first of all, were not restraining their words and, secondly, that backing away from the European conference allowed Russia to declare war on Turkey, without having secured an agreement for this beforehand with the European powers. This audacious comment demanded either an equally rude response addressing the London Council with consideration of future consequences, such as calling back our ambassador from London and ceasing diplomatic relations, or simply not responding, considering it *non avenue*.[78] Not a single political voice supported the first option. . . . Prince Gorchakov advised the Sovereign Emperor of the second; the advice was taken, and the defiant reprimand that England made to Russia received neither attention nor consequences. But England was not content with this. Our ambassador to London, Count Shuvalov, arrived in Petersburg and brought with him a new note from the St. James Council, which categorically listed all the points of inviolability that England demanded from Russia, threatening, in case of any disagreement on the part of Russia, to recognize each violation of the listed points as *casus belli*.[79]

The points were as follows: Suez Canal, Egypt, Bosporus and Dardanelles Straits, Constantinople, and, finally, the Persian Gulf.

Unfortunately, in response to the English Council's new antics, Prince Gorchakov acted incoherently and, fearing a break with England, even sacrificed Russia's assets. It would be so straightforward—following the model of Russia's initial response, in which the Russian government carried itself with dignity—to not reply anything or else to reply that Russia would act as required by her interests in relation to each of the European governments, and with this, end all of England's interference with our affairs. But Prince Gorchakov considered it necessary to respond to the London Council with a long missive, in which without any consideration of Russia's dignity, he gave England the responsibility for deciding Russia's commitments, going through each point separately.

England acknowledged Russia's declaration as satisfactory, but, alas, Russia's interests couldn't be satisfied by it; quite the opposite, Russia's interests were flouted long ago precisely because of their relationship to the primary goal: the freedom of our military operations in the war with Turkey. This declaration was the Achilles' heel for Russia in the war they'd undertaken. Two years later, everything sorrowful and degrading for Russia happened within the walls of Constantinople at first and at the Berlin Congress afterward, and this was the unavoidable consequence of the unhappy declaration that Prince Gorchakov made when declaring war.

This was the outright establishment of the idea of trusteeship, not only of Europe, but of England directly over Russia in the war with Turkey.

In some part, I suppose, especially with this sorrowful episode in the history of our diplomatic relations with Europe in general and with England in particular at the start of the war, I ought to explain the noteworthy expression: Military exercise, which I heard uttered so many times during the first part of the war, on the one hand with such lightheartedness despite costing us such terrifyingly bloody and irreparable sacrifices, but on the other hand, it did not correlate with all the passionate military patriotism that appeared then in newspaper articles, in poetic work, in military songs, where the battle cry was Constantinople and Sophia.

In Prince Gorchakov's office it was planned like this: Russia enters Bulgaria with several of its own corps, with no need of help from either the Serbian or the Romanian troops or the Bulgarian people; the Russian troops would reach the Balkans by the end of summer, and Turkey would propose peace, which we would accept. . . . We must try not to scare Europe with too many Russian troops on the Balkan peninsula and, at the same time, not draw Slavic troops into military action, avoiding a Slavic fire—that is what our diplomats approximately repeated at the moment our army set off for the Danube.

The plans for war were so unassuming, like the conditions of peace which our diplomats prepared in case the Sultan, frightened by the invasion of our troops, inquired about peace upon their approach to the Balkans.

The conditions were as follows: Bulgaria will be incorporated by Serbia, that is made a Turkish vassal principality, with a right to autonomy within the government. Serbia and Montenegro will receive an increase in territory. Southern Bulgarians and other Christians will receive better governance, and the improvement in Bosnia and Herzegovina will be provided by Austria. These modest conditions that the Russian diplomat planned to present to Turkey after a successful military exercise in Bulgaria required soldiers and money. This being said, it's necessary to remember that in the text of these provisionally planned conditions for future peace in the office of Prince Gorchakov, the phrase "under the guardianship of Europe, in agreement with Europe" was added everywhere, so the implication of all these conditions was that we not only entered into war with Turkey under the stewardship of Europe but also that we undertook this war under all of Europe's authority. Terrible sacrifices were made on our behalf, and on Europe's behalf, only one: the agreement that we offer Turkey the conditions of peace. This in particular explains the unbelievable political peculiarity that, having unsheathed the sword to deliver our Bulgarian brethren from their Turkish yoke, with a pen we gave up two nations of heroes, Bosnia and Herzegovina, to the Austrian yoke.

To lift our spirits and for moral sentiment during the start of the war in particular, the name of the commander in chief signified a great deal.

One can unmistakably say that the Sovereign Emperor's choice of Prince Nikolas Nikolaevich as commander in chief of the army was suggested to him by all of Russia, as he was a favorite not only among the troops but also among all classes of the Russian people, which, apart from his deeply sympathetic qualities of simplicity, directness, honesty, and cordiality, furthered his charming appearance, reminding everyone of the majestic presence of Nicholas I. Thanks to his name, the spirit of the troops was excellent, and no one doubted the folk hero-soldier's military feats.

But, alas, this splendid mood elicited by sympathy for the identity of the prince commander in chief suffered from the very beginning from unfortunate choices he made early on when assigning his closest assistants. Two names spread through Russia, surprising many and making many, as it happened, uncomfortable. These names were: Nepokojchitsky and Levitsky. Both were Polish. The first received the most important and crucial post as the chief of the headquarters, the second received the post of his assistant. Both names were irreproachable and respected. Both generals were figures against whom no one could make the slightest accusation or even cast any shadow of doubt; these were honest, trustworthy, and good people, but everything was about nationality. To pick a Polish national as chief of the headquarters wasn't worth mentioning, as they said then that they didn't find anyone worthy among Russian generals to fill this important post. It couldn't have been coincidence that from the large number of Russian generals not one was found, but from the modest number of Polish nationals two were taken: both the chief of the headquarters and his assistant.

Then, as soon as the military action started, there was the question of whether the Sovereign Emperor should go visit the active forces. It was more than clear that the Sovereign Emperor was drawn to the place where there would be fighting with his troop's enemy, where there would be injuries and death. As an example, there was Emperor William the Elder, who was always present with his army in all previous wars and who could influence his sovereign nephew.

Selections from Leo Tolstoy, *Anna Karenina*

This selection from Anna Karenina *highlights a high-society gathering after an opera at the home of Princess Betsy. The interactions between characters, including the role of the hostess, are similar to what one would find at a literary evening in the late nineteenth century. The novel was initially published in serial form in* Russian Messenger *between 1875 and 1877. The selections from part one and part two both came out in volume 115, February 1875.*

Source: Leo Tolstoy, *Anna Karenina*, trans. Constance Garnett (1878; Project Gutenberg, 2025), https://gutenberg.org/ebooks/1399.

Part One, Chapter 22

The ball was only just beginning as Kitty and her mother walked up the great staircase, flooded with light, and lined with flowers and footmen in powder and red coats. From the rooms came a constant, steady hum, as from a hive, and the rustle of movement; and while on the landing between trees they gave last touches to their hair and dresses before the mirror, they heard from the ballroom the careful, distinct notes of the fiddles of the orchestra beginning the first waltz. A little old man in civilian dress, arranging his gray curls before another mirror, and diffusing an odor of scent, stumbled against them on the stairs, and stood aside, evidently admiring Kitty, whom he did not know. A beardless youth, one of those society youths whom the old Prince Shtcherbatsky called "young bucks," in an exceedingly open waistcoat, straightening his white tie as he went, bowed to them, and after running by, came back to ask Kitty for a quadrille. As the first quadrille had already been given to Vronsky, she had to promise this youth the second. An officer, buttoning his glove, stood aside in the doorway, and stroking his mustache, admired rosy Kitty.

Although her dress, her coiffure, and all the preparations for the ball had cost Kitty great trouble and consideration, at this moment she walked into the ballroom in her elaborate tulle dress over a pink slip as easily and simply as though all the rosettes and lace, all the minute details of her attire, had not cost her or her family a moment's attention, as though she had been born in that tulle and lace, with her hair done up high on her head, and a rose and two leaves on the top of it.

When, just before entering the ballroom, the princess, her mother, tried to turn right side out of the ribbon of her sash, Kitty had drawn back a little. She felt that everything must be right of itself, and graceful, and nothing could need setting straight.

It was one of Kitty's best days. Her dress was not uncomfortable anywhere; her lace berthe did not droop anywhere; her rosettes were not crushed nor torn off; her pink slippers with high, hollowed-out heels did not pinch, but gladdened her feet; and the thick rolls of fair chignon kept up on her head as if they were her own hair. All the three buttons buttoned up without tearing on the long glove that covered her hand without concealing its lines. The black velvet of her locket nestled with special softness round her neck. That velvet was delicious; at home, looking at her neck in the looking-glass, Kitty had felt that that velvet was speaking. About all the rest there might be a doubt, but the velvet was delicious. Kitty smiled here too, at the ball, when she glanced at it in the glass. Her bare shoulders and arms gave Kitty a sense of chill marble, a feeling she particularly liked. Her eyes sparkled, and her rosy lips could not keep from smiling from the consciousness of her own attractiveness. She had scarcely entered the ballroom and reached the throng of ladies, all tulle, ribbons, lace, and flowers, waiting to be asked to dance—Kitty was never one of that throng—when she was asked for a waltz, and asked by the best partner, the first star in the hierarchy of the ballroom, a renowned director of dances, a married man, handsome and well-built, Yegorushka Korsunsky. He had only just left the Countess Bonina, with whom he had danced the first half of the waltz, and, scanning his kingdom—that is to say, a few couples who had started dancing—he caught sight of Kitty, entering, and flew up to her with that peculiar, easy amble which is confined to directors of balls. Without even asking her if she cared to dance, he put out his arm to encircle her slender waist. She looked round for someone to give her fan to, and their hostess, smiling to her, took it.

"How nice you've come in good time," he said to her, embracing her waist; "such a bad habit to be late." Bending her left hand, she laid it on his shoulder, and her little feet in their pink slippers began swiftly, lightly, and rhythmically moving over the slippery floor in time to the music.

"It's a rest to waltz with you," he said to her, as they fell into the first slow steps of the waltz. "It's exquisite—such lightness, precision." He said to her the same thing he said to almost all his partners whom he knew well.

She smiled at his praise, and continued to look about the room over his shoulder. She was not like a girl at her first ball, for whom all faces in the ballroom melt into one vision of fairyland. And she was not a girl who had gone the stale round of balls till every face in the ballroom was familiar and tiresome. But she was in the middle stage between these two; she was excited, and at the same time she had sufficient self-possession to be able to observe. In the left corner of the ballroom she saw the cream of society gathered together. There—incredibly naked—was the beauty Lidi, Korsunsky's wife; there was the lady of the house; there shone the bald head of Krivin, always to be found where the best people were. In that direction gazed the young men, not venturing to approach. There, too, she descried Stiva, and there she saw the exquisite figure and head of Anna in a black velvet gown. And he was there. Kitty had not seen him since the evening she refused Levin. With her long-sighted eyes, she knew him at once, and was even aware that he was looking at her.

"Another turn, eh? You're not tired?" said Korsunsky, a little out of breath.

"No, thank you!"

"Where shall I take you?"

"Madame Karenina's here, I think . . . take me to her."

"Wherever you command."

And Korsunsky began waltzing with measured

steps straight towards the group in the left corner, continually saying, "Pardon, mesdames, pardon, pardon, mesdames"; and steering his course through the sea of lace, tulle, and ribbon, and not disarranging a feather, he turned his partner sharply round, so that her slim ankles, in light transparent stockings, were exposed to view, and her train floated out in fan shape and covered Krivin's knees. Korsunsky bowed, set straight his open shirt front, and gave her his arm to conduct her to Anna Arkadyevna. Kitty, flushed, took her train from Krivin's knees, and, a little giddy, looked round, seeking Anna. Anna was not in lilac, as Kitty had so urgently wished, but in a black, low-cut, velvet gown, showing her full throat and shoulders, that looked as though carved in old ivory, and her rounded arms, with tiny, slender wrists. The whole gown was trimmed with Venetian guipure. On her head, among her black hair—her own, with no false additions—was a little wreath of pansies, and a bouquet of the same in the black ribbon of her sash among white lace. Her coiffure was not striking. All that was noticeable was the little willful tendrils of her curly hair that would always break free about her neck and temples. Round her well-cut, strong neck was a thread of pearls.

Kitty had been seeing Anna every day; she adored her, and had pictured her invariably in lilac. But now seeing her in black, she felt that she had not fully seen her charm. She saw her now as someone quite new and surprising to her. Now she understood that Anna could not have been in lilac, and that her charm was just that she always stood out against her attire, that her dress could never be noticeable on her. And her black dress, with its sumptuous lace, was not noticeable on her; it was only the frame, and all that was seen was she—simple, natural, elegant, and at the same time gay and eager.

She was standing holding herself, as always, very erect, and when Kitty drew near the group she was speaking to the master of the house, her head slightly turned towards him.

"No, I don't throw stones," she was saying, in answer to something, "though I can't understand it," she went on, shrugging her shoulders, and she turned at once with a soft smile of protection towards Kitty. With a flying, feminine glance she scanned her attire, and made a movement of her head, hardly perceptible, but understood by Kitty, signifying approval of her dress and her looks. "You came into the room dancing," she added.

"This is one of my most faithful supporters," said Korsunsky, bowing to Anna Arkadyevna, whom he had not yet seen. "The princess helps to make balls happy and successful. Anna Arkadyevna, a waltz?" he said, bending down to her.

"Why, have you met?" inquired their host.

"Is there anyone we have not met? My wife and I are like white wolves—everyone knows us," answered Korsunsky. "A waltz, Anna Arkadyevna?"

"I don't dance when it's possible not to dance," she said.

"But tonight it's impossible," answered Korsunsky.

At that instant Vronsky came up.

"Well, since it's impossible tonight, let us start," she said, not noticing Vronsky's bow, and she hastily put her hand on Korsunsky's shoulder.

"What is she vexed with him about?" thought Kitty, discerning that Anna had intentionally not responded to Vronsky's bow. Vronsky went up to Kitty reminding her of the first quadrille, and expressing his regret that he had not seen her all this time. Kitty gazed in admiration at Anna waltzing, and listened to him. She expected him to ask her for a waltz, but he did not, and she glanced wonderingly at him. He flushed slightly, and hurriedly asked her to waltz, but he had only just put his arm round her waist and taken the first step when the music suddenly stopped. Kitty looked into his face, which was so close to her own, and long afterwards—for several years after—that look, full of love, to which he made no response, cut her to the heart with an agony of shame.

"*Pardon! pardon!* Waltz! waltz!" shouted Korsunsky from the other side of the room, and seizing the first young lady he came across he began dancing himself.

Chapter 23

Vronsky and Kitty waltzed several times round the room. After the first waltz Kitty went to her mother, and she had hardly time to say a few words to Countess Nordston when Vronsky came up again for the first quadrille. During the quadrille nothing of any significance was said: there was disjointed talk between them of the Korsunskys, husband and wife, whom he described very amusingly, as delightful children at forty, and of the future town theater; and only once the conversation touched her to the quick, when he asked her about Levin, whether he was here, and added that he liked him so much. But Kitty did not expect much from the quadrille. She looked forward with a thrill at her heart to the mazurka. She fancied that in the mazurka everything must be decided. The fact that he did not during the quadrille ask her for the mazurka did not trouble her. She felt sure she would dance the mazurka with him as she had done at former balls, and refused five young men, saying she was engaged for the mazurka. The whole ball up to the last quadrille was for Kitty an enchanted vision of delightful colors, sounds, and motions. She only sat down when she felt too tired and begged for a rest. But as she was dancing the last quadrille with one of the tiresome young men whom she could not refuse, she chanced to be *vis-à-vis* with Vronsky and Anna. She had not been near Anna again since the beginning of the evening, and now again she saw her suddenly quite new and surprising. She saw in her the signs of that excitement of success she knew so well in herself; she saw that she was intoxicated with the delighted admiration she was exciting. She knew that feeling and knew its signs, and saw them in Anna; saw the quivering, flashing light in her eyes, and the smile of happiness and excitement unconsciously playing on her lips, and the deliberate grace, precision, and lightness of her movements.

"Who?" she asked herself. "All or one?" And not assisting the harassed young man she was dancing with in the conversation, the thread of which he had lost and could not pick up again, she obeyed with external liveliness the peremptory shouts of Korsunsky starting them all into the *grand rond*, and then into the *chaîne*, and at the same time she kept watch with a growing pang at her heart. "No, it's not the admiration of the crowd has intoxicated her, but the adoration of one. And that one? can it be he?" Every time he spoke to Anna the joyous light flashed into her eyes, and the smile of happiness curved her red lips. She seemed to make an effort to control herself, to try not to show these signs of delight, but they came out on her face of themselves. "But what of him?" Kitty looked at him and was filled with terror. What was pictured so clearly to Kitty in the mirror of Anna's face she saw in him. What had become of his always self-possessed resolute manner, and the carelessly serene expression of his face? Now every time he turned to her, he bent his head, as though he would have fallen at her feet, and in his eyes there was nothing but humble submission and dread. "I would not offend you," his eyes seemed every time to be saying, "but I want to save myself, and I don't know how." On his face was a look such as Kitty had never seen before.

They were speaking of common acquaintances, keeping up the most trivial conversation, but to Kitty it seemed that every word they said was determining their fate and hers. And strange it was that they were actually talking of how absurd Ivan Ivanovitch was with his French, and how the Eletsky girl might have made a better match, yet these words had all the while consequence for them, and they were feeling just as Kitty did. The whole ball, the whole world, everything seemed lost in fog in Kitty's soul. Nothing but the stern discipline of her bringing-up supported her and forced her to do what was expected of her, that is, to dance, to answer questions, to talk, even to smile. But before the mazurka, when they were beginning to rearrange the chairs and a few couples moved out of the smaller rooms into the big room, a moment of despair and horror came for Kitty. She had refused five partners, and now she was not dancing the mazurka. She had not even a hope of being asked for it, because she was so successful in society that the idea would never occur to anyone that she had remained disengaged till now. She would have to tell her mother she felt ill and go home, but she had not the strength to do this. She felt crushed. She went to the furthest end of the little drawing-room and sank into a low chair. Her light, transparent skirts rose like a cloud about her slender waist; one bare, thin, soft, girlish arm, hanging listlessly, was lost in the folds of her pink tunic; in the other she held her fan, and with rapid, short strokes fanned her burning face. But while she looked like a butterfly, clinging to a blade of grass, and just about to open its rainbow wings for fresh flight, her heart ached with a horrible despair.

"But perhaps I am wrong, perhaps it was not so?" And again she recalled all she had seen.

"Kitty, what is it?" said Countess Nordston, stepping noiselessly over the carpet towards her. "I don't understand it."

Kitty's lower lip began to quiver; she got up quickly.

"Kitty, you're not dancing the mazurka?"

"No, no," said Kitty in a voice shaking with tears.

"He asked her for the mazurka before me," said Countess Nordston, knowing Kitty would understand who were "he" and "her." "She said: 'Why, aren't you going to dance it with Princess Shtcherbatskaya?'"

"Oh, I don't care!" answered Kitty.

No one but she herself understood her position; no one knew that she had just refused the man whom perhaps she loved, and refused him because she had put her faith in another.

Countess Nordston found Korsunsky, with whom she was to dance the mazurka, and told him to ask Kitty.

Kitty danced in the first couple, and luckily for her she had not to talk, because Korsunsky was all the time running about directing the figure. Vronsky and Anna sat almost opposite her. She saw them with her long-sighted eyes, and saw them, too, close by, when they met in the figures, and the more she saw of them the more convinced was she that her unhappiness was complete. She saw that they felt themselves alone in that crowded room. And on Vronsky's face, always so firm and independent, she saw that look that had struck her, of bewilderment and humble submissiveness, like the expression of an intelligent dog when it has done wrong.

Anna smiled, and her smile was reflected by him. She grew thoughtful, and he became serious. Some supernatural force drew Kitty's eyes to Anna's face. She was fascinating in her simple black dress, fascinating were her round arms with their bracelets, fascinating was her firm neck with its thread of pearls, fascinating the straying curls of her loose hair, fascinating the graceful, light movements of her little feet and hands, fascinating was that lovely face in its eagerness, but there was something terrible and cruel in her fascination.

Kitty admired her more than ever, and more and more acute was her suffering. Kitty felt overwhelmed, and her face showed it. When Vronsky saw her, coming across her in the mazurka, he did not at once recognize her, she was so changed.

"Delightful ball!" he said to her, for the sake of saying something.

"Yes," she answered.

In the middle of the mazurka, repeating a complicated figure, newly invented by Korsunsky, Anna came forward into the center of the circle, chose two gentlemen, and summoned a lady and Kitty. Kitty gazed at her in dismay as she went up. Anna looked at her with drooping eyelids, and smiled, pressing her hand. But, noticing that Kitty only responded to her smile by a look of despair and amazement, she turned away from her, and began gaily talking to the other lady.

"Yes, there is something uncanny, devilish and fascinating in her," Kitty said to herself.

Anna did not mean to stay to supper, but the master of the house began to press her to do so.

"Nonsense, Anna Arkadyevna," said Korsunsky, drawing her bare arm under the sleeve of his dress coat, "I've such an idea for a cotillion! *Un bijou!*"

And he moved gradually on, trying to draw her along with him. Their host smiled approvingly.

"No, I am not going to stay," answered Anna, smiling, but in spite of her smile, both Korsunsky and the master of the house saw from her resolute tone that she would not stay.

"No; why, as it is, I have danced more at your ball in Moscow than I have all the winter in Petersburg," said Anna, looking round at Vronsky, who stood near her. "I must rest a little before my journey."

"Are you certainly going tomorrow then?" asked Vronsky.

"Yes, I suppose so," answered Anna, as it were wondering at the boldness of his question; but the irrepressible, quivering brilliance of her eyes and her smile set him on fire as she said it.

Anna Arkadyevna did not stay to supper, but went home.

Part Two, Chapter 6

Princess Betsy drove home from the theater, without waiting for the end of the last act. She had only just time to go into her dressing-room, sprinkle her long, pale face with powder, rub it, set her dress to rights, and order tea in the big drawing-room, when one after another carriages drove up to her huge house in Bolshaia Morskaia. Her guests stepped out at the wide entrance, and the stout porter, who used to read the newspapers in the mornings behind the glass door, to the edification of the passers-by, noiselessly opened the immense door, letting the visitors pass by him into the house.

Almost at the same instant the hostess, with freshly arranged coiffure and freshened face, walked in at one door and her guests at the other door of the drawing-room, a large room with dark walls, downy rugs, and a brightly lighted table, gleaming with the light of candles, white cloth, silver samovar, and transparent china tea-things.

The hostess sat down at the table and took off her gloves. Chairs were set with the aid of footmen, moving almost imperceptibly about the room; the party settled itself, divided into two groups: one round the samovar near the hostess, the other at the opposite end of the drawing-room, round the handsome wife of an ambassador, in black velvet, with sharply defined black eyebrows. In both groups conversation wavered, as it always does, for the first few minutes, broken up by meetings, greetings, offers of tea, and as it were, feeling about for something to rest upon.

"She's exceptionally good as an actress; one can see she's studied Kaulbach," said a diplomatic attaché in the group round the ambassador's wife. "Did you notice how she fell down? . . ."

"Oh, please, don't let us talk about Nilsson! No one can possibly say anything new about her," said a fat, red-faced, flaxen-headed lady, without eyebrows and chignon, wearing an old silk dress. This was Princess Myakaya, noted for her simplicity and the roughness of her manners, and nicknamed *enfant terrible*. Princess Myakaya, sitting in the middle between the two groups, and listening to both, took part in the conversation first of one and then of the other. "Three people have used that very phrase about Kaulbach to me today already, just as though they had made a compact about it. And I can't see why they liked that remark so."

The conversation was cut short by this observation, and a new subject had to be thought of again.

"Do tell me something amusing but not spiteful," said the ambassador's wife, a great proficient in the art of that elegant conversation called by the English *small talk*. She addressed the attaché, who was at a loss now what to begin upon.

"They say that that's a difficult task, that nothing's amusing that isn't spiteful," he began with a smile. "But I'll try. Get me a subject. It all lies in the subject. If a subject's given me, it's easy to spin something round it. I often think that the celebrated talkers of the last century would have found it difficult to talk cleverly now. Everything clever is so stale. . . ."

"That has been said long ago," the ambassador's wife interrupted him, laughing.

The conversation began amiably, but just because it was too amiable, it came to a stop again. They had to have recourse to the sure, never-failing topic—gossip.

"Don't you think there's something Louis Quinze about Tushkevitch?" he said, glancing towards a handsome, fair-haired young man, standing at the table.

"Oh, yes! He's in the same style as the drawing-room and that's why it is he's so often here."

This conversation was maintained, since it rested

on allusions to what could not be talked of in that room—that is to say, of the relations of Tushkevitch with their hostess.

Round the samovar and the hostess the conversation had been meanwhile vacillating in just the same way between three inevitable topics: the latest piece of public news, the theater, and scandal. It, too, came finally to rest on the last topic, that is, ill-natured gossip.

"Have you heard the Maltishtcheva woman—the mother, not the daughter—has ordered a costume in *diable rose* color?"

"Nonsense! No, that's too lovely!"

"I wonder that with her sense—for she's not a fool, you know—that she doesn't see how funny she is."

Everyone had something to say in censure or ridicule of the luckless Madame Maltishtcheva, and the conversation crackled merrily, like a burning faggot-stack.

The husband of Princess Betsy, a good-natured fat man, an ardent collector of engravings, hearing that his wife had visitors, came into the drawing-room before going to his club. Stepping noiselessly over the thick rugs, he went up to Princess Myakaya.

"How did you like Nilsson?" he asked.

"Oh, how can you steal upon anyone like that! How you startled me!" she responded. "Please don't talk to me about the opera; you know nothing about music. I'd better meet you on your own ground, and talk about your majolica and engravings. Come now, what treasure have you been buying lately at the old curiosity shops?"

"Would you like me to show you? But you don't understand such things."

"Oh, do show me! I've been learning about them at those—what's their names? . . . the bankers . . . they've some splendid engravings. They showed them to us."

"Why, have you been at the Schützburgs?" asked the hostess from the samovar.

"Yes, *ma chère*. They asked my husband and me to dinner, and told us the sauce at that dinner cost a hundred pounds," Princess Myakaya said, speaking loudly, and conscious everyone was listening; "and very nasty sauce it was, some green mess. We had to ask them, and I made them sauce for eighteen pence, and everybody was very much pleased with it. I can't run to hundred-pound sauces."

"She's unique!" said the lady of the house.

"Marvelous!" said someone.

The sensation produced by Princess Myakaya's speeches was always unique, and the secret of the sensation she produced lay in the fact that though she spoke not always appropriately, as now, she said simple things with some sense in them. In the society in which she lived such plain statements produced the effect of the wittiest epigram. Princess Myakaya could never see why it had that effect, but she knew it had, and took advantage of it.

As everyone had been listening while Princess Myakaya spoke, and so the conversation around the ambassador's wife had dropped, Princess Betsy tried to bring the whole party together, and turned to the ambassador's wife.

"Will you really not have tea? You should come over here by us."

"No, we're very happy here," the ambassador's wife responded with a smile, and she went on with the conversation that had been begun.

It was a very agreeable conversation. They were criticizing the Karenins, husband and wife.

"Anna is quite changed since her stay in Moscow. There's something strange about her," said her friend.

"The great change is that she brought back with her the shadow of Alexey Vronsky," said the ambassador's wife.

"Well, what of it? There's a fable of Grimm's about a man without a shadow, a man who's lost his shadow. And that's his punishment for something. I never could understand how it was a punishment. But a woman must dislike being without a shadow."

"Yes, but women with a shadow usually come to a bad end," said Anna's friend.

"Bad luck to your tongue!" said Princess Myakaya suddenly. "Madame Karenina's a splendid woman. I don't like her husband, but I like her very much."

"Why don't you like her husband? He's such a remarkable man," said the ambassador's wife. "My husband says there are few statesmen like him in Europe."

"And my husband tells me just the same, but I don't believe it," said Princess Myakaya. "If our husbands didn't talk to us, we should see the facts as they are. Alexey Alexandrovitch, to my thinking, is simply a fool. I say it in a whisper . . . but doesn't it really make everything clear? Before, when I was told to consider him clever, I kept looking for his ability, and thought myself a fool for not seeing it; but directly I said, he's a fool, though only in a whisper, everything's explained, isn't it?"

"How spiteful you are today!"

"Not a bit. I'd no other way out of it. One of the two had to be a fool. And, well, you know one can't say that of oneself."

"'No one is satisfied with his fortune, and everyone is satisfied with his wit.'" The attaché repeated the French saying.

"That's just it, just it," Princess Myakaya turned to him. "But the point is that I won't abandon Anna to your mercies. She's so nice, so charming. How can she help it if they're all in love with her, and follow her about like shadows?"

"Oh, I had no idea of blaming her for it," Anna's friend said in self-defense.

"If no one follows us about like a shadow, that's no proof that we've any right to blame her."

And having duly disposed of Anna's friend, the Princess Myakaya got up, and together with the ambassador's wife, joined the group at the table, where the conversation was dealing with the king of Prussia.

"What wicked gossip were you talking over there?" asked Betsy.

"About the Karenins. The princess gave us a sketch of Alexey Alexandrovitch," said the ambassador's wife with a smile, as she sat down at the table.

"Pity we didn't hear it!" said Princess Betsy, glancing towards the door. "Ah, here you are at last!" she said, turning with a smile to Vronsky, as he came in.

Vronsky was not merely acquainted with all the persons whom he was meeting here; he saw them all every day; and so he came in with the quiet manner with which one enters a room full of people from whom one has only just parted.

"Where do I come from?" he said, in answer to a question from the ambassador's wife. "Well, there's no help for it, I must confess. From the *opera bouffe*. I do believe I've seen it a hundred times, and always with fresh enjoyment. It's exquisite! I know it's disgraceful, but I go to sleep at the opera, and I sit out the *opera bouffe* to the last minute, and enjoy it. This evening. . . ."

He mentioned a French actress, and was going to tell something about her; but the ambassador's wife, with playful horror, cut him short.

"Please don't tell us about that horror."

"All right, I won't especially as everyone knows those horrors."

"And we should all go to see them if it were accepted as the correct thing, like the opera," chimed in Princess Myakaya.

Fyodor Dostoevsky, "The Grand Inquisitor"

"The Grand Inquisitor" was originally published as an embedded narrative in Brothers Karamazov, *which was published in serial form from 1879 to 1880 in Katkov's* Russian Messenger. *"The Grand Inquisitor" can be found in volume 141, June 1879. At the time, the story was read as part of the novel, but partway through the twentieth century the text began to be read separately and published independently.*

Source: Fyodor Dostoevsky, "The Grand Inquisitor," trans. H. P. Blavatsky (1880; Project Gutenberg, 2020), https://gutenberg.org/ebooks/8578.

[Dedicated by the Translator to those sceptics who clamour so loudly, both in print and private letters—"Show us the wonder-working 'Brothers,' let them come out publicly—and we will believe in them!"]

[The following is an extract from M. Dostoevsky's celebrated novel, *The Brothers Karamazof*, the last publication from the pen of the great Russian novelist, who died a few months ago, just as the concluding chapters appeared in print. Dostoevsky is beginning to be recognized as one of the ablest and profoundest among Russian writers. His characters are invariably typical portraits drawn from various classes of Russian society, strikingly life-like and realistic to the highest degree. The following extract is a cutting satire on modern theology generally and the Roman Catholic religion in particular. The idea is that Christ revisits earth, coming to Spain at the period of the Inquisition, and is at once arrested as a heretic by the Grand Inquisitor. One of the three brothers of the story, Ivan, a rank materialist and an atheist of the new school, is supposed to throw this conception into the form of a poem, which he describes to Alyosha—the youngest of the brothers, a young Christian mystic brought up by a "saint" in a monastery—as follows: (—Ed. *Theosophist*, Nov. 1881)

"Quite impossible, as you see, to start without an introduction," laughed Ivan. "Well, then, I mean to place the event described in the poem in the sixteenth century, an age—as you must have been told at school—when it was the great fashion among poets to make the denizens and powers of higher worlds descend on earth and mix freely with mortals. . . . In France all the notaries' clerks, and the monks in the cloisters as well, used to give grand performances, dramatic plays in which long scenes were enacted by the Madonna, the angels, the saints, Christ, and even by God Himself. In those days, everything was very artless and primitive. An instance of it may be found in Victor Hugo's drama, Notre Dame de Paris, where, at the Municipal Hall, a play called *Le Bon Jugement de la Tres-sainte et Gracièuse Vierge Marie*, is enacted in honour of Louis XI, in which the Virgin appears personally to pronounce her 'good judgment.' In Moscow, during the pre-petrean period, performances of nearly the same character, chosen especially from the Old Testament, were also in great favour. Apart from such plays, the world was overflooded with mystical writings, 'verses'—the heroes of which were always selected from the ranks of angels, saints and other heavenly citizens answering to the devotional purposes of the age. The recluses of our monasteries, like the Roman Catholic monks, passed their time in translating, copying, and even producing original compositions upon such subjects, and that, remember, during the Tarter period! . . . In this connection, I am reminded of a poem compiled in a convent—a translation from the Greek, of course—called, 'The Travels of the Mother of God among the Damned,' with fitting illustrations and a boldness of conception inferior nowise to that of Dante. The 'Mother of God' visits hell, in company with the archangel Michael as her cicerone to guide her through the legions of the 'damned.' She sees them all, and is witness to their multifarious tortures. Among the many other exceedingly remarkably varieties of torments—every category of sinners having its own—there is one especially worthy of notice, namely a class of the 'damned' sentenced to gradually sink in a burning lake of brimstone and fire. Those whose sins cause them to sink so low that they no longer can rise to the surface are for ever forgotten by God, i.e., they fade out from the omniscient memory, says the poem—an expression, by the way, of an extraordinary profundity of thought, when closely analysed. The Virgin is terribly shocked, and falling down upon her knees in tears before the throne of God, begs that all she has seen in hell—all, all without exception, should have their sentences remitted to them. Her dialogue with God is colossally interesting. She supplicates, she will not leave Him. And when God, pointing to the pierced hands and feet of her Son, cries, 'How can I forgive His executioners?' She then commands that all the saints, martyrs, angels and archangels, should prostrate themselves with her before the Immutable and Changeless One and implore Him to change His wrath into mercy and—forgive them all. The poem closes upon her obtaining from God a compromise, a kind of yearly respite of tortures between Good Friday and Trinity, a chorus of the 'damned' singing loud praises to God from their 'bottomless pit,' thanking and telling Him:

Thou art right, O Lord, very right,
Thou hast condemned us justly.

"My poem is of the same character.

"In it, it is Christ who appears on the scene. True, He says nothing, but only appears and passes out of sight. Fifteen centuries have elapsed since He left the world with the distinct promise to return 'with power and great glory'; fifteen long centuries since His prophet cried, 'Prepare ye the way of the Lord!' since He Himself had foretold, while yet on earth, 'Of that day and hour knoweth no man, no, not the angels of heaven but my Father only.' But Christendom expects Him still. . . .

"It waits for Him with the same old faith and the same emotion; aye, with a far greater faith, for fifteen centuries have rolled away since the last sign from heaven was sent to man,

And blind faith remained alone
To lull the trusting heart,
As heav'n would send a sign no more.

"True, again, we have all heard of miracles being wrought ever since the 'age of miracles' passed away to return no more. We had, and still have, our saints credited with performing the most miraculous cures; and, if we can believe their biographers, there have been those among them who have been personally visited by the Queen of Heaven. But Satan sleepeth not, and the first germs of doubt, and ever-increasing unbelief in such wonders, already had begun to sprout in Christendom as early as the sixteenth century. It was just at that time that a new and terrible heresy first made its appearance in the north of Germany.* [*Luther's reform] A great star 'shining as it were a lamp . . . fell upon the fountains waters' . . . and 'they were made bitter.' This 'heresy' blasphemously denied 'miracles.' But those who had remained faithful believed all the more ardently, the tears of mankind ascended to Him as heretofore, and the Christian world was expecting Him as confidently as ever; they loved Him and hoped in Him, thirsted and hungered to suffer and die for Him just as many of them had done before. . . . So many centuries had weak, trusting humanity implored Him, crying with ardent faith and fervour: 'How long, O Lord, holy and true, dost Thou not come!' So many long centuries hath it vainly appealed to Him, that at last, in His inexhaustible compassion, He consenteth to answer the prayer. . . . He decideth that once more, if it were but for one short hour, the people—His long-suffering, tortured, fatally sinful, his loving and child-like, trusting people—shall behold Him again. The scene of action is placed by me in Spain, at Seville, during that terrible period of the Inquisition, when, for the greater glory of God, stakes were flaming all over the country.

Burning wicked heretics,
In grand auto-da-fes.

"This particular visit has, of course, nothing to do with the promised Advent, when, according to the programme, 'after the tribulation of those days,' He will appear 'coming in the clouds of heaven.' For, that 'coming of the Son of Man,' as we are informed, will take place as suddenly 'as the lightning cometh out of the east and shineth even unto the west.' No; this once, He desired to come unknown, and appear among His children, just when the bones of the heretics, sentenced to be burnt alive, had commenced crackling at the flaming stakes. Owing to His limitless mercy, He mixes once more with mortals and in the same form in which He was wont to appear fifteen centuries ago. He descends, just at the very moment when before king, courtiers, knights, cardinals, and the fairest dames of court, before the whole population of Seville, upwards of a hundred wicked heretics are being roasted, in a magnificent *auto-da-fe ad majorem Dei gloriam*, by the order of the powerful Cardinal Grand Inquisitor.

"He comes silently and unannounced; yet all—how strange—yea, all recognize Him, at once! The population rushes towards Him as if propelled by some irresistible force; it surrounds, throngs, and presses around, it follows Him. . . . Silently, and with a smile of boundless compassion upon His lips, He crosses the dense crowd, and moves softly on. The Sun of Love burns in His heart, and warm rays of Light, Wisdom and Power beam forth from His eyes, and pour down their waves upon the swarming multitudes of the rabble assembled around, making their hearts vibrate with returning love. He extends His hands over their heads, blesses them, and from mere contact with Him, aye, even with His garments, a healing power goes forth. An old man, blind from his birth, cries, 'Lord, heal me, that I may see Thee!' and the scales falling off the closed eyes, the blind man beholds Him. . . . The crowd weeps for joy, and kisses the ground upon which He treads. Children strew flowers along His path and sing to Him, 'Hosanna!' It is He, it is Himself, they say to each other, it must be He, it can be none other but He! He pauses at the portal of the old cathedral, just as a wee white coffin is carried in, with tears and great lamentations. The lid is off, and in the coffin lies the body of a fair-child, seven years old, the only child of an eminent citizen of the city. The little corpse lies buried in flowers. 'He will raise the child to life!' confidently shouts the crowd to the weeping mother. The officiating priest who had come to meet the funeral procession, looks perplexed, and frowns. A loud cry is suddenly heard, and the bereaved mother prostrates herself at His feet. 'If it be Thou, then bring back my child to life!' she cries beseechingly. The procession halts, and the little coffin is gently lowered at his feet. Divine compassion beams forth from His eyes, and as He looks at the child, His lips are heard to whisper once more, '*Talitha Cumi*'—and 'straightway the damsel arose.' The child rises in her coffin. Her little hands still hold the nosegay of white roses which after death was placed in them, and, looking round with large astonished eyes she smiles sweetly. . . . The crowd is violently excited. A terrible commotion rages among them, the populace shouts and loudly weeps, when suddenly, before the cathedral door, appears the Cardinal Grand Inquisitor himself. . . . He is a tall, gaunt-looking old man of nearly four-score years and ten, with a stern, withered face, and deeply sunken eyes, from the cavity of which glitter two fiery sparks. He has laid aside his gorgeous cardinal's robes in which he had appeared before the people at the auto da-fe of the enemies of the Romish Church, and is now clad in his old, rough, monkish cassock. His sullen assistants and slaves of the 'holy guard' are following at a distance. He pauses before the crowd and observes. He has seen all. He has witnessed the placing of the little coffin at His feet, the calling back to life. And now, his dark, grim face has grown still darker; his bushy grey eyebrows nearly meet, and his sunken eye flashes with sinister light. Slowly raising his finger, he commands his minions to arrest Him. . . .

"Such is his power over the well-disciplined, submissive and now trembling people, that the thick crowds immediately give way, and scattering before the guard, amid dead silence and without one breath of protest, allow them to lay their sacrilegious hands upon the stranger and lead Him away. . . . That same populace, like one man, now bows its head to the ground before the old Inquisitor, who blesses it and slowly moves onward. The guards conduct their prisoner to the ancient building of the Holy Tribunal; pushing Him into a narrow, gloomy, vaulted prison-cell, they lock Him in and retire. . . .

"The day wanes, and night—a dark, hot breathless Spanish night—creeps on and settles upon the city of Seville. The air smells of laurels and orange blossoms. In the Cimmerian darkness of the old Tribunal Hall the iron door of the cell is suddenly thrown open, and the Grand Inquisitor, holding a dark lantern, slowly stalks into the dungeon. He is alone, and, as the heavy door closes behind him, he pauses at the threshold, and, for a minute or two, silently and gloomily scrutinizes the Face before him. At last approaching with measured steps, he sets his lantern down upon the table and addresses Him in these words:

"'It is Thou! . . . Thou!' . . . Receiving no reply, he rapidly continues: 'Nay, answer not; be silent! . . . And what couldst Thou say? . . . I know but too well Thy answer. . . . Besides, Thou hast no right to add one syllable to that which was already uttered by Thee before. . . . Why shouldst Thou now return, to impede us in our work? For Thou hast come but for that only, and Thou knowest it well. But art Thou as well aware of what awaits Thee in the morning? I do not know, nor do I care to know who thou mayest be:

be it Thou or only thine image, to-morrow I will condemn and burn Thee on the stake, as the most wicked of all the heretics; and that same people, who to-day were kissing Thy feet, to-morrow at one bend of my finger, will rush to add fuel to Thy funeral pile. . . . Wert Thou aware of this?' he adds, speaking as if in solemn thought, and never for one instant taking his piercing glance off the meek Face before him." . . .

"I can hardly realize the situation described—what is all this, Ivan?" suddenly interrupted Alyosha, who had remained silently listening to his brother. "Is this an extravagant fancy, or some mistake of the old man, an impossible quid pro quo?"

"Let it be the latter, if you like," laughed Ivan, "since modern realism has so perverted your taste that you feel unable to realize anything from the world of fancy. . . . Let it be a quid pro quo, if you so choose it. Again, the Inquisitor is ninety years old, and he might have easily gone mad with his one *idee fixe* of power; or, it might have as well been a delirious vision, called forth by dying fancy, overheated by the auto-da-fe of the hundred heretics in that forenoon. . . . But what matters for the poem, whether it was a quid pro quo or an uncontrollable fancy? The question is, that the old man has to open his heart; that he must give out his thought at last; and that the hour has come when he does speak it out, and says loudly that which for ninety years he has kept secret within his own breast."

"And his prisoner, does He never reply? Does He keep silent, looking at him, without saying a word?"

"Of course; and it could not well be otherwise," again retorted Ivan. "The Grand Inquisitor begins from his very first words by telling Him that He has no right to add one syllable to that which He had said before. To make the situation clear at once, the above preliminary monologue is intended to convey to the reader the very fundamental idea which underlies Roman Catholicism—as well as I can convey it, his words mean, in short: 'Everything was given over by Thee to the Pope, and everything now rests with him alone; Thou hast no business to return and thus hinder us in our work.' In this sense the Jesuits not only talk but write likewise.

"'Hast thou the right to divulge to us a single one of the mysteries of that world whence Thou comest?' enquires of Him my old Inquisitor, and forthwith answers for Him. 'Nay, Thou has no such right. For, that would be adding to that which was already said by Thee before; hence depriving people of that freedom for which Thou hast so stoutly stood up while yet on earth. . . . Anything new that Thou would now proclaim would have to be regarded as an attempt to interfere with that freedom of choice, as it would come as a new and a miraculous revelation superseding the old revelation of fifteen hundred years ago, when Thou didst so repeatedly tell the people: "The truth shall make you free." Behold then, Thy "free" people now!' adds the old man with sombre irony. 'Yea! . . . it has cost us dearly,' he continues, sternly looking at his victim. 'But we have at last accomplished our task, and—in Thy name. . . . For fifteen long centuries we had to toil and suffer owing to that "freedom": but now we have prevailed and our work is done, and well and strongly it is done. . . . Believest not Thou it is so very strong? . . . And why should Thou look at me so meekly as if I were not worthy even of Thy indignation? . . . Know then, that now, and only now, Thy people feel fully sure and satisfied of their freedom; and that only since they have themselves and of their own free will delivered that freedom unto our hands by placing it submissively at our feet. But then, that is what we have done. Is it that which Thou has striven for? Is this the kind of "freedom" Thou has promised them?'"

"Now again, I do not understand," interrupted Alyosha. "Does the old man mock and laugh?"

"Not in the least. He seriously regards it as a great service done by himself, his brother monks and Jesuits, to humanity, to have conquered and subjected unto their authority that freedom, and boasts that it was done but for the good of the world. 'For only now,' he says (speaking of the Inquisition) 'has it become possible to us, for the first time, to give a serious thought to human happiness. Man is born a rebel, and can rebels be ever happy? . . . Thou has been fairly warned of it, but evidently to no use, since Thou hast rejected the only means which could make mankind happy; fortunately at Thy departure Thou hast delivered the task to us. . . . Thou has promised, ratifying the pledge by Thy own words, in words giving us the right to bind and unbind . . . and surely, Thou couldst not think of depriving us of it now!'"

"But what can he mean by the words, 'Thou has been fairly warned'?" asked Alexis.

"These words give the key to what the old man has to say for his justification . . . But listen—

"'The terrible and wise spirit, the spirit of self-annihilation and non-being,' goes on the Inquisitor, 'the great spirit of negation conversed with Thee in the wilderness, and we are told that he "tempted" Thee. . . . Was it so? And if it were so, then it is impossible to utter anything more truthful than what is contained in his three offers, which Thou didst reject, and which are usually called "temptations." Yea; if ever there was on earth a genuine striking wonder produced, it was on that day of Thy three temptations, and it is precisely in these three short sentences that the marvelous miracle is contained. If it were possible that they should vanish and disappear for ever, without leaving any trace, from the record and from the memory of man, and that it should become necessary again to devise, invent, and make them reappear in Thy history once more, thinkest Thou that all the world's sages, all the legislators, initiates, philosophers and thinkers, if called upon to frame three questions which should, like these, besides answering the magnitude of the event, express in three short sentences the whole future history of this our world and of mankind—dost Thou believe, I ask Thee, that all their combined efforts could ever create anything equal in power and depth of thought to the three propositions offered Thee by the powerful and all-wise spirit in the wilderness? Judging of them by their marvelous aptness alone, one can at once perceive that they emanated not from a finite, terrestrial intellect, but indeed, from the Eternal and the Absolute. In these three offers we find, blended into one and foretold to us, the complete subsequent history of man; we are shown three images, so to say, uniting in them all the future axiomatic, insoluble problems and contradictions of human nature, the world over. In those days, the wondrous wisdom contained in them was not made so apparent as it is now, for futurity remained still veiled; but now, when fifteen centuries have elapsed, we see that everything in these three questions is so marvelously foreseen and foretold, that to add to, or to take away from, the prophecy one jot, would be absolutely impossible!

"'Decide then thyself,' sternly proceeded the Inquisitor, 'which of ye twain was right: Thou who didst reject, or he who offered? Remember the subtle meaning of question the first, which runs thus: Wouldst Thou go into the world empty-handed? Would Thou venture thither with Thy vague and undefined promise of freedom, which men, dull and unruly as they are by nature, are unable so much as to understand, which they avoid and fear?—for never was there anything more unbearable to the human race than personal freedom! Dost Thou see these stones in the desolate and glaring wilderness? Command that these stones be made bread—and mankind will run after Thee, obedient and grateful like a herd of cattle. But even then it will be ever diffident and trembling, lest Thou should take away Thy hand, and they lose thereby their bread! Thou didst refuse to accept the offer for fear of depriving men of their free choice; for where is there freedom of choice where men are bribed with bread? Man shall not live by bread alone—was Thine answer. Thou knewest not, it seems, that it was precisely in the name of that earthly bread that the terrestrial spirit would one day rise against, struggle with, and finally conquer Thee, followed by the hungry multitudes shouting: "Who is like unto that Beast, who maketh fire come down from heaven upon the earth!" Knowest Thou not that, but a few centuries hence, and the whole of mankind will have proclaimed in its wisdom and through its mouthpiece, Science, that there is no more crime, hence no more sin on earth, but only hungry people? "Feed us first and then command us to be virtuous!" will be the words written upon the banner lifted against Thee—a banner which shall destroy Thy Church to its very foundations, and in the place of Thy Temple shall raise once more the terrible Tower of Babel; and though its building be left unfinished, as was that of the first one, yet the fact will remain recorded that Thou couldst, but wouldst not, prevent the attempt to build that new tower by accepting the offer, and thus saving mankind a millennium of useless suffering on earth. And it is to us that the people will return again. They will search for us catacombs, as we shall once more be persecuted and martyred—and they will begin crying unto us: "Feed us, for they who promised us the fire from heaven have deceived us!" It is then that we will finish building their tower for them. For they alone who feed them shall finish it, and we shall feed them in Thy name, and lying to them that it is in that name. Oh, never, never, will they learn to feed themselves without our help! No science will ever give them bread so long as they remain free, so long as they refuse to lay that freedom at our feet, and say: "Enslave, but feed us!" That day must come when men will understand that freedom and daily bread enough to satisfy all are unthinkable and can never be had together, as men will never be able to fairly divide the two among themselves. And they will also learn that they can never be free, for they are weak, vicious, miserable nonentities born wicked and rebellious. Thou has promised to them the bread of life, the bread of heaven; but I ask Thee again, can that bread ever equal in the sight of the weak and the vicious, the ever ungrateful human race, their daily bread on earth? And even supposing that thousands and tens of thousands follow Thee in the name of, and for the sake of, Thy heavenly bread, what will become of the millions and hundreds of millions of human beings too weak to scorn the earthly for the sake of Thy heavenly bread? Or is it but those tens of thousands chosen among the great and the mighty, that are so dear to Thee, while the remaining millions, innumerable as the grains of sand in the seas, the weak and the loving, have to be used as material for the former? No, no! In our sight and for our purpose the weak and the lowly are the more dear to us. True, they are vicious and rebellious, but we will force them into obedience, and it is they who will admire us the most. They will regard us as gods, and feel grateful to those who have consented to lead the masses and bear their burden of freedom by ruling over them—so terrible will that freedom at last appear to men! Then we will tell them that it is in obedience to Thy will and in Thy name that we rule over them. We will deceive them once more and lie to them once again—for never, never more will we allow Thee to come among us. In this deception we will find our suffering, for we must needs lie eternally, and never cease to lie!

"Such is the secret meaning of "temptation" the first, and that is what Thou didst reject in the wilderness for the sake of that freedom which Thou didst prize above all. Meanwhile Thy tempter's offer contained another great world-mystery. By accepting the "bread," Thou wouldst have satisfied and answered a universal craving, a ceaseless longing alive in the heart of every individual human being, lurking in the breast of collective mankind, that most perplexing problem—"whom or what shall we worship?" There exists no greater or more painful anxiety for a man who has freed himself from all religious bias, than how he shall soonest find a new object or idea to worship. But man seeks to bow before that only which is recognized by the greater majority, if not by all his fellow-men, as having a right to be worshipped; whose rights are so unquestionable that men agree unanimously to bow down to it. For the chief concern of these miserable creatures is not to find and worship the idol of their own choice, but to discover that which all others will believe in, and consent to bow down to in a mass. It is that instinctive need of having a worship in common that is the chief suffering of every man, the chief concern of mankind from the beginning of times. It is for that universality of religious worship that people destroyed each other by sword. Creating gods unto themselves, they forthwith began appealing to each other: "Abandon your deities, come and bow down to ours, or death to ye and your idols!" And so will they do till the end of this world; they will do so even then, when all the gods themselves have disappeared, for then men will prostrate themselves before and worship some idea. Thou didst know, Thou couldst not be ignorant of, that mysterious fundamental principle in human nature, and still thou hast rejected the only absolute banner offered Thee, to which all the nations would remain true, and before which all would have bowed—the banner of earthly bread, rejected in the name of freedom and of "bread in the kingdom of God"! Behold, then, what Thou hast done furthermore for that "freedom's" sake! I repeat to Thee, man has no greater anxiety in life than to find some one to whom he can make over that gift of freedom with which the unfortunate creature is born. But he alone will prove capable of silencing and quieting their consciences, that shall succeed in possessing himself of the freedom of men. With "daily bread" an irresistible power was offered Thee: show a man "bread" and he will follow Thee, for what can he resist less than the attraction of bread? But if, at the same time, another succeed in possessing himself of his conscience—oh! then even Thy bread will be forgotten, and man will follow him who seduced his conscience. So far Thou wert right. For the mystery of human being does not solely rest in the desire to live, but in the problem—for what should one live at all? Without a clear perception of his reasons for living, man will never consent to live, and will rather destroy himself than tarry on earth, though he be surrounded with bread. This is the truth. But what has happened? Instead of getting hold of man's freedom, Thou has enlarged it still more! Hast Thou again forgotten that to man rest and even death are preferable to a free choice between the knowledge of Good and Evil? Nothing seems more seductive in his eyes than freedom of conscience, and nothing proves more painful. And behold! instead of laying a firm foundation whereon to rest once for all man's conscience, Thou hast chosen to stir up in him all that is abnormal, mysterious, and indefinite, all that is beyond human strength, and has acted as if Thou never hadst any love for him, and yet Thou wert He who came to "lay down His life for His friends!" Thou hast burdened man's soul with anxieties hitherto unknown to him. Thirsting for human love freely given, seeking to enable man, seduced and charmed by Thee, to follow Thy path of his own free-will, instead of the old and wise law which held him in subjection, Thou hast given him the right henceforth to choose and freely decide what is good and bad for him, guided but by Thine image in his heart. But hast Thou never dreamt of the probability, nay, of the certainty, of that same man one day rejected finally, and controverting even Thine image and Thy truth, once he would find himself laden with such a terrible burden as freedom of choice? That a time would surely come when men would exclaim that Truth and Light cannot be in Thee, for no one could have left them in a greater perplexity and mental suffering than Thou has done, lading them with so many cares and insoluble problems. Thus, it is Thyself who hast laid the foundation for the destruction of Thine own kingdom and no one but Thou is to be blamed for it.

"'Meantime, every chance of success was offered Thee. There are three Powers, three unique Forces upon earth, capable of conquering for ever by charming the conscience of these weak rebels—men—for their own good; and these Forces are: Miracle, Mystery and Authority. Thou hast rejected all the three, and thus wert the first to set them an example. When the terrible and all-wise spirit placed Thee on a pinnacle of the temple and said unto Thee, "If Thou be the son of God, cast Thyself down, for it is written, He shall give His angels charge concerning Thee: and in their hands they shall bear Thee up, lest at any time Thou dash Thy foot against a stone!"—for thus Thy faith in Thy father should have been made evident, Thou didst refuse to accept his suggestion and didst not follow it. Oh, undoubtedly, Thou didst act in this with all the magnificent pride of a god, but then men—that weak and rebel race—are they also gods, to understand Thy refusal? Of course, Thou didst well know that by taking one single step forward, by making the slightest motion to throw Thyself down, Thou wouldst have tempted "the Lord Thy God," lost suddenly all faith in Him, and dashed Thyself to atoms against that same earth which Thou camest to save, and thus wouldst have allowed the wise spirit which tempted Thee to triumph and rejoice. But, then, how many such as Thee are to be found on this globe, I ask Thee? Couldst Thou ever for a moment imagine that men would have the same strength to resist such a temptation? Is human nature calculated to reject miracle, and trust, during the most terrible moments in life, when the most momentous, painful and perplexing problems struggle within man's soul, to the free decisions of his heart for the true solution? Oh, Thou knewest well that that action of Thine would remain recorded in books for ages to come, reaching to the confines of the globe, and Thy hope was, that following Thy example, man would remain true to his God, without needing any miracle to keep his faith alive! But Thou knewest not, it seems, that no sooner would man reject miracle than he would reject God likewise, for he seeketh less God than "a sign" from Him. And thus, as it is beyond the power of man to remain without miracles, so, rather than live without, he will create for himself new wonders of his own making; and he will bow to and worship the soothsayer's miracles, the old witch's sorcery, were he a rebel, a heretic, and an atheist a hundred times over. Thy refusal to come down from the cross when people, mocking and wagging their heads were saying to Thee—"Save Thyself if Thou be the son of God, and we will believe in Thee," was due to the same determination—not to enslave man through miracle, but to obtain faith in Thee freely and apart from any miraculous influence. Thou thirstest for free and uninfluenced love, and refuses the passionate adoration of the slave before a Potency which would have subjected his will once for ever. Thou judgest of men too highly here, again, for though rebels they be, they are born slaves and nothing more. Behold, and judge of them once more, now that fifteen centuries have elapsed since that moment. Look at them, whom Thou didst try to elevate unto Thee! I swear man is weaker and lower than Thou hast ever imagined him to be! Can he ever do that which Thou art said to have accomplished? By valuing him so highly Thou hast acted as if there were no love for him in Thine heart, for Thou hast demanded of him more than he could ever give—Thou, who lovest him more than Thyself! Hadst Thou esteemed him less, less wouldst Thou have demanded of him, and that would have been more like love, for his burden would have been made thereby lighter. Man is weak and cowardly. What matters it, if he now riots and rebels throughout the world against our will and power, and prides himself upon that rebellion? It is but the petty pride and vanity of a school-boy. It is the rioting of little children, getting up a mutiny in the classroom and driving their schoolmaster out of it. But it will not last long, and when the day of their triumph is over, they will have to pay dearly for it. They will destroy the temples and raze them to the ground, flooding the earth with blood. But the foolish children will have to learn some day that, rebels though they be and riotous from nature, they are too weak to maintain the spirit of mutiny for any length of time. Suffused with idiotic tears, they will confess that He who created them rebellious undoubtedly did so but to mock them. They will pronounce these words in despair, and such blasphemous utterances will but add to their misery—for human nature cannot endure blasphemy, and takes her own revenge in the end.

"'And thus, after all Thou has suffered for mankind and its freedom, the present fate of men may be summed up in three words: Unrest, Confusion, Misery! Thy great prophet John records in his vision, that he saw, during the first resurrection of the chosen servants of God—"the number of them which were sealed" in their foreheads, "twelve thousand" of every tribe. But were they, indeed, as many? Then they must have been gods, not men. They had shared Thy Cross for long years, suffered scores of years' hunger and thirst in dreary wildernesses and deserts, feeding upon locusts and roots—and of these children of free love for Thee, and self-sacrifice in Thy name, Thou mayest well feel proud. But remember that these are but a few thousands—of gods, not men; and how about all others? And why should the weakest be held guilty for not being able to endure what the strongest have endured? Why should a soul incapable of containing such terrible gifts be punished for its weakness? Didst Thou really come to, and for, the "elect" alone? If so, then the mystery will remain forever mysterious to our finite minds. And if a mystery, then were we right to proclaim it as one, and preach it, teaching them that neither their freely given love to Thee nor freedom of conscience were essential, but only that incomprehensible mystery which they must blindly obey even against the dictates of their conscience. Thus did we. We corrected and improved Thy teaching and based it upon "Miracle, Mystery, and Authority." And men rejoiced at finding themselves led once more like a herd of cattle, and at finding their hearts at last delivered of the terrible burden laid upon them by Thee, which caused them so much suffering. Tell me, were we right in doing as we did. Did not we show our great love for humanity, by realizing in such a humble spirit its helplessness, by so mercifully lightening its great burden, and by permitting and remitting for its weak nature every sin, provided it be committed with our authorization? For what, then, hast Thou come again to trouble us in our work? And why lookest Thou at me so penetratingly with Thy meek eyes, and in such a silence? Rather shouldst Thou feel wroth, for I need not Thy love, I reject it, and love Thee not, myself. Why should I conceal the truth from Thee? I know but too well with whom I am now talking! What I had to say was known to Thee before, I read it in Thine eye. How should I conceal from Thee our secret? If perchance Thou wouldst hear it from my own lips, then listen: We are not with Thee, but with him, and that is our secret! For centuries have we abandoned Thee to follow him, yes—eight centuries. Eight hundred years now since we accepted from him the gift rejected by Thee with indignation; that last gift which he offered Thee from the high mountain when, showing all the kingdoms of the world and the glory of them, he saith unto Thee: "All these things will I give Thee, if Thou will fall down and worship me!" We took Rome from him and the glaive of Caesar, and declared ourselves alone the kings of this earth, its sole kings, though our work is not yet fully accomplished. But who is to blame for it? Our work is but in its incipient stage, but it is nevertheless started. We may have long to wait until its culmination, and mankind have to suffer much, but we shall reach the goal some day, and become sole Caesars, and then will be the time to think of universal happiness for men.

"'Thou couldst accept the glaive of Caesar Thyself; why didst Thou reject the offer? By accepting from the powerful spirit his third offer Thou would have realized every aspiration man seeketh for himself on earth; man would have found a constant object for worship; one to deliver his conscience up to, and one that should unite all together into one common and harmonious ant-hill; for an innate necessity for universal union constitutes the third and final affliction of mankind. Humanity as a whole has ever aspired to unite itself universally. Many were, the great nations with great histories, but the greater they were, the more unhappy they felt, as they felt the stronger necessity of a universal union among men. Great conquerors, like Timoor and Tchengis-Khan, passed like a cyclone upon the face of the earth in their efforts to conquer the universe, but even they, albeit unconsciously, expressed the same aspiration towards universal and common union. In accepting the kingdom of the world and Caesar's purple, one would found a universal kingdom and secure to mankind eternal peace. And who can rule mankind better than those who have possessed themselves of man's conscience, and hold in their hand man's daily bread? Having accepted Caesar's glaive and purple, we had, of course, but to deny Thee, to henceforth follow him alone. Oh, centuries of intellectual riot and rebellious free thought are yet before us, and their science will end by anthropophagy, for having begun to build their Babylonian tower without our help they will have to end by anthropophagy. But it is precisely at that time that the Beast will crawl up to us in full submission, and lick the soles of our feet, and sprinkle them with tears of blood and we shall sit upon the scarlet-colored Beast, and lifting up high the golden cup "full of abomination and filthiness," shall show written upon it the word "Mystery"! But it is only then that men will see the beginning of a kingdom of peace and happiness. Thou art proud of Thine own elect, but Thou has none other but these elect, and we—we will give rest to all. But that is not the end. Many are those among thine elect and the laborers of Thy vineyard, who, tired of waiting for Thy coming, already have carried and will yet carry, the great fervor of their hearts and their spiritual strength into another field, and will end by lifting up against Thee Thine own banner of freedom. But it is Thyself Thou hast to thank. Under our rule and sway all will be happy, and will neither rebel nor destroy each other as they did while under Thy free banner. Oh, we will take good care to prove to them that they will become absolutely free only when they have abjured their freedom in our favor and submit to us absolutely. Thinkest Thou we shall be right or still lying? They will convince themselves of our rightness, for they will see what a depth of degrading slavery and strife that liberty of Thine has led them into. Liberty, Freedom of Thought and Conscience, and Science will lead them into such impassable chasms, place them face to face before such wonders and insoluble mysteries, that some of them—more rebellious and ferocious than the rest—will destroy themselves; others—rebellious but weak—will destroy each other; while the remainder, weak, helpless and miserable, will crawl back to our feet and cry: "'Yes; right were ye, oh Fathers of Jesus; ye alone are in possession of His mystery, and we return to you, praying that ye save us from ourselves!" Receiving their bread from us, they will clearly see that we take the bread from them, the bread made by their own hands, but to give it back to them in equal shares and that without any miracle; and having ascertained that, though we have not changed stones into bread, yet bread they have, while every other bread turned verily in their own hands into stones, they will be only too glad to have it so. Until that day, they will never be happy. And who is it that helped the most to blind them, tell me? Who separated the flock and scattered it over ways unknown if it be not Thee? But we will gather the sheep once more and subject them to our will for ever. We will prove to them their own weakness and make them humble again, whilst with Thee they have learnt but pride, for Thou hast made more of them than they ever were worth. We will give them that quiet, humble happiness, which alone benefits such weak, foolish creatures as they are, and having once had proved to them their weakness, they will become timid and obedient, and gather around us as chickens around their hen. They will wonder at and feel a superstitious admiration for us, and feel proud to be led by men so powerful and wise that a handful of them can subject a flock a thousand millions strong. Gradually men will begin to fear us. They will nervously dread our slightest anger, their intellects will weaken, their eyes become as easily accessible to tears as those of children and women; but we will teach them an easy transition from grief and tears to laughter, childish joy and mirthful song. Yes; we will make them work like slaves, but during their recreation hours they shall have an innocent child-like life, full of play and merry laughter. We will even permit them sin, for, weak and helpless, they will feel the more love for us for permitting them to indulge in it. We will tell them that every kind of sin will be remitted to them, so long as it is done with our permission; that we take all these sins upon ourselves, for we so love the world, that we are even willing to sacrifice our souls for its satisfaction. And, appearing before them in the light of their scapegoats and redeemers, we shall be adored the more for it. They will have no secrets from us. It will rest with us to permit them to live with their wives and concubines, or to forbid them, to have children or remain childless, either way depending on the degree of their obedience to us; and they will submit most joyfully to us the most agonizing secrets of their souls—all, all will they lay down at our feet, and we will authorize and remit them all in Thy name, and they will believe us and accept our mediation with rapture, as it will deliver them from their greatest anxiety and torture—that of having to decide freely for themselves. And all will be happy, all except the one or two hundred thousands of their rulers. For it is but we, we the keepers of the great Mystery who will be miserable. There will be thousands of millions of happy infants, and one hundred thousand martyrs who have taken upon themselves the curse of knowledge of good and evil. Peaceable will be their end, and peacefully will they die, in Thy name, to find behind the portals of the grave—but death. But we will keep the secret inviolate, and deceive them for their own good with the mirage of life eternal in Thy kingdom. For, were there really anything like life beyond the grave, surely it would never fall to the lot of such as they! People tell us and prophesy of Thy coming and triumphing once more on earth; of Thy appearing with the army of Thy elect, with Thy proud and mighty ones; but we will answer Thee that they have saved but themselves while we have saved all. We are also threatened with the great disgrace which awaits the whore, "Babylon the great, the mother of harlots"—who sits upon the Beast, holding in her hands the Mystery, the word written upon her forehead; and we are told that the weak ones, the lambs shall rebel against her and shall make her desolate and naked. But then will I arise, and point out to Thee the thousands of millions of happy infants free from any sin. And we who have taken their sins upon us, for their own good, shall stand before Thee and say: "Judge us if Thou canst and darest!" Know then that I fear Thee not. Know that I too have lived in the dreary wilderness, where I fed upon locusts and roots, that I too have blessed freedom with which thou hast blessed men, and that I too have once prepared to join the ranks of Thy elect, the proud and the mighty. But I awoke from my delusion and refused since then to serve insanity. I returned to join the legion of those who corrected Thy mistakes. I left the proud and returned to the really humble, and for their own happiness. What I now tell thee will come to pass, and our kingdom shall be built, I tell Thee not later than to-morrow Thou shalt see that obedient flock which at one simple motion of my hand will rush to add burning coals to Thy stake, on which I will burn Thee for having dared to come and trouble us in our work. For, if there ever was one who deserved more than any of the others our inquisitorial fires—it is Thee! To-morrow I will burn Thee. *Dixi.*"

Ivan paused. He had entered into the situation and had spoken with great animation, but now he suddenly burst out laughing.

"But all that is absurd!" suddenly exclaimed Alyosha, who had hitherto listened perplexed and agitated but in profound silence. "Your poem is a glorification of Christ, not an accusation, as you, perhaps, meant to be. And who will believe you when you speak of 'freedom'? Is it thus that we Christians must understand it? It is Rome (not all Rome, for that would be unjust), but the worst of the Roman Catholics, the Inquisitors and Jesuits, that you have been exposing! Your Inquisitor is an impossible character. What are these sins they are taking upon themselves? Who are those keepers of mystery who took upon themselves a curse for the good of mankind? Who ever met them? We all know the Jesuits, and no one has a good word to say in their favor; but when were they as you depict them? Never, never! The Jesuits are merely a Romish army making ready for their future temporal kingdom, with a mitred emperor—a Roman high priest at their head. That is their ideal and object, without any mystery or elevated suffering. The most prosaic thirsting for power, for the sake of the mean and earthly pleasures of life, a desire to enslave their fellow-men, something like our late system of serfs, with themselves at the head as landed proprietors—that is all that they can be accused of. They may not believe in God, that is also possible, but your suffering Inquisitor is simply—a fancy!"

"Hold, hold!" interrupted Ivan, smiling. "Do not be so excited. A fancy, you say; be it so! Of course, it is a fancy. But stop. Do you really imagine that all this Catholic movement during the last centuries is naught but a desire for power for the mere purpose of 'mean pleasures'? Is this what your Father Paissiy taught you?"

"No, no, quite the reverse, for Father Paissiy once told me something very similar to what you yourself say, though, of course, not that—something quite different," suddenly added Alexis, blushing.

"A precious piece of information, notwithstanding your 'not that.' I ask you, why should the Inquisitors and the Jesuits of your imagination live but for the attainment of 'mean material pleasures?' Why should there not be found among them one single genuine martyr suffering under a great and holy idea and loving humanity with all his heart? Now let us suppose that among all these Jesuits thirsting and hungering but after 'mean material pleasures' there may be one, just one like my old Inquisitor, who had himself fed upon roots in the wilderness, suffered the tortures of damnation while trying to conquer flesh, in order to become free and perfect, but who had never ceased to love humanity, and who one day prophetically beheld the truth; who saw as plain as he could see that the bulk of humanity could never be happy under the old system, that it was not for them that the great Idealist had come and died and dreamt of His Universal Harmony. Having realized that truth, he returned into the world and joined—intelligent and practical people. Is this so impossible?"

"Joined whom? What intelligent and practical people?" exclaimed Alyosha quite excited. "Why should they be more intelligent than other men, and what secrets and mysteries can they have? They have neither. Atheism and infidelity is all the secret they have. Your Inquisitor does not believe in God, and that is all the Mystery there is in it!"

"It may be so. You have guessed rightly there. And it is so, and that is his whole secret; but is this not the acutest sufferings for such a man as he, who killed all his young life in asceticism in the desert, and yet could not cure himself of his love towards his fellow-men? Toward the end of his life he becomes convinced that it is only by following the advice of the great and terrible spirit that the fate of these millions of weak rebels, these 'half-finished samples of humanity created in mockery' can be made tolerable. And once convinced of it, he sees as clearly that to achieve that object, one must follow blindly the guidance of the wise spirit, the fearful spirit of death and destruction, hence accept a system of lies and deception and lead humanity consciously this time toward death and destruction, and moreover, be deceiving them all the while in order to prevent them from realizing where they are being led, and so force the miserable blind men to feel happy, at least while here on earth. And note this: a wholesale deception in the name of Him, in whose ideal the old man had so passionately, so fervently, believed during nearly his whole life! Is this no suffering? And were such a solitary exception found amidst, and at the head of, that army 'that thirsts for power but for the sake of the mean pleasures of life,' think you one such man would not suffice to bring on a tragedy? Moreover, one single man like my Inquisitor as a principal leader, would prove sufficient to discover the real guiding idea of the Romish system with all its armies of Jesuits, the greatest and chiefest conviction that the solitary type described in my poem has at no time ever disappeared from among the chief leaders of that movement. Who knows but that terrible old man, loving humanity so stubbornly and in such an original way, exists even in our days in the shape of a whole host of such solitary exceptions, whose existence is not due to mere chance, but to a well-defined association born of mutual consent, to a secret league, organized several centuries back, in order to guard the Mystery from the indiscreet eyes of the miserable and weak people, and only in view of their own happiness? And so it is; it cannot be otherwise. I suspect that even Masons have some such Mystery underlying the basis of their organization, and that it is just the reason why the Roman Catholic clergy hate them so, dreading to find in them rivals, competition, the dismemberment of the unity of the idea, for the realization of which one flock and one Shepherd are needed. However, in defending my idea, I look like an author whose production is unable to stand criticism. Enough of this."

"You are, perhaps, a Mason yourself!" exclaimed Alyosha. "You do not believe in God," he added, with a note of profound sadness in his voice. But suddenly remarking that his brother was looking at him with mockery, "How do you mean then to bring your poem to a close?" he unexpectedly enquired, casting his eyes downward, "or does it break off here?"

"My intention is to end it with the following scene: Having disburdened his heart, the Inquisitor waits for some time to hear his prisoner speak in His turn. His silence weighs upon him. He has seen that his captive has been attentively listening to him all the time, with His eyes fixed penetratingly and softly on the face of his jailer, and evidently bent upon not replying to him. The old man longs to hear His voice, to hear Him reply; better words of bitterness and scorn than His silence. Suddenly He rises; slowly and silently approaching the Inquisitor, He bends towards him and softly kisses the bloodless, four-score-and-ten-year-old lips. That is all the answer. The Grand Inquisitor shudders. There is a convulsive twitch at the corner of his mouth. He goes to the door, opens it, and addressing Him, 'Go,' he says, 'go, and return no more . . . do not come again . . . never, never!' and—lets Him out into the dark night. The prisoner vanishes."

"And the old man?"

"The kiss burns his heart, but the old man remains firm in his own ideas and unbelief."

"And you, together with him? You too!" despairingly exclaimed Alyosha, while Ivan burst into a still louder fit of laughter.

Acknowledgments

My students were an integral part of writing and developing this game. I am especially grateful to the students in my spring 2016 Reacting to the Past class, who volunteered to playtest this game for extra credit. Their enthusiasm astounded me—they spent nearly an hour giving me feedback and brainstorming revisions with me. Some students—Imogen Sealy, Haley Williams, and Greta Unger—weren't even in the class, but they came just for their love of Reacting to the Past. The feedback from this group, and all my subsequent classes, has guided this game into its final format. Special thanks to Haley Price, who went above and beyond in her summer research assistant position. In particular, she authored the Alexandra Volkova sheet, wrote the historical bulletins, and designed an interactive video game for the materials.

The Reacting to the Past community at the Summer Institute and Game Development conferences has been a constant source of inspiration. I received valuable feedback early on at the GDC, particularly from Mark Carnes and Jenn Worth. Deep thanks to Nick Proctor for advising me on the game design process and to Paula Lazarus for her insightful comments. I am indebted to Maria Gapotchenko, who was the first person other than me to playtest this game and proofread the gamebook, including several of my translations. One of her students, Isabella Durso, wrote an outstanding role sheet for Anatolii Koni that I incorporated into the game.

I am grateful to the Liberal Arts Honors Program at The University of Texas at Austin, where Larry Carver and Paul Sullivan first introduced me to Reacting to the Past. My colleagues Stacey Amorous, Julie Casey, Michael Johnson, and Elon Lang have encouraged me in too many ways to list. Marc Musick, director of LAH, has been wonderfully supportive of all my endeavors. Finally, my sincere thanks to the Center of Teaching and Learning at The University of Texas at Austin for awarding me a teaching grant in the summer of 2020 that allowed me to hire a research assistant and revise and enhance the game mechanics; to Liberal Arts Honors for funding conference travel; and to the College of Liberal Arts for a subvention grant to cover copyright permissions.

None of this would have come into existence without my husband and his excitement for this project. Thank you for everything—spending lunch hours discussing Russian literary journals, Populists, and Slavophiles; imagining ways to integrate board game mechanics; making reading suggestions; and always believing in me.

Appendix
Russian Names

Understanding Russian names is important for following character and plot development in the readings, while using them correctly is essential for interacting with other characters at literary salons. Russian names typically have three parts, signify gender, and carry formal and informal versions.

To better understand how names work, we'll look at some of the names from the game:

Gleb Ivanovich Uspensky
Vladimir Sergeevich Solovyov
Nadezhda Stepanovna Sokhanskaya
Elena Ivanovna Apreleva

The three parts comprising a Russian name are the first name, a patronymic name, and a last name. The first name is given at birth. The patronymic name comes from the first name of one's father. The last name is the family name, also passed down from one's father and shared with siblings and other relatives. Women, when married, typically will change their last name to their husband's last name, but their patronymic remains the same.

Patronymic and last names are both gendered, meaning they have different endings for females and males. Patronymic endings will be *-ovna/-evna* for women and *-ovich/-evich* for men. This use of *o* or *e* simply depends on spelling rules. But because of the gendered names, Gleb Uspensky has "Ivanovich" as his patronymic, while Elena Apreleva, whose father was also named Ivan, has "Ivanovna."

Last names are also gendered, with women's names usually ending in *-a* or *-aya* and men's last names ending in *-y* or a consonant.

To address someone formally, use their first name and their patronymic: "Vladimir Sergeevich" or "Nadezhda Stepanovna." In the nineteenth century, where our game takes place, Russians would use this formal address with someone they just met, someone they don't know very well, or anytime they want to be very polite. If you meet someone at the literary salon for the first time or are speaking to someone older than you, use the formal form of address. In our nineteenth-century novels, you may even notice husbands and wives using formal names with each other as a sign of respect. Formal or informal types of address may also indicate a difference in class. A servant or person in a lower social class would address their employer or member of the nobility using the formal version, while a member of the upper class would typically refer to an employee using the informal version.

If a Russian uses an informal form of address with someone they don't know very well, the implied intimacy will likely cause offense. To be informal, you may use just the first name. First names may be shortened to a nickname or made more affectionate with the addition of a diminutive. For example, "Elena" may be shortened to the friendly "Lena" and then show special fondness with the diminutive "Lenochka." Diminutives are used in very particular situations—between close friends, a parent and child, or a couple. More examples of nicknames and their diminutives can be found at Russian Language Lessons, www.russianlessons.net/vocabulary/russian_names.php.

Notes

INTRODUCTION

1. Pushkin and Dewey, "Bronze Horseman."

HISTORICAL BACKGROUND

1. Lincoln, *Sunlight at Midnight*, 18.
2. Bater, "Between Old and New," 45-46.
3. Bater, "Between Old and New," 45-46.
4. Bater, "Between Old and New," 47-48.
5. Bater, "Between Old and New," 50-51.
6. Bater, "Between Old and New," 65.
7. Shevzov, "Letting the People into the Church: Reflections on Orthodoxy and Community in Late Imperial Russia," 69.
8. Avrutin, *Jews and the Imperial State*, 7-9.
9. Westwood, *Endurance and Endeavor*, 81-84.
10. Afanas'ev, "Jurors and Jury Trials in Imperial Russia, 1866-1885," 214-30.
11. Lincoln, *Sunlight at Midnight*, 122.
12. Martinsen, *Literary Journals in Imperial Russia*, 101.
13. Martinsen, *Literary Journals in Imperial Russia*, 103.
14. Lincoln, *Sunlight at Midnight*, 130.
15. Brooks, *When Russia Learned to Read*, 4.
16. Terras, *Handbook of Russian Literature*, 243.
17. Terras, *Handbook of Russian Literature*, 281.
18. Lincoln, *Sunlight at Midnight*, 150-51.
19. Lincoln, *Sunlight at Midnight*, 149-52.
20. Venturi, *Roots of Revolution*, 574.
21. Venturi, *Roots of Revolution*, 595-96.
22. Venturi, *Roots of Revolution*, 334-35.
23. Venturi, *Roots of Revolution*, 336.
24. Radzinsky, *Alexander II*, 176-78.
25. Venturi, *Roots of Revolution*, 347-50.
26. Engel and Rosenthal, *Five Sisters*, 7-10.
27. Terras, *Handbook of Russian Literature*, 303.
28. Engel and Rosenthal, *Five Sisters*, xxx.
29. Engel and Rosenthal, *Five Sisters*, xx.
30. Whittaker, "Women's Movement," 35-69.
31. Engel, *Mothers and Daughters*, 114-24, 176-78.
32. Polunov, *Russia in the Nineteenth Century*, 163-65.
33. Polunov, *Russia in the Nineteenth Century*, 165.
34. Westwood, *Endurance and Endeavor*, 101-3.
35. Heraclides and Dialla, *Humanitarian Intervention in the Long Nineteenth Century*, 176.
36. Brooks, *When Russia Learned to Read*, 60-61.
37. Brooks, *When Russia Learned to Read*, 112.
38. Brooks, *When Russia Learned to Read*, 92.
39. Brooks, *When Russia Learned to Read*, 109.
40. Mirsky, *History of Russian Literature*, 172-76.
41. Terras, *Handbook of Russian Literature*, 81, 444-45.
42. Martinsen, *Literary Journals in Imperial Russia*, 114.
43. Mirsky, *History of Russian Literature*, 276-77.
44. Mirsky, *History of Russian Literature*, 177-82.
45. Bartlett, *Leo Tolstoy*, 233-37.
46. Mirsky, *History of Russian Literature*, 273.
47. Moss, A History of Russia, 427.

CORE TEXTS

1. A lengthy footnote on legislative technicalities has been omitted. Unless otherwise indicated, the notes in this chapter are from the source. Notes preceded by "*AN:*" are mine.
2. Postmaster Spekin is a character from Nikolai Gogol's play *The Inspector General*.
3. The epigraph, slightly misquoted, is from volume 2 of Gogol's *Dead Souls*.
4. Onegin: hero of Pushkin's novel in verse, *Eugene Onegin*.
5. Zakhar: Oblomov's personal servant, a serf. The "three hundred Zakhars" are the serfs owned by Oblomov as part of his estate.
6. *Barshchina*: obligation of the serfs to work on the landowners' land and perform various services. During the first half of the nineteenth century the customary obligation was three days a week, though this was often exceeded. Equivalent to the French *corvèe* before 1789.
7. *Ekonomicheskii Ukazatel'* (*Economic Guide*): a St. Petersburg economic journal of laissez-faire leanings.
8. Kvas is a fermented drink, made from bread.
9. A pud equals 36 pounds.
10. A desiatina equals 2.7 acres.
11. Source: "Slovoboiazn," *Kolokol*, l.16, June 1, 1858; 13:281-82, 563.

12. Prince Alexander Mikhailovich Gorchakov (1798-1883) was appointed minister of foreign affairs in 1856.

13. Source: "1 iulia 1858," *Kolokol*, l.18, July 1, 1858; 13:293-98, 569-70.

14. From a poem called "The Old Barrel Organ (Remembering the Unforgettable One)" ("*Staraia Sharmanka. K vospominaniem o Nezabvennom*"), probably by V. R. Zotov, which circulated in Petersburg and Moscow, and was published in *The Bell* on November 1, 1857. The "Unforgettable One" is the late tsar, Nicholas I.

15. Count Viktor N. Panin (1801-74), minister of justice from 1841 to 1862.

16. Prince Alexey F. Orlov (1786-1862), head of the Third Department from 1844 to 1856, from 1856 chair of the State Council and Committee of Ministers, and from 1857 chair of the Secret and then Main Committee to examine the question of serfdom.

17. While still heir to the throne, Alexander II traveled to the Caucasus and visited military units actively engaged in combat, for which he was awarded the Order of St. George, fourth degree.

18. Konstantin I. Arseniev (1789-1865) was a statistician, historian, and geographer, who tutored the future tsar from 1828 to 1835.

19. In November 1857, the tsar instructed Vladimir I. Nazimov (governor of Vilna, Kovno, and Grodno) to allow local gentry to form committees to discuss how the serfs might be freed; copies of the rescript were sent to all the other governors, and it was published. The "Secret Committee" Alexander set up in January 1857 to examine the emancipation question was renamed the Main Committee early the following year.

20. Herzen: "There are many who reproach *The Bell*, among them the Prussian Kreuz Zeitung, with a disrespectful tone and familiar air toward people who, although they stand in the way of any improvement and are major scoundrels, still belong to the highest ranks. [. . .] In the ringing of our *Bell* there is a howl that arises from the jail cells, barracks, and stables, from the landowners' fields and the censor's slaughterhouse—*The Bell* definitely belongs to bad society, which is why it lacks the clerk's manners and the secretary's courtesy."

21. Grigory B. Blank (1811-89), a Tambov landowner, strongly supported serfdom. Nikolay A. Bezobrazov (1816-67), leader of the St. Petersburg gentry, wrote brochures about gentry rights.

22. Herzen refers to articles published in *The Bell* in 1857 and 1858, exposing crimes against serfs and others, and the absence of punishment for their tormenters.

23. Source: "Peterburgskii universitet zakryt!," *Kolokol*, 1.109. October 15, 1861; 15:164-65, 394.

24. Ismail I. Sreznevsky (1812-80) was a philologist who taught in Kharkov, and, beginning in 1847, was a professor at St. Petersburg University.

25. Grigory I. Filipson (1809-83) was a lieutenant-general, senator, and in 1861-62, trustee of the Petersburg education district; Count Pavel N. Ignatiev (1797-1879), governor-general of Vitebsk, Mogilev, and Smolensk, and from 1854 to 1861, military governor-general of St. Petersburg.

26. Count Petr A. Shuvalov (1827-89) was an adjutant-general who held high offices in the St. Petersburg police, the Ministry of the Interior, and in 1861 in the Third Department.

27. Source: "Pis'mo k Imperatoru Aleksandru II," *Kolokol*, l.221, June 1, 1866; 19:81-82, 392-93.

28. Muravyov did this to discourage radical young women from continuing to display distinctive hair styles and wear unconventional clothes (Verhoeven, *The Odd Man Karakozov*, 114-17).

29. Source: "Iz Peterburga," *Kolokol*, l.221, June 1, 1866; 19:84-88, 393.

30. Fyodor F. Trepov (1812-89) became chief of police in St. Petersburg in April 1866.

31. Journals that received warnings, like *The Contemporary* and *The Russian Word*, saw their subscriptions decline.

32. Orlov-Davydov spoke at the January 9, 1865, meeting of the Moscow Assembly of the Nobility.

33. Source: "Ot gosudaria Kniaziu P.P. Gagarinu," *Kolokol*, l.222, June 15, 1866; 19:95-101, 396-98. Prince Pavel P. Gagarin (1789-1872), a senator, served on the commission investigating the Petrashevsky Circle, the emancipation committee, and was chairman of the court that tried Karakozov.

34. Herzen: "In all probability, Gagarin wrote this letter 'to himself.' This is all a continuation of the system set up after the infamous fire in Petersburg, the system of intimidation of the sovereign. He is assured and frightened, and he assures and frightens himself, and signs, like a future constitutional monarch, not knowing what it is—*il regne, mais ne gouverne pas*."

35. The initial draft of the manifesto by Yu. Samarin and N. Milyutin was profoundly altered by the Moscow metropolitan Filaret.

36. Herzen: "It stands to reason that not a single serious social teaching has ever attacked property rights from the viewpoint of theft." Herzen goes on to call Gagarin's view that serfs should not receive any post-emancipation allotment as an endorsement of theft as the foundation of landowners' rights.

37. This quote from Psalm 113 (115 in the King James version) appeared on Russian coins under Paul I and later on 1812 war medals.

38. In Denis Fonvizin's 1782 play *The Minor*.

39. Loosely quoted by Chernyshevsky from Part III of Hegel's Introduction in his *Vorlesungen uber die Aesthetik* (pages 54–55 in the Berlin, 1842, edition).—TRANS.

40. In French in the original. Translation: That says everything.

41. *AN:* Masha and Olya are likely Elena Shtakenshneider's younger sisters.

42. *AN:* This quote references a poem by Fyodor Ivanovich Tyutchev (1803–73), dated November 21, 1864: "O this South, o this Nice! . . . / O, how their glitter troubles me! / Life, like a shot bird, / wants to rise—and cannot . . . / The broken wings just hang, / There is no flight, nor spread / All of it, clinging to the earth / Shakes from pain and powerlessness."

43. Shcherbina died April 10, 1869, from an abscess in his throat. *AN:* Nikolai Fyodorovich Shcherbina (1829–69) was a Russian poet and satirist, known for his collection *Greek Poems*, who worked in the Ministry of Internal Affairs in the main department for printing.

44. *AN:* The original word *khokhol* is considered an ethnic slur for Ukrainians, referring to Ukrainian men's traditional topknot of hair.

45. *AN:* Nizhyn, a town in Ukraine, was a large city in the nineteenth century with a significant Jewish population. Milesian refers to Miletus, the birthplace of one of the earliest schools of pre-Socratic Greek philosophy.

46. The text of the epigram does not correspond with the published version, where we read: "Tell us, why do you shorten your pathetic time / with childlike malice?"

47. Mikhail Fyordorovich Negreskul, the son-in-law of Peter Lavrov, married to his daughter Maria Petrovna, was born around 1843 and actively participated in the student protests from 1868–69. On December 4, 1869, he was arrested in connection with the Nechaev affair, imprisoned in the Petropavlosk Fortress for five months, and in May 1870, released to live under home arrest because of illness. On February 12, 1871, he died of consumption.

48. *AN:* The 14th Line is a street on Vaskilevsky Island in St. Petersburg.

49. *AN:* Manya refers to Maria Petrovna Negreskul, his wife, who is pregnant at the time.

50. Only three editions came out: October, November, and December in 1869. "A. Strugovshchikov" was named the editor. More detailed background on this journal, the editors, and its staff are covered in N. F. Belchikov's work "The Journal *Bibliograph*" in the collection *Journalism in the 60s* (Academia, 1930), 132–235.

51. Translation: outright.

52. The court composition was fairly diverse: There was the journalist Andrei Aleksandrovich Kraevsky (1810–89), at one point the publisher of the newspaper *The Voice* (he had already handed over *Notes of the Fatherland* to Nekrasov); the philosopher Vladimir Viktorovich Lesevich (1837–1905); the attorney-at-law and literary scholar Viktor Pavlovich Gaevsky (1826–88); doctor and poet Nikolai Stepanovich Kurochkin (1830–84); Nikolai Adrianovich Neklyudov (1840–96), one of the ringleaders from the student movement in 1861, a former justice of the peace from 1869, who later became Chief Prosecutor of the Senate; and Konstantin Konstantinovich Arseniev (1837–1919), who then became a publicist for *Messenger of Europe*, having been an attorney-at-law.

53. Luka Nikolaevich Antropov (1843–84) was a journalist for *Moscow News* and author of the play *Will O' the Wisp* (1878).

54. Yurii Fyodorovich Samarin (1819–76) was a Slavophile writer and a social activist. His essay "The Periphery of Russia" came out in Berlin in 1868–76.

55. *AN:* Mikhail Katkov, the influential messenger of *Russian Messenger*, was politically conservative and a staunch supporter of the tsar.

56. M. P. Pokrovsky in 1861 was one of the leaders of the student movement, and in 1869 he became a follower of Katkov.

57. The Imperial surgeon Pavel Andreevich Naranovich (1801–74) was the head of the Medical Surgical Academy from 1867 to 1869, which sympathized with higher education for women, and he used his connections to support the efforts for women's higher education.

58. When the minister of public education, Mr. Dmitri Tolstoy, proposed to arrange lectures open to the general public "on the basis of existing regulations for lectures" instead of the access to the universities that women requested, representatives of the bourgeois wing of the women's movement led by Stasova and Trubinkova decided to accept this proposal, although the more radically inclined women were against it. "The opposition was terrible!" Stasova wrote. Among the most "ardent" opponents, she listed Tkacheva, Veber, Tsetsina, and others.

59. Saturdays were inconvenient for deputies from the opposition, who, for the most part, belonged to the working intelligentsia.

60. This happened the day before, that is, on November 30. Alexander Alexandrovich Cherkesov (1839–1908) was the son of a landowner, a graduate of the Tsarskoe Selo lyceum. In 1865 upon returning from abroad, he was arrested because of his relationship with Herzen but was released after two months. He entered the book trade; aside from a library and bookstore in Petersburg, he had a bookstore in Moscow, where the head was P. G. Uspensky, around whom the Moscow Nechaev Circle gathered.

61. In the record from December 5, a correction is entered—not Ushakova, but Evreinova, a friend of Sophia Kovalevskaya's. But Ushakova also existed. Kovalevskaya recalls in her own memoirs (see *Voice of the Past*, 1916, no. 4, p. 93) about her Heidelberg friend, Sonechka Ushakova.

62. *AN:* This chain, a symbol for those who served as magistrates, was created by Alexander II in 1865 as part of his 1864 judicial reforms that created the office of magistrates. The chain consisted of a medal suspended from flat, heavy links made of gilded bronze.

63. The earliest information about the establishment of the Society for Expanding Women's Labor is found in the entry dated April 19, 1863, by E. A. Shtakenshneider, which turned out to be more forward-looking than Lavrov: she anticipates that uniting the representatives of two different social groups having the label "aristocrat" and "nihilist" would not succeed. She, who Lavrov counted among the centrists, considered herself in 1864 more closely associated with the "nihilists," but later in her evaluation of the women's movement and practical activity, drew closer to the bourgeoise arm of the women's movement, led by the triumvirate of M. V. Trubnikova (1845–97), N. V. Stasova (1822–95), and A. P. Filosofova (1837–1912). Her own involvement in the women's movement, where she put the most energy, even though it was in peripheral roles, is reflected minimally in her diary. For example, she completely fails to recall that in her apartment, chemistry lessons were taught by Professor Nikolai Pavlovich Fyodorov and only mentions in passing lectures given by the architect Rossi. For more about the women's movement, see the book on N. V. Stasova by Vladimir Stasov (1899), on A. V. Filosofova by Tyrkova, and also *Materials on the History of Women's Education in Russia* by E. Likhachev, vol. 3 (1901).

64. The dating is not precise: In reality, E. I. Konrady submitted her notes for the "First Congress of Naturalists" on January 2, 1868. These "notes," in the words of A. V. Tyrkova, "created an era in the history of Russian women's education." They were read aloud and provoked incessant applause. "The congress," said A. P. Filosofova, "shows we are prepared to help, but refused to take the initiative in this matter that is, of course, completely alien to the social goals of this congress. Konrady's brave stunt unified all the women and all the best women's thoughts and gave them the opportunity to move around." This note-petition by E. I. Konrady was published in the *Proceedings of the First Congress of Russian Naturalists* and in V. I. Stasov's book *N. V. Stasova*, 166–69.

65. *AN:* Evgenia Ivanovna Konrady (1838–98) was a publicist and a translator; from 1868 to 1874 she edited the publication *The Weekly*.

66. Ekaterina Aleksandrovna Solodovnikova was a spokesperson of the left wing of the women's movement during these years. She and her group arranged a concert for Lavrovskaya, raised money, and on April 1, 1869, they opened the so-called Alarchinsky courses.

67. At the affair on November 26, 1878, Dmitri Andreevich Tolstoy, minister of public education, told the emissaries that "this is entirely unnecessary for women, they should get married and set all science aside" and so on (see Stasov, *N. V. Stasova*, 182–83).

68. After ten years of hard work, the champions of higher education for women could finally triumph: On September 20, 1878, the Bestuzhev courses were opened. The committee of founders, considered unnecessary, was abolished. Filosofova was elected chair of the new society at the general meeting on November 4.

69. The name of the brochure by Tsitovich, the professor for Novorosiisky University, is not transcribed accurately. It was called "A Response to the Letter for Educated People" (Odessa, 1879). This brochure takes issue with

N. K. Mikhailovsky's article "Letters to Educated People" where he ridiculed Tsitovich's views on communal land ownership. This brochure was written very viciously and cynically, but it especially sharply attacked women's equality. Tsitovcih describes the new woman as follows: "The outward appearance is some kind of hermaphrodite, the inner—a true daughter of Cain." Tsitovich does not believe that the mutual pursuit of knowledge by men and women can "be managed without sin." Tsitovich's brochure expressed the views of the most reactionary circles.

70. *AN:* "Gospodin" is roughly the equivalent of "mister" in late nineteenth-century Russia.

71. *AN:* Scylla and Charybdis are two sea monsters from Greek mythology. Located on opposite sides of the Strait of Messina, between Sicily and mainland Italy, they were considered a hazard that sailors must pass through.

72. *AN:* "Tsargrad" is the Slavic name for Constantinople that was popular among Slavophiles.

73. *AN:* The word "cent" appears as *grosh* in the original, which refers to a half kopeck coin used between 1838 and 1917.

74. *AN:* Translation: My dear, peace before anything; war must be avoided at any cost.

75. *AN:* Translation: Peace at any cost; my dear, war is unavoidable.

76. *AN:* The Porte refers to the central government of the Ottoman Empire.

77. *AN:* In this sentence "estate," the translation from the original *soslovie*, refers to social groups that existed in Russia and determined one's social and political rights and obligations. The social classification was inherited from one's parents and passed down through generations.

78. *AN:* Translation: void.

79. *AN:* Translation: cause for declaration of war.

Bibliography

Afanas'ev, Alexander. "Jurors and Jury Trials in Imperial Russia, 1866–1885." Translated by William Sunderland. In *Russia's Great Reforms, 1855–1881*, edited by Ben Eklof, John Bushnell, and Larissa Zakharova, 270–90. Bloomington: Indiana University Press, 1994.

Andrew, Joe, ed. and trans. *Russian Women's Shorter Fiction: An Anthology, 1835–1860*. New York: Oxford University Press, 1996.

Avrutin, Eugene M. *Jews and the Imperial State*. Ithaca, NY: Cornell University Press, 2010.

Bartlett, Rosamund. *Leo Tolstoy*. Boston: Houghton Mifflin Harcourt, 2011.

Bater, James H. "Between Old and New: St. Petersburg in the Late Imperial Era." In *The City in Late Imperial Russia*, edited by Michael F. Hamm, 45–46. Bloomington: Indiana University Press, 1986.

Berlin, Isaiah. *Russian Thinkers*. New York: Penguin Books, 1979.

Brooks, Jeffrey. *When Russia Learned to Read*. Evanston, IL: Northwestern University Press, 2003.

Chernyshevsky, Nikolai. *The Aesthetic Relations of Art to Reality*. In *Russian Philosophy*, vol. 2, *The Nihilist, the Populists: Critics of Religion and Culture*, edited by James M. Edie, James P. Scanlan, and Mary-Barbara Zeldin, with the collaboration of George L. Kline, 16–28. Knoxville: University of Tennessee Press, 1976.

Engel, Barbara Alpern. *Mothers and Daughters: Women of the Intelligentsia in Nineteenth-Century Russia*. New York: Cambridge University Press, 1983.

Engel, Barbara Alpern, and Clifford N. Rosenthal, eds. and trans. *Five Sisters: Women against the Tsar*. DeKalb: Northern Illinois University Press, 2013.

Engelstein, Laura. *Slavophile Empire: Imperial Russia's Illiberal Path*. Ithaca, NY: Cornell University Press, 2009.

Fedyashin, Anton. *Liberals Under Autocracy: Modernization and Civil Society, 1866–1904*. Chapel Hill: University of North Carolina Press, 2020.

Frank, Joseph. *Dostoevsky: A Writer in His Time*. Princeton, NJ: Princeton University Press, 2010.

Frank, Joseph. *Dostoevsky: The Mantle of the Prophet, 1871–1881*. Princeton, NJ: Princeton University Press, 2002.

Gerstein, Linda. *Nikolaj Strakhov: Philosopher, Man of Letters, Social Critic*. Cambridge, MA: Harvard University Press, 1971.

Heraclides, Alexis, and Ada Dialla. *Humanitarian Intervention in the Long Nineteenth Century*. Manchester, UK: Manchester University Press, 2015.

Herzen, Alexander. *A Herzen Reader*. Edited and translated by Kathleen Parthé. Evanston, IL: Northwestern University Press, 2012.

Katz, Michael. *Michael Katkov: A Political Biography, 1818–1887*. The Hague: Mouton, 1966.

Kornblatt, Judith. *Divine Sophia*. Ithaca, NY: Cornell University Press, 2009.

Lavrov, Pyotr Lavrovich. *Historical Letters*. Moscow: Academia, 1912.

Lincoln, W. Bruce. *The Great Reforms: Autocracy, Bureaucracy, and the Politics of Change in Imperial Russia*. DeKalb: Northern Illinois University Press, 1990.

Lincoln, W. Bruce. *Sunlight at Midnight: St. Petersburg and the Rise of Modern Russia*. New York: Basic Books, 2000.

Lukashevich, Stephan. *Ivan Aksakov, 1823–1886: A Study in Russian Thought and Politics*. Cambridge, MA: Harvard University Press, 1965.

Martinsen, Deborah, ed. *Literary Journals in Imperial Russia*. New York: Cambridge University Press, 1997.

McLean, Hugh. *Nikolai Leskov: The Man and His Art*. Cambridge, MA: Harvard University Press, 2014.

Mirsky, D. S. Prince. *A History of Russian Literature: From Its Beginnings to 1900*. Edited by Francis J. Whitfield. New York: Vintage Books, 1958.

Monas, Sydney. *The Third Section: Police and Society in Russia under Nicholas I*. Cambridge, MA: Harvard University Press, 2013.

Moss, Walter. *A History of Russia, Vol. I: to 1917*. New York: McGraw Hill, 1997.

Moss, Walter. *Russia in the Age of Alexander II, Tolstoy, and Dostoevsky*. London: Anthem, 2002.

Nepomnyashchy, Catherine T. "Katkov and the

Emergence of the Russian Messenger." *Ulbandus Review* 1, no. 1 (1977): 59-89.

Nikitenko, Alexander. *The Diary of a Russian Censor*. Abridged, edited, and translated by Helen Saltz Jacobson. Amherst: University of Massachusetts Press, 1975.

Polunov, Alexander. *Russia in the Nineteenth Century: Autocracy, Reform, and Social Change, 1814-1914*. Edited by Thomas C. Owen and Larissa G. Zakharova. Translated by Marshall S. Shatz. Armonk, NY: M. E. Sharpe, 2005.

Pushkin, A. S., and John Dewey. "The Bronze Horseman: A St Petersburg Story." *Translation and Literature* 7, no. 1 (1998): 59-71. http://www.jstor.org/stable/40339775.

Radzinsky, Edvard. *Alexander II: The Last Great Tsar*. Translated by Antonina Boius. New York: Free Press, 2005.

Rieber, Alfred J. *Merchants and Entrepreneurs in Imperial Russia*. Chapel Hill: University of North Carolina Press, 1982.

Shein, Louis J., ed. and trans. *Readings in Russian Philosophical Thought*. Waterloo, ON: Wilfrid Laurier University Press, 1977.

Shevzov, Vera. "Letting the People into the Church: Reflections on Orthodoxy and Community in Late Imperial Russia." In *Orthodox Russia: Belief and Practice Under the Tsars*, edited by Valerie Kivelson and Robert H. Greene, 59-80. University Park: Pennsylvania State University Press, 2003.

Shtakenshneider, Elena Andreevna. *Dnevnik i zapiski (1854-1886)*. Edited by I. N. Rozanov. M. -L: Academia, 1934. https://coollib.net/b/443919/read#t15.

Stites, Richard. *The Women's Liberation Movement in Russia: Feminism, Nihilism, and Bolshevism, 1860-1930*. Princeton, NJ: Princeton University Press, 1991.

Terras, Victor, ed. *Handbook of Russian Literature*. New Haven, CT: Yale University Press, 1985.

Ulianova, Galina. *Female Entrepreneurs in Nineteenth-Century Russia*. London: Pickering and Chatto, 2009.

Uspensky, Gleb. "A Village Diary." In *Readings in Russian Civilization*. Vol. 2, *Imperial Russia, 1700-1917*, edited by Thomas Riha, 358-67. Chicago: University of Chicago Press, 1969.

Venturi, Franco. *Roots of Revolution: A History of the Populist and Socialist Movements in Nineteenth Century Russia*. Translated by Francis Haskell. New York: Grosset & Dunlap, 1960.

Walicki, Andrzej. *A History of Russian Thought from the Enlightenment to Marxism*. Translated by Hilda Andrews-Rusiecka. Stanford, CA: Stanford University Press, 1979.

Westwood, J. N. *Endurance and Endeavor: Russian History, 1812-2001*. New York: Oxford University Press, 2002.

Whittaker, Cynthia H. "The Women's Movement during the Reign of Alexander II: A Case Study in Liberalism." *Journal of Modern History* 48, no. 2 (June 1976): 35-69.

www.ingramcontent.com/pod-product-compliance
Lightning Source LLC
Chambersburg PA
CBHW080635230426
43663CB00016B/2884